A Life Impossible

A Life Impossible

Living with ALS:

Finding Peace and Wisdom

Within a Fragile Existence

STEVE GLEASON

With Jeff Duncan

ALFRED A. KNOPF   New York

2024

THIS IS A BORZOI BOOK
PUBLISHED BY ALFRED A. KNOPF

Copyright © 2024 by Steve Gleason

All rights reserved. Published in the United States by Alfred A. Knopf,
a division of Penguin Random House LLC, New York, and distributed
in Canada by Penguin Random House Canada Limited, Toronto.

www.aaknopf.com

Knopf, Borzoi Books, and the colophon are registered trademarks
of Penguin Random House LLC.

Library of Congress Cataloging-in-Publication Data
Names: Gleason, Steve, [date]- author. | Duncan, Jeff, author.
Title: A life impossible: living with ALS: finding peace and wisdom
within a fragile existence / Steve Gleason with Jeff Duncan.
Description: First edition. | New York: Alfred A. Knopf, 2024.
Identifiers: LCCN 2023048917 | ISBN 9780593536810 (hardcover) |
ISBN 9780593536827 (ebook)
Subjects: LCSH: Gleason, Steve, 1977—Health. |
Amyotrophic lateral sclerosis—Patients—Biography. |
Football players—United States—Biography.
Classification: LCC RC406.A24 G54 2024 |
DDC 616.8/39—dc23/eng/20231214
LC record available at https://lccn.loc.gov/2023048917

Jacket photograph by Aleksandra Konoplia/Getty Images
Spine-of-jacket photograph: Creativ Studio Heinemann/Getty Images
Back-of-jacket photographs: (left) Michael Hebert;
(right) James Shaw for Dear World

Jacket design by Linda Huang

Manufactured in the United States of America
First Edition

May all the caregivers of the Universe,
and at least one "Scheduler and godfather,"
be infinitely blessed.

For all the families working to live with ALS
and anyone who has experienced hardship and suffering.
May you know you are not alone.

For the Varisco family.
Without you, there is no New Orleans.
I'm the luckiest son-in-law (brother-in-law) ever.

For my parents.
Thank you for pouring the foundation to make me smart,
strong, humble, and courageous.

For Gray and Rivers.
May you know you are unconditionally loved.
Embrace the adventurous journey to endlessly discover
a clearer view of truth.

For Michel.
We're an epic fucking team.
That boy has disappeared.
Admiration, friendship, and love remain.
The greatest things you'll ever know are invisible.
May you know you are free.

I know I was born, and I know that I'll die.
The in-between is mine.

—EDDIE VEDDER

Contents

A Life Impossible

1

Naked Tears

Tears water our growth.
—AUTHOR UNKNOWN

I sat naked in the shower while a twenty-four-year-old man washed my armpits.

Across the bathroom, my three-year-old daughter, Gray, sat in the middle of the floor, cross-legged like the Buddha, with one difference. She was wailing hysterically and incessantly. Inconsolable. And I was incapable of helping her.

Only minutes earlier, my wife, Michel, marched through my bedroom holding a screaming Gray, set her down in the middle of the bathroom floor, and quickly left without any explanation. All I knew was that we were getting ready to fly to Chicago, and Michel was trying to pack.

The shower is the final phase of what I call my morning "workout," the routine I conduct with my care crew to prepare me for each day.

In many ways, the workout functions like the pregame warmup I performed during my eight-year playing career with the New Orleans Saints. There is one major difference, though: These days I am completely reliant on caregivers to perform these tasks for me because I can no longer move, talk, or breathe.

On January 5, 2011, I was diagnosed with amyotrophic lateral sclerosis, a rare neurodegenerative disease that damages the nerves that control voluntary muscle movement. ALS, commonly known as Lou Gehrig's disease, is relentless and humiliating. It progressively robs people of their motor skills and, in turn, destroys their quality of life. Although your senses and brain remain sharp, you gradually lose the ability to walk, talk, swallow, and breathe.

Today, I'm well past the point of being able to move, talk, or breathe on my own. The powerful legs I once used to race downfield on National Football League kickoffs now are withered. My arms, once muscled and ripped, are frail and motionless. My 5-foot-11 frame, once a strapping 210 pounds, is now an emaciated meat sack of flesh and bones. I've lived in a wheelchair for more than a decade. I've lived on a ventilator since 2014.

Lou Gehrig, the famous Major League Baseball (MLB) player for whom the disease is named, died two years after he was diagnosed. Most people diagnosed with ALS follow in Gehrig's steps— death comes a few years after diagnosis. I'm clearly biased, but I'd say I don't look too shabby for being more than ten years past my expiration date.

Each morning my care crew and I go through the same routine. In the early years, the process took about two hours to complete. Through trial and error, we have streamlined it to a very efficient forty-five to sixty minutes. Those early years of this workout, being naked and silent, and feeling a brutal powerlessness and vulnerability, were a time of great suffering. I decided to call it a *workout* to clarify my mindset and find ways to enjoy the process, just like I'd enjoyed difficult workouts in the NFL. For me, the difference between suffering and difficult is all in my mindset. Now, my day usually begins at 6 a.m. with two hours of meditation and mental training, while in bed.

During this mental training, I "eat" breakfast—a syringe of meds, coffee, and a smoothie—through a feeding tube that has been surgically inserted into my stomach. Then my caregivers stretch me for fifteen to thirty minutes to work my muscles and keep my body limber. After I stretch, I'm given an enema to encourage a bowel movement and lifted by a caregiver out of bed and carried

onto an aluminum plastic shower chair. Being carried by someone else, while not breathing, is a profoundly vulnerable step that
requires radical acceptance. To begin the bowel program, one of
them pushes his or her fist into my torso to force poop out of my
body and into a garbage bag and bucket positioned below the seat.

Over the years, this part of the workout has evolved greatly.
Like every single aspect of life with ALS, it's an exploration of the
unknown and there's no handbook. Up until about a year ago, it
was something like a poop war. I would encourage caregivers to
push so hard around my large intestinal tract, some of them would
initially be scared they were touching my spine and hurting me.
Since then, it has become more of a dance. We are patient, and
let my gut do what it does. When caregivers push, it's now a light
coaxing, a serenade.

Normally, I communicate with people, including my caregivers,
using eye-tracking technology on my computer tablet. But because
I am without my tablet during my workout process, I use a simple
nonverbal system to let them know what I need. Using eye and
facial movements, I guide them:

"Eyebrows up" for harder.

"Blinking" for softer.

"Look to the left" for move left.

"Look to the right" for move right.

If I need something out of the ordinary, I use an ingenious no-
tech communication system perfected by musician Jason Becker,
and his father, Gary. Jason was diagnosed with ALS in 1989. Gary
developed the Becker communication system in 1997 after Jason
lost the ability to talk. This "letter board," as we call it, has six
boxes with a group of four letters in each—three boxes on top and
three more on the bottom. The ingenious aspect is that each letter
can be communicated in two eye movements. The first eye movement indicates the box, and the second one identifies the specific
letter within that box. I use this letter board all the time, especially
in my workout and when I'm outside during the day because the
ultraviolet light from the sun kills the infrared eye tracker that follows my eyes. I'm infinitely grateful to the Beckers!

———

WHILE WE'RE PERFORMING the bowel program, a cough machine blows air deep into my lungs and blows mucus out of my nose, my mouth, and the surgically placed tracheostomy hole in my neck. The bowel process can sometimes take twenty minutes to complete and is admittedly gnarly to witness. The physical pressure on my body often causes me to wince and drool. But as barbaric as it looks, I have grown to really love my daily "exorcism." I feel reborn afterward.

Next, a caregiver takes my remaining clothes off and wheels me into the adjacent bathroom for my shower, which is administered through a handheld showerhead. To facilitate the process, I'm briefly taken off the ventilator. I'm no longer able to "hold my breath," but over the past nine years of living with a ventilator, we now know that I can be off the vent for around ninety seconds and be OK. It's one of a handful of times during the day that I am not connected to the machine that breathes for me and makes this impossible life possible. It's like a practice of dying, which invigorates me. I do not take one glorious, oxygen-rich, ineffable breath for granted.

I am most vulnerable during the daily shower—naked in every way, physically and emotionally. This nakedness can be an incoherently isolating experience. But through a process of surrender and trust in the meticulous system we have created, this dance with the caregivers has been perfected over time. It is now beautifully choreographed and executed.

During my shower, I face the large bathroom mirror and cabinets in our bathroom. For Christmas a couple of years ago, I asked for a picture of Thich Quang Duc to be hung in the bathroom. Thich Quang Duc was the Vietnamese Buddhist monk who famously burned himself to death at a busy Saigon intersection in 1963. He did this in protest of governmental religious persecution. The worldwide recognition of this image and the actions of Quang Duc ultimately led to a government regime change. David Halberstam documented the event for the *New York Times*: "As he burned he never moved a muscle, never uttered a sound, his outward composure in sharp contrast to the wailing people around him."

My responsibility is to stay poised throughout the workout. When I see Quang Duc, I marvel at his ability to remain calm while burning to death. I find it miraculous.

Quang Duc inspires and motivates me every morning. How trained and powerful is that dude's mind? If this monk can be this equanimous in the midst of flames, can I do the same in my life?

Life with ALS prevents me from enjoying some of the things that ordinary people might take for granted. One of the realities of my life is that I've never hugged our kids, or more importantly, Rivers and Gray have never been hugged by their dad. Ever. If you saw your daughter weeping in the middle of your bathroom floor, wouldn't you pick her up? Or raise your voice and call your spouse to find out what was going on? If you were my wife, wouldn't you like to hand off your crying three-year-old to your able-bodied husband for some respite?

We learned Michel was pregnant a few weeks after I was diagnosed with ALS. Our children, Gray and Rivers, motivate me to continue. Being an active and involved parent has been the most important commitment in my life, but in addition to enormous joy and inspiration, it can be a deep source of exhaustion and pain. So one of my mantras is *Be passionately committed, and completely unattached.*

At times, like during Gray's meltdown, there is fear that I am not a good enough dad, that I am somehow unworthy. The desire to do something to prove my value has been a theme in my life, even before ALS. Social scientist Arthur Brooks calls this "the striver's curse." It's almost universal that people think they have to accomplish more and more to gain the approval of others in order to be happy and feel valued. This is an exhausting and futile approach to life. I learned that I was inadequate, or unworthy of love, early in life through my Christian fundamentalist upbringing, and my parents' adherence to those beliefs. I call these "constructed core beliefs." These are typically so deeply embedded in our psyche we don't even recognize them. I sense that many people in our world, especially in the West, experience this same inadequacy and instinct to prove their worth.

I expressed this tension between wanting to do more as a father and loving unconditionally to one of my mentors and teachers, Peter Crone, known as the Mind Architect. Peter insightfully responded, "Steve, your presence is enough." Hearing those words, a massive emotional burden was lifted. I decided that being present is my purpose. I know it's not true that I am not worthy or that I don't matter. *My presence IS enough.* I live from this place.

But . . .

Not always.

That summer day in 2022, as Gray wept helplessly on the cold bathroom floor, my naked, silent, unmoving *presence* certainly didn't feel like enough. I felt woefully inadequate as a father. I was powerless to do *anything.*

As Beau Baker, the twenty-four-year-old caregiver working with me that morning, dried my lower body, I felt a guilt and humiliation that shattered my mind. I allowed myself to get attached to the delusion that my life should somehow be different. Beau is a rising star on our care staff, but he's a relative kid himself. Screaming toddlers are not yet his field of expertise and my daughter was howling uncontrollably. I couldn't hold her, comfort her, or help. I couldn't even talk to her. I only sat there, like some stone-faced statue.

I wept, my tears matching Gray's. While she wailed audibly, my heart wailed silently, deep inside my chest. I tried to scream from the depths of my pain. Nothing. A second effort. Silence. My emotions had no outlet. In addition to the human desire to prove ourselves, it's also normal for humans to distract ourselves or to take flight in order to escape our pain. But . . . there is no escape for me.

As fast as she'd brought Gray in, Michel returned to the bathroom, swept her back into her arms, and left without a glance. I lost it. I felt only shame and inadequacy as a husband and father. Through tears, I used the letter board and spelled to Beau "I-M U-S-E-L-E-S-S."

This is life with ALS. It is a tenuous and tumultuous roller-coaster ride of setbacks. Each day brings enormous challenges—not just for the person afflicted by the disease but for everyone in their orbit.

Beau was on this roller coaster right at my side. When I had finished spelling my message, he resiliently replied, "That's not true."

Michel and I have lived and moved through so much anguish together, we have learned to communicate quite well. We have compassion and understanding for each other's pain. After this morning's workout, she talked through what happened with me and Beau. She explained that she simply needed a few minutes of reprieve, as all parents do.

We are challenged daily. Michel is essentially a single mother, and every day can be taxing for both of us. When I try to communicate with Gray, Michel, or our son, Rivers, it can take so long that the moment passes before they are engaged. Multiple times a day, I'll be typing something to say to one of them, or to anyone, but they're out of the room by the time I'm finished. For some reason, I still say what I typed, just to release it. The effort it takes for me to connect with my people can be difficult and exhausting—unimaginably fucking exhausting. And so often the effort is unsuccessful or, because there's no inflection in my synthetic voice, it completely backfires. This has happened countless times over the years. It's no one's fault; it's the reality of this life. Accepting these moments and leaving them behind can feel impossible. It is heart crushing. I feel disappointment and failure that would have been inconceivable before ALS.

And yet, I'm learning to explore acceptance. As reported in the Kimsuka Sutta, Siddhartha Gautama (the Buddha) said, "Whatever has the nature of arising has the nature of ceasing." And I know this. Times like that day on the bathroom floor are impermanent moments. Emotions such as uselessness are transitory. Therefore I can accept them, without attachment to how I think life *should* be. This wisdom is simple to understand, but it ain't easy to live. It's the practice of a lifetime.

Fortunately, I was inspired by Gray. Ten minutes after Michel took her, I watched her run into my room with a big smile on her face. "Daddy, are you ready to go fly in the airplane?!" She had quickly left her pain behind, as toddlers so miraculously do. Is this what Jesus meant when he said, "Unless you change and become like little children, you will never enter the kingdom of heaven"? I was humbled.

It can be tough for people to snap out of negative moods, but Gray helped me recognize the circumstance of my life. Do I need a reason to be happy? I'm a decade past my expiration date, and I'm alive! I have an opportunity to grow stronger, be better, and begin again.

Through tears I am baptized.

Reborn.

My body is a prison. I face insurmountable adversity each day, yet my family and I are able to survive and live within this miraculous, wonderful life. I have learned to accept things that are out of my control, to transform suffering into strength. I move through fear to discover the extraordinary on the other side. We all face the impossible at some point in our lives. By exploring acceptance, love, and the power of the human spirit, I recognize the innate peace in the midst of chaos. There is light in the darkness. The light within all of us. Every day. Every precious moment. I know it. I live it.

2

Roots

Be it no concern, point of no return
Go forward in reverse
This I will recall. Everytime I fall . . .
. . . I'm free
Setting forth in the universe
—EDDIE VEDDER, "Setting Forth"

I was born in Spokane, Washington. Growing up in this picturesque river town in eastern Washington about twenty miles
from the Idaho border shaped and formed my life.

It's a midsize, family-friendly town, with a fairly strong history
of professional athletes, like John Stockton and Ryne Sandberg, but
more than anything, Spokane is a nature lover's paradise. Being on
the east side of the state, the landscape is more or less a high desert
with pretty extreme temperatures. It's a short drive to reach the
surrounding mountains, forests, lakes, and rivers. For those who
are aware, it can be a playground for hikers, bikers, skiers, and water
sports enthusiasts. Starting from sixth grade, I have fond memories
of riding bikes with my younger brother, Kyle, on scorching summer days to the 7 Mile Bridge and making the twenty-five-foot leap
into the ice-cold, crystal-clear water of the Spokane River. I was
lucky to have family friends who had lake houses and ski condos,
so I made the most of living in Spokane. Every chance I got, I went

skiing, sledding, and snowboarding in the winters and boating, fishing, and water-skiing in the summers.

I also was formed by my upbringing. My dad, Michael, was a hustler. Without a college degree, he had a number of odd jobs, including pouring concrete and selling cars at a Ford dealership. He started to sell real estate when I was around six and did that until he retired.

My mom, Gail, was an academic, a lifelong teacher. More than anyone, my mom taught me how to explore, not only the exterior world, but also the interior world of my mind. I've loved to travel since I was young. Every summer, Mom would drive me and Kyle to Redwood City, California, to stay with her parents for a month. As an English teacher, and a huge fan of France, she would always tell us, "The root of the word 'travel' comes from the French word *travail*, which means struggle. Travel isn't always easy, but the struggles we face can help us in real life." Mom romanticized about the adversity associated with travel. Flat tires, car trouble, and sold-out motels were all part of the adventure for her.

For the entire time I was growing up, we lived in middle-class neighborhoods on the north side of town. We were poor in my early years. We moved from rental to rental six or seven times before I was three. Our first stable home was a modest rented one-floor brick house on West Cora Avenue, right across the street from Audubon Park, where I spent countless hours playing under the giant pine trees. I would lie at the base of the trees, looking up, and my youthful four-year-old eyes imagined that the very tops of the pines touched the sky.

When I was six, my parents bought an older house about a mile away on North Howard Street, a classic 1940s-era fixer-upper that my dad got for a $1,500 down payment. The roof leaked so we kept a bucket in the living room to catch the dripping water from the ceiling. When my parents removed the old carpet on the first floor, swaths of it fell apart in their hands. Mom and Dad remodeled the entire house over the next few years. My brother and I put a lot of hard work into the renovation, too. I vividly remember painting the interior and exterior of the house, and even getting to go on the roof to pull off the shingles in the blazing upper-90-degree temperatures.

My dad was a single-minded tough guy, the product of a strict Catholic upbringing. He went to Catholic grade schools where they taught that fear is the path to love. He was an extremely restless kid, so the structure and rigidity of the school was difficult. One of the nuns would slap him in the face until she could make him cry, except he was so defiant that he wouldn't cry. Finally, the tears streamed down, but from her eyes, not his. She wept while slapping him. In that environment, he never developed solid coping skills and wasn't shown the language of love. His father was rarely home because he was a long-haul truck driver; he had grown up poor on a farm in northern Wisconsin. Grandpa Gleason was so ashamed of his family that he left home at the age of twelve to seek a better way to live. My dad said he learned the value of putting in a hard day's work from his father and worked to instill that same work ethic in me and Kyle. He also introduced self-discipline that I've been able to implement in many aspects of my life. I wouldn't say I learned discipline directly from my dad, but rather his constant, scornful criticism and the punishment of spankings indirectly, and perhaps traumatically, allowed me to acquire the life skills of acceptance, self-control, and discipline.

My mom was the quiet, cerebral one in the family. She had a master's degree in teaching and an undergraduate degree in art history. My mom came from a large family similar to my wife Michel's. Her father, Jim Matthiesen, "Grandpa Matt," was a pilot in the military, then later flew commercially for American Airlines. He traveled all over the world for his job. All the kids and grandkids loved Grandpa Matt. But some members of my mom's family could be prideful and stubborn. They often struggled to admit fault or acknowledge when bad things happened. They seemed to live in denial. My mom certainly carried that trait. I have similar characteristics, and I'm lucky to be aware of this tendency. I work to be transparent and express my shortcomings and vulnerabilities, of which there are many.

Grandpa Matt was my undisputed childhood hero. Certainly

a flawed hero, as my dad frequently pointed out to me and my brother. He drank beer often in his retirement years and likely had PTSD, but he was never judgmental or mean to us when he drank. A veteran pilot of World War II and Korea, he earned the Distinguished Flying Cross. He flew the B-17, B-24, and P-51 among others, got shot down over Norway, then test-flew the first round of Boeing 707s. He would take me, my brother, and my cousin flying a few times a year and was the most badass dude I knew. I seriously considered being a pilot as I grew up.

My parents met in a nondenominational fundamentalist church, the First Community Church, which was about as close to a cult as you could get. The church was dominated by its pastor, called Grandpa Bob, who controlled everything, including the parishioners' minds. Anything that wasn't within his interpretation of the Bible was considered evil. The church didn't believe in dating or listening to secular music. It didn't officially arrange my parents' marriage, but Grandpa Bob and the leaders told my mom and dad they had to get married because it was "the will of God."

Every marriage goes through its share of trials, but my parents' relationship was particularly rocky, even rageful. Their behavior certainly didn't qualify as "Christian." Fortunately, they did their best to love me and my brother, Kyle, based upon the ideas they followed. As long as we followed their rules, something I learned to do at an early age, we'd be fine.

When I was four or five and we were living in our house on West Cora Avenue, a handful of kids from our church were playing in the water from our sprinkler in the front yard. I was walking behind a girl and made a sly comment about her butt. My dad heard me, grabbed my arm, and yanked me to my room, pulled down my pants, and spanked me. This wasn't uncommon. Both my parents spanked me and my brother. I don't remember being angry at them. I figured this was perfectly normal for everyone, based on what they told us about obedience. Dad often quoted Proverbs: "He that spareth his rod hateth his son." I chose obedience. On the downside, I also learned I had to be the "good boy" and prove my worthiness to be loved. Kyle was four years younger, but bolder than I was.

I was mostly a quiet observer. Kyle would try to intervene with my parents, and that often ended in physical violence, with my brother getting the worst of it. My dad wasn't taught how to be tactful. His personal beliefs were the only truth. He was direct and blunt to a fault, but fortunately he was also transparent, quick to acknowledge failure and could easily say "I'm sorry." I have heard him apologize repeatedly throughout my life, usually with tears of regret. These were the times I was most proud of him. I would tell Kyle, "He's doing his best." Learning to forgive other people at an early age laid a solid foundation for me. My mom was the opposite. She was easy to be with. Dad was judgmental, so I never knew when something I did or said would set him off. While Mom was quiet, a listener, and would offer guidance when asked, she tended to suppress her painful feelings, thoughts, and words.

In their case, opposites did *not* attract. It was not conducive to a healthy marriage. They never seemed to work toward a resolution. Instead, they dug in, stood their ground, and were stuck in the same conversation year after year. They blamed each other and rarely tried to understand the other's point of view or deal with their issues. Sometimes they went at each other for hours at a time. I hated this. I needed some place to release these intense, burning emotions, so I'd leave the house, crying, trying to hide the tears with my hands or my shirt and murmuring, "Please just stop this!"

During times like this, I often escaped to what I considered sacred places. Places outdoors, the more secluded from people the better, so I could release, feel the peace in nature, and rest. When I was three or four, those places were the sandbox in our backyard right next to the garage, or the orange circular rope swing hanging from the tall ponderosa pine in Audubon Park across the street. When I grew older and we moved to Howard Avenue, I would escape to the tree we had in the front yard. On dry, hot summer days, typical of the high desert plains in eastern Washington, my brother and I would sit in the shade of that tree with our dog, Rico, reading a book, taking a nap, or simply watching the clouds come and go in the sky. These sacred places were the first of many in my life. I've always sought out, or been called to, places like these where I could nurture myself and heal. For me, they illuminate the mystery and vitality of life.

I've also always enjoyed exploring how much I can extend and expand the frontiers of my physical and mental boundaries. Exploring fear and the unknown. Is this in our DNA? Do all of us humans have this?

ONE OF MY MOST VIVID and elaborate memories is of a day when I was six years old at our house on West Cora Avenue. It was a sunny afternoon, on a hot midsummer day. We had a massive 1977 gold Buick that was parked by the curb in front of our house. I don't remember exactly why, but I climbed in the Buick to get something. The windows were rolled up, except for the driver's-side window, which was cracked at the top to let in a bit of air. When I got in the gold boat of a car, everything was blazing; even the gold velour seats were hot. I immediately felt individual beads of sweat dripping down my forehead. I don't know why, but I didn't wipe them away. For some reason, I liked the physical sensation of having them drip onto my cheeks and temples. It was like being in a Buick sauna and I decided to stay in until I could not possibly continue.

The heat and sweat seemed to increase exponentially. I felt perspiration in places I'd never felt before, like my ankles and the tops of my feet. My breathing became vigorous and effortful, and the hot dry air felt like it was baking my lungs. There were several points where I noticed my body was buzzing, or screaming, especially my feet and hands. My lungs were burning. I wanted to get out because it was so unbearably hot. In uncharted territory, I was afraid, but also curious. I'm not sure why, or what possessed me, but my soul, if that is what it is, pushed and pulled me to explore whatever was on the other side. The other side of my fear. At some point, there was a shift. The effort seemed to disappear; it no longer felt anything like effort. It just *was*. A beautiful surrender. I could simply observe myself in the car, and I continued to do so until my hair, face, and clothes were drenched and dripping. Then, I finally got out of the gold sauna.

As I walked around outside, I remember feeling cleansed, energized, or maybe just empty. Perhaps "eclipsed" is the proper term. The sky was crisper and brighter, and the trees, with their spectacular greens and browns, were more vivid. I turned toward the sun, closed my eyes, and was cradled in its light and warmth. I remember thinking *God is everything, everywhere.* I was a new person, with clear eyes, clearer thoughts, and a mind at peace. I felt the goodness and perfection within my body and the world.

The nondenominational, fundamentalist church in which I was raised taught that we were all failed sinners who needed to be saved by something outside of us. They taught all the standard fire and brimstone, fear and judgment as the path to heaven: Other than the singing, I typically experienced only fear and unworthiness. In the gold sauna, somehow I experienced love, union, and heaven right where I was. This was not in a book or a building, but right within me. Of course, at that age I didn't conceptualize it this way.

Strangely, I never did try the gold sauna again, but I continued to seek out the sacredness of nature and the thrill of pushing the boundaries of my physical and mental limits. I continued to be curious about what and who I truly am, and what I could experience on the other side of, and within, my own fear.

3

Growth

It takes courage to grow up and become who you really are.

—E. E. CUMMINGS

I was pretty sheltered from life during my grade-school years. Maybe that's why my brother, Kyle, lovingly called me "an awkward fuck." From first through sixth grade, I went to a private school associated with our church. Cocooned in this unconventional school, I didn't have any real social skills.

There were only around twenty kids in the entire school. By third grade, I was one of two students in my grade. My mom was the principal and one of two or three teachers. By sixth grade, I was the only student in my class, and most of my classes were VHS video sessions from some Florida Christian school.

After sixth grade, my life drastically changed. We'd been living in a small house in a lower-middle-class neighborhood. My dad had a number of successful years as a realtor, so we were able to move to a really cool house in Five Mile Heights, an upper-middle-class neighborhood on the north side of Spokane County. The house was on a steep hill leading up to Five Mile Prairie, which is a 400-foot-high, 3,400-acre granite and lava mesa. Circular in outline, Five Mile Prairie is surrounded almost entirely by basalt cliffs. It rises abruptly on the north, east, and west, but slopes gently on the south, providing a spectacular view of the whole city.

I spent countless hours with Kyle and friends, or just alone, exploring, writing, singing, napping, dreaming, listening to music, or kissing girls up on the prairie. It was one of my favorite places of all time. Another sacred place. Our home life was fairly oppressive because of our parents' dysfunctional marriage. The outdoors was our escape.

The land across the street from my house was too steep for construction. It led to the top of the prairie. Kyle and I would make the long, steep climb up the basalt rock covered with sagebrush, pretending we were army soldiers; when we got to the top, we would sit and gaze on the land, city, and people. I was twelve and in both a real and symbolic way, this expanded view represented the next six years of my life. I grew from being an isolated child with no real exposure to the outside world to an interconnected member of a generous, flourishing community. That community formed me, just like this land had formed the prairie we were sitting on.

As a young boy I loved being alone in nature. I never felt lonely. Over the next six years, I still loved experiencing nature by myself, but sports, beginning with soccer, which I began playing competitively at age eight, allowed me to grow from an awkward, shy kid into a quiet explorer of the outside world, the social world, and the vast inner cosmos.

During this period, I made lifelong friends, companions who still challenge me to this day to be the best version of myself. I loved and had my heart broken by love. I learned to share my fears and vulnerability. I cried, was baptized by tears and lifted up by friends.

Athletics was the engine that gave me the confidence to do everything I did. My success in athletics allowed me to shed my shyness and social awkwardness.

My reaching that point, though, was quite improbable.

I was born with a disorder that turned the bottoms of my feet inward toward each other. Metatarsus adductus is a foot deformity believed to result from a baby's positioning inside the mother's womb. In my case, the tendons on the outsides of my feet were longer than those on the insides, causing the soles of my feet to point toward each other instead of down.

Metatarsus adductus occurs in about one or two per thousand

live births and is more common in firstborn children like me. Fortunately, the disorder is correctable with proper care and treatment.

From the get-go, my mom would stretch my feet each time she
changed my diaper. She would tie my baby shoes tight to coax the
bones to grow straight. I had to wear them on the opposite foot—
left shoe on the right foot, right shoe on the left foot—to help correct the problem. I even wore casts on my lower legs when I was six
months old. My mom decided to get rid of them after I somehow
kicked one of the knee-to-toe plaster casts off, resulting in a pool
of blood and skin. My mom feared that I might be severely disabled, and my dad was worried about my athletic future. Eventually,
the bones straightened, and the tendons in my inner calves and
ankles mostly corrected. My feet ended up with a slight bow, or C
shape, so I walked on the outsides of my feet, would wear out shoes
quickly, and rolled my ankles constantly. Otherwise, I experienced
no major issues with the condition after it was corrected.

Both of my parents had athletic backgrounds, but as a teacher,
my mom wasn't into sports like my dad. He was obsessed, especially
with football and baseball.

My dad was naturally athletic. At 6-foot-1, 190 pounds, he was
taller and lankier than I was. He used to brag that he could run
the 40-yard dash in 4.6 seconds without any training. He played
baseball and football at Gonzaga Prep and was drafted in the 13th
round of the Major League Baseball draft by the California Angels.
Football, though, was his first love. At the time, his parents were
not in a good relationship, and football allowed him to express his
anger on the field. He was a running back and defensive back at
Gonzaga Preparatory School, where in seventh grade, while flipping through his senior year book, I learned his nickname was
"Psycho." He earned a football scholarship to the University of
Washington, but his playing career lasted just two years because of
an undiagnosed pelvic rotational injury.

I was built more like my mother, shorter and stockier. My mater-
nal grandmother, Patricia Matthiesen, was an accomplished swimmer in her day. She had a room full of medals and a 25-meter pool

at her home in Redwood City, California. She swam daily until she was about ninety-four, and when we visited her, she always made us swim laps before allowing us to play in the water. We learned kick turns and all the strokes: freestyle, backstroke, butterfly, and breaststroke. At the time, I didn't love lap swimming, I just wanted to play. But the mandatory laps eventually became enjoyable and made me into a strong swimmer. They helped develop the body positioning and endurance that allowed me to become a better all-around athlete.

At an early age, my dad bought me balls for multiple sports and taught me the basics of each one. One of my dad's favorite stories is about the first time he showed me how to swing a plastic wiffle-ball bat. I was five, and I don't remember the details, but Dad said he took me into the backyard of the house we rented near Audubon Park and instructed me on the basics of how to swing. Then he threw me a pitch, and I blasted the plastic ball across the yard and over the roof of our house. Dad later said he realized at that moment that he might have something special on his hands.

Sports became my social outlet, my only real exposure to the outside world. I wasn't aware of it at the time, but when I look back, kids seemed to like me because I was good at sports. Consequently, I made friends quickly.

Soccer was the perfect sport for me. I wasn't a particularly big kid but I was naturally fast, quick, and agile. I started playing in the third grade and took to the sport immediately. The team consisted of a bunch of kids from a different part of town, who I didn't know. I came to the team with a couple of church friends. This was the first time I started being called Steve instead of Stephen. Our team colors were red so we fittingly were called the Red Rockets.

I vividly remember my first game at the North Sports Complex, where I would spend an inordinate amount of my life over the next five to six years. Soccer, at this age, was just a bunch of kids buzzing around the ball like bees to a hive. Early in the game, I got the ball, was able to break away from the swarm, and smoke past everyone for half the field to score. I remember the breakaway more fondly than the goal. I can still see the brown and green of the dying grass and remember how thrilling it felt to pull away from the kids pursuing me. The memory remains branded in my mind forty years later.

I played for the Red Rockets for three years and eventually developed into one of the better junior players in the city. I made a select team in our region and was invited to try out for the local premier team, the highest-level team for kids my age. I made it and was a key player for two years.

By the time I reached seventh grade, the church school had fallen apart, so I transferred to Assumption Catholic, a private kindergarten-through-eighth-grade school in the northwest Spokane suburbs within walking distance of our house in Five Mile Heights. My mom got a teaching position there and was also my homeroom teacher that year. I joined the seventh-grade class, which had more than thirty kids. All of this was a huge transition. Suddenly, there were cute girls and big boys everywhere I turned. The newness of it all was both exciting and scary.

My worldview expanded greatly during this time. I got in a fight with a guy who became one of my best friends in the class. I blossomed into an all-star baseball player. I started alpine skiing, a sport I pursued as long as I was able. I had my first girlfriend. I regularly snuck out of our new house and walked to my friends' houses, where we would roam the neighborhood for miles, playing and exploring. These adventures were pretty innocent but could turn mischievous. We set up construction barriers from road repair sites and put them in the middle of a highway, so people driving would have to move them. When I was thirteen, on one of these adventures I had my first beer at one of our neighborhood parks.

All the while, sports was hastening my development. I learned that putting yourself out there and making yourself vulnerable to other people is an important key to a happy and successful life.

There were also some rough learning experiences along the way. I was extremely competitive and sometimes I struggled with my emotions. Early on, when I was eight or nine, I'd cry on the sidelines after we lost a game in a soccer tournament. In eighth-grade baseball, I got kicked out of a game because I yelled at the umpire and told him he sucked.

Gradually, though, I started to mature and learn to manage my emotions in athletics.

I was introduced to football in the eighth grade. To that point, I had only played baseball and soccer. My friend and soccer team-mate Jason Mark persuaded me to go out for the football team. I was hesitant, but he begged me to attend one practice just to see if I liked it. I still remember that first practice. I didn't realize it at the time, but I was pretty big for a thirteen-year-old, about 5-foot-11 and 140 pounds. The coach started practice with hitting drills. I laid into some guy and knocked him on his back, "flatbacked" in football parlance. I felt an adrenaline rush I had never experienced before. I thought, *Man, this is amazing!*

Up until then, soccer was my passion. At the levels I was play-ing, soccer was exponentially harder than football, because football required far less endurance. In soccer, I would be running nonstop for forty-five minutes each half of the game. In football, I'd run for five to ten seconds, then stand in a huddle for a couple minutes. I remember thinking, *Man this is easy!* The afternoon after my first football practice, I went to soccer practice. We ended the workout with our regular three-mile run, and I was exhausted. My feet and ankles were killing me. I mentioned this to my mom, so she put my feet in an ice bucket to ease the pain. At our next practice, before our final tournament of the season, I mentioned to my coach that I was planning to play football. He absorbed this for a moment then told me that three sports would be too much; I should choose between football and soccer. That night, I called him and told him I was withdrawing from soccer after that weekend's tournament.

I played the entire football season during my eighth-grade year and really enjoyed it. Assumption was a small parochial school, so we had to join forces with another school in the area, St. Charles Catholic, to have enough players to field a football team. This team made it to the playoffs and lost in the championship.

On the first play of the first football game I ever played, I ran down on a kickoff and hit a guy so hard that I knocked myself silly. I didn't lose consciousness, but I felt a lot of pain throughout my entire body, along with a massive buzz of adrenaline. I loved it. For some reason, I found a process where I would really focus my attention right in the place I felt pain. Almost, like I would become the pain. I didn't conceptualize it this way in eighth grade, but over the course of my football career, I found the process of moving closer and closer to physical pain so fascinating, because through this intimate focus, it was no longer pain. I started to flourish on the football field. I enjoyed its combination of mental and physical toughness. I had loved soccer, but once football took over, I never missed it.

Toward the end of my eighth-grade year, I had to decide where I'd go to high school. About half of the kids in my Assumption class were planning to attend Gonzaga Preparatory, a private Jesuit school located in northeast Spokane. Prep, as it was known, competed in the top sports division in the state and featured historically strong baseball and football programs, my two main sports. The choice was obvious, but there was a problem. Tuition was $3,000 a year, which was a lot of money for us. My dad said he would pay for me to go to Gonzaga Prep, but I was on my own to pay for college. I wanted to enjoy the next four years, and I was confident that I would figure out what to do after that.

Gonzaga Prep's football teams have always been legendary, but the school also encouraged students to lose "yourself" in the practice of serving others. They also emphasized developing strong social relationships and spiritual exploration for their students. This culminates in a weekend retreat called Search. The details of Search are secret, but it was my first experience of understanding that everyone has faults and deep pain. I didn't grow up Catholic, but the loving, open-minded, and welcoming Prep community was exactly what I needed to feel at that stage of my teenage life.

My sophomore year was one of exponential change and growth. My parents' marriage reached a fever-pitched level of dysfunction.

After years of yelling and screaming for hours and hours, their fighting escalated to the point where they got physically violent with each other and finally decided to separate. I felt enormous relief when dad moved out. Their split, and eventual divorce, was the best thing for everyone. It was refreshing to live in a quiet house, without the constant turmoil. As painful as their marriage was on me and my brother, it helped me see that I wanted something better in my relationships and marriage.

Later that year, I started dating a girl one year younger than me, Jen Austin. During our first conversation, in the cafeteria amongst the noise and laughter, I remember Jen seemed to have an authenticity to her. She was transparent and real. We added our laughter to the room. I dated Jen for the rest of my time at Prep, with a couple of breakups. One absolutely crushed me, and I think one crushed her. But our relationship would shape my perspective on friendship and love, or more specifically, romantic love, for the rest of my life.

I certainly did not emerge from Gonzaga Prep spotless. I was caught cheating in biology class. Once, while serving as our basketball team's mascot, a "Bullpup," I got ejected from the game and watched the second half of our district finals from the top row of the Spokane Coliseum. Who knew you could be ejected for stealing the other mascot's head and tossing it into the stands? I also might have tried to stuff a freshman or two into a garbage can. I had plenty of jock moments, with all the good and bad that come with that.

But all in all, my time there was good; in fact, I'd say "glorious."

Academically, I did well. I enjoyed language arts and physics and saying yes to things other than sports, like acting in plays.

I was taught to think for myself, which disgruntled my parents, to say the least. I learned to love my neighbor, and even my so-called enemies, as myself. In so many ways, the school didn't just shape my boyhood; it formed me into the man I am today. The friends I made there are still my best friends. They support and challenge me to be the best version of myself. Five of them served as groomsmen in my wedding, thirteen years after our graduation.

———

AND MAKE NO MISTAKE, I was mostly unformed before Gonzaga Prep. At freshman orientation in the fall of 1990, my dad had to explain how the combination to my locker worked. And he had to do it over and over again. I was a clueless, formless boy just beginning to take shape.

4

Sports

Everything negative—pressure, challenges—
is all an opportunity for me to rise.

—KOBE BRYANT

Gonzaga Prep was a longtime high school football power in Washington State. They regularly won the Greater Spokane League (GSL) title and produced some of the state's top players. If you were a young football player in Spokane, you aspired to one day play for the Bullpups. The program is so well established that most of the two-deep roster is always dominated by upperclassmen. I was one of the rare sophomores to start on the varsity teams.

I learned to play the game with intelligence and passion. Playing alongside one of my lifelong best friends, Jim Salters, we dominated opponents defensively. Jim lived with our family when my parents divorced and played linebacker next to me for three years at Gonzaga Prep. He was the valedictorian of my senior class and went on to star as a linebacker for Princeton University. I became a team captain as both a junior and senior and won the GSL Defensive MVP award both years.

By my junior year, I had started to garner attention from college football programs. The recruiting experience was quite an adventure. I didn't receive a lot of interest early on, in part because I didn't attend any of the summer camps, where you can make a name for yourself with college scouts. I was either at the lake with my friends or busy with baseball. Also I was 5-foot-11, 195 pounds, which is tiny by major college standards for my position, linebacker.

In baseball, I was Gonzaga Prep's starting center fielder for three seasons and was named the Most Valuable Player of the Greater Spokane League during my senior season. I broke the league's home-run record in the last game of my senior year, hitting opposite-field home runs. I also wanted to consider colleges with good baseball programs.

My dad and I thought baseball would eventually prove to be my best avenue to professional sports, because we both figured I was too small to play in the NFL. The idea was to get a football scholarship, since it paid the full price of tuition, room, and board, and play both sports, with the goal of ultimately trying to make it to the major leagues as a professional baseball player.

I was interested in the University of Washington, where my dad played, and was invited to their "junior day" in the spring before my senior year. There were a bunch of top football prospects on campus that day, and I was the smallest linebacker by far in the group. UW stopped recruiting me after that.

In the end, my recruitment boiled down to three Pacific-10 schools: the University of Oregon, Stanford, and Washington State.

But, this was before Oregon became OREGON. At the time, they weren't sponsored by Nike and had yet to grow into a major football power competing for national championships. Also, they didn't have a baseball program at the time, so the Ducks were strictly a fallback option for us.

Stanford was my dream school. It checked all the boxes: a prestigious academic institution, which was the ultimate focus for me. They also had a great football tradition, stemming from a legendary head coach: Bill Walsh. The odds of my playing professional sports were microscopic, so I wanted to get the kind of elite education that would help me flourish after athletics and graduation.

What's more, several Gonzaga Prep players had gone on to play there. One of them was Justin Strand, who I played with during my sophomore season, when he was a senior. Justin was a blue-chip recruit, a 6-foot-2, 220-pound linebacker; every major school in the country had recruited him. He was also a great dude. Stanford's recruiting coordinator noticed me on tape while he was evaluating game film of Justin. I happened to be at school when the recruiter was visiting and he told me that he thought I had better instincts at the position than Justin, and that Stanford would be monitoring my progress. Our linebacker coach, Mark Machtolf, was also my head baseball coach at Gonzaga Prep and the person I most respected athletically. Mark had gone to Stanford on a football scholarship and played baseball there as well. He ended up switching to baseball full-time and wound up becoming the College World Series MVP. My intention was to follow a similar path.

During the recruiting process, I received handwritten letters and phone calls from Coach Walsh. These letters made a huge impression on me. He was considered one of the best coaches in football history, having led the San Francisco 49ers to three Super Bowl championships during his ten-year tenure in the NFL. He was now back for a second stint at Stanford, the place where he had launched his head coaching career in 1977. In one of his letters, he invited me to visit their campus in Palo Alto, California, and wrote that he would offer me a scholarship when I was there. I read that letter sitting alone in the basement of our house on Dell Drive, looking out the large glass sliding door in silent solitude. *Holy shit balls . . . This is really happening. I'm going to go to one of the most prestigious academic institutions in the world, and learn from one of the greatest coaches in the history of this game.*

Things changed on November 28, 1994, when Coach Walsh abruptly resigned. Tyrone Willingham, an assistant coach at Notre Dame, was hired as his replacement two weeks later. The recruiting coordinator, who was one of the few members of Walsh's staff that Willingham kept, reassured me that the scholarship was still in place, and Stanford flew me and my dad down for an official recruiting visit in December.

I was a little nervous before the trip to Palo Alto. There were about fifteen recruits on the visit. One of our first stops was the team meeting room. We walked in and saw fifteen Stanford Cardinal jerseys hanging on the stage of the amphitheater-style room. Each one had a recruit's high school number and last name on it. I was in awe seeing my number, 34, and "Gleason" on the back of the jersey. Justin Strand was my host for the visit. We went to a couple of fraternity parties, ending the night on a balcony at a frat house that overlooked Greek row. As I surveyed the scene, it started to sink in: I would be on this campus next year, starting a whole new chapter in my life.

The next day was the final day of the trip, and I was scheduled to meet with Coach Willingham. This was standard operating procedure for every recruit, the time when the official scholarship offer would happen. I was no longer nervous. I felt confident, envisioning the coach saying, "Steve, on behalf of Stanford University, and our football team, I would like to offer you a full scholarship."

We were escorted to Coach Willingham's office, which was narrow and lined with windows along the left side. He got up from behind his massive wooden desk on the other side of the room. He was stoic during the introductory formalities, and we all sat down. Things moved quickly, as expected. Willingham said, "Steve, I've watched your film, and I've made the decision that you won't be a good fit here at Stanford." After a moment of stunned, tense silence, he added, "We don't think you have the toughness to be a linebacker here."

Shock.

What the fuck?! Am I dreaming?

I was trying to process the words coming out of this man's mouth. There was further silence and tension. My mind raced. I didn't know what to do or say. My dad spoke up: "Did you say that Stephen isn't tough enough to play here?!" He paused in disbelief. "Then, you definitely haven't watched film on him."

I am not the type of person who's going to argue or beg for anything, so I just stood up, shook his hand, and said, "OK, thanks, Coach. I'll see you down the road. . . . But my dad's right." We walked out of the office.

Just like that, a dream derailed.

On the ride back to the hotel, my dad did most of the talking.

I was absolutely crushed, but I didn't have anything to say. I felt like I was the victim of a prank that everyone else was in on, so I remained unemotional on the outside, despite my internal anguish.

The following Monday back at Gonzaga Prep, I met with Coach Machtolf in the football office. I stayed reasonably composed because I respected him so much, but I mostly felt embarrassed that I'd thought I could do what he had done.

Later that afternoon when school let out, Chris Pettigrew, one of my closest friends in high school, met me at my locker and asked me how I was doing. He knew I was struggling. Senior hall was empty other than the two of us standing in the afternoon shadows. I trusted Chris. The tsunami of emotions that had been swelling within me over the past twenty-four hours finally crashed through. Full of tears, I told him that I was embarrassed, felt rejected and so fucking hurt. Chris listened to it all, like the great friend that he was, and still is today.

In the end, I accepted a scholarship offer to Washington State University (WSU), in Pullman, Washington, about seventy-five miles south of Spokane. Coach Mike Price was the first Pac-10 coach to offer me a scholarship, and I intended to reward his loyalty. He believed in me when a lot of other coaches didn't. Plus, the defensive coach, Bill Doba, had created a position in the Washington State defensive scheme that was perfectly suited to my size, speed, and skill set.

It turned out to be a perfect place for me. It was far enough away from Spokane for me to be independent, yet close enough to home for me to be comfortable and still see friends and family. My family was able to watch every home game from the stands at Martin Stadium. I was able to play football and baseball and attract attention from both the NFL and MLB. I lived with friends from Spokane whom I'd known since the seventh grade. As a continuation of my world's expansion, I also became close friends with a more diverse group of teammates than I'd ever experienced. Guys from major California cities, who had literally raised themselves. They had seen family members shot and killed. Some of them were the first in their family to attend college.

The first day we were on campus, there was something of an orientation. In the afternoon, we met with the WSU sports psychologist to talk about how we were raised, where we were from, our experience with racial issues and violence. We sat on the floor of the WSU gymnastics room, and each player introduced himself and shared his background and life experience. There was a wide array of kids. Everyone was pretty transparent. Several players were similar to me, from a nondiverse city where race was seen as a side issue, unless, of course, you were a racial or ethnic minority. When Mike Schwartz's turn to speak came up, he started off by saying he was from Chehalis, Washington, a town of 7,439 people on the west side of the state about ninety miles south of Seattle. He was hesitant initially, then said, "I'm from a small town. There weren't really any racial issues." He paused for an awkward moment and seemed reluctant to talk. Finally, he turned to the player next to him, looked him in the eyes, and said, "I've never actually been this close to a Black person before." The group of us detonated with laughter. Any tension in the group evaporated. We weren't Black or White; we were all just kids embarking into unknown territory. We were now family.

I SAT OUT my freshman season after I had arthroscopic surgery for a meniscus tear in my knee a couple weeks before the opening game. It was a humbling experience, the first time in years where I wasn't the focus and key part of a team.

I joined the Alpha Tau Omega fraternity and lived in the frat house during my freshman year while studying architecture. I loved the subject and thought it was something I could enjoy in the future. During the spring semester, I went to class, then headed to spring football practice, and after that, I would play a baseball game. Then I'd study, and try to participate in fraternity activities. By the end of the semester, I was worn out. Something had to give. I felt like I had three full-time jobs—plus I was partying way too much. I had to really think about who I wanted to become and what goals to pursue. Playing two sports forced me to be disciplined and responsible. I moved out of the fraternity house, and switched from architecture to management information systems, which is still a tough major, but not nearly as time-intensive as architecture.

The next few years, I spent in a "live out" house just west of campus. The house was a block from the fraternity, so I could join the madness if I wanted, but it was far enough from the epicenter that I could focus and rest. I found this to be my style—close enough to the culture, but outside the wake.

During my red-shirt freshman season, I finally got back on the football field, playing mostly on special teams, the units that are on the field during kicking plays. On an idyllic fall day in the home opener against the no. 25–ranked Oregon Ducks, I was playing the 5 spot on the opening kickoff. The 5 position is basically "the Dude" on kickoff coverage, the spot coaches assign to their best tacklers. Kickoff coverage is the most intense, focused, and dangerous play in football. It's basically a high-speed human demolition derby, with every player running full speed for more than fifty yards before hitting or tackling someone. That day, I raced downfield, and flew past all the blockers. I had the kick returner in my sights and was coming at a perfect angle of attack toward him. Life moved in slow motion. I was in the flow. *Keep this angle. He doesn't see you. Tighten the angle. He's committed. He doesn't fucking see you! Get some!!* I blindsided the returner. I had waited a year for this. I jumped up and celebrated with the fans. After a year on the sideline, it was glorious.

The next morning, before our team review of the film, the defensive backs coach, Craig Bray, pulled me to the side in the hallway outside the film room. Coach Bray was one of the most direct, critical, no-nonsense coaches I've been around.

"Steve," he said, "I have coached for a long time, including years in the NFL. I'll tell you that if you can play special teams like you did yesterday, there are NFL teams that will keep you around. In fact, you could last a long time at the next level."

I kept that comment in mind throughout my college career. It helped shape my entire approach to training and playing. It truly gave me the confidence that I could one day play in the NFL.

I was small by Pac-10 linebacker standards, 5-foot-11, 214 pounds. The average linebacker in our league was 6-2, 232 pounds. But I was able to compensate by using my intelligence, speed, and technique to anticipate plays before they happened. Plus, I was playing a position that accentuated my strengths and hid my lack of size. The weak side, aka "Willy," linebacker position in the defensive scheme run by our defensive coordinator, Coach Bill Doba, was created for rangy players who could make plays from one side of the field to the other. Coach Doba was one of the architects of the Palouse Posse, the great WSU defense that led the nation in total defense in 1994. In this scheme, I rarely had to take on big offensive linemen and was freed to pursue ball carriers using my speed and instincts.

I became a starter as a sophomore and led our team in tackles (100) and tackles for loss, including one particularly memorable stick in a 38–28 win against Stanford, right on the Cardinal sideline, at the feet of Coach Tyrone Willingham. As I got up and ran back to the huddle, I gave him a wink, "Hi, Coach." That year, I helped lead Wazzu to the Rose Bowl for the first time in sixty-seven years. It's still considered the greatest season in the history of the football program. We had some great players. Quarterback Ryan Leaf was a Heisman Trophy candidate and the no. 2 overall pick in the 1998 NFL draft. Our defensive line also had two second-round picks: tackle Leon Bender and defensive end Dorian Boose, who both died young, tragically; one of a seizure and one by suicide.

We played the unbeaten and no. 1–ranked Michigan Wolverines. Their roster was loaded with future NFL players Charles Woodson, Brian Griese, Chris Howard, Dhani Jones, Tai Streets, and Anthony Thomas. A crowd of 101,219 packed the stadium. We played them down to the wire, but they ultimately prevailed 21–16. I finished with a game-high nine tackles.

That same year, I started in center field for the WSU baseball team. I finished the year hitting .290 with six home runs and six triples, one short of a school record.

We weren't as successful in my junior and senior football seasons, but I was able to flourish individually. I became a team captain and continued to rank among the team leaders in tackles. I made the All-Pac-10 Conference team and the league's all-academic team. I also lettered both years in baseball as the team's starting center fielder.

I learned some essential life lessons during my time at Washington State. I began to understand that our power resides not in our physical strength or appearance. Our true power is in our mindset. I learned that sharing weakness with teammates and friends ultimately makes a stronger squad. I learned that being fully prepared can open your eyes to opportunities where others only see defeat. That is something in which I have continued to trust.

5

Saints

Impossible is not a fact. It's an opinion.
Impossible is not a declaration. It's a dare.
Impossible is nothing.

—MUHAMMED ALI

M y NFL draft prospects as a college senior boiled down to this: I was a microscopic long shot.

Just before the spring before the 2000 NFL draft, I heard comments from NFL scouts similar to those I had heard from college coaches as a high school prospect: *You're a great football player, and love your tenacity on the field, but you're too small.* They were just being honest. I knew the odds.

A handful of scouts told me that I was on their draft board as a strong safety, potentially a late pick in the fifth, sixth, or seventh round. That kind of made sense. My time of 4.46 seconds in the 40-yard dash was easily fast enough to be a safety, but there was one problem: the number of times I'd played safety in my life was exactly zero.

When draft weekend arrived on April 15–16, I didn't even watch or follow along the first day. While the top prospects were invited to the big event the league staged at Madison Square Garden in New York City, I stayed in Pullman and monitored things from my apartment. My agent, Ken Staninger, had given me a good read on where my prospects stood, so I had no expectations. The entire draft lasted just two days back then, with the first three rounds of selections on Saturday and the final four rounds on Sunday. A handful of scouts called me to say that they were looking at me on day 2, but they had a lot of other guys they were also considering. My agent and I updated each other periodically, but I wasn't surprised when I didn't get picked at all. In all, thirty-one linebackers and twenty safeties were drafted over those two days. My agent and I knew that if I had any chance to make the NFL, it would be on special teams, just like Coach Bray had told me a few years earlier.

Scouts for the New York Jets, Oakland Raiders, and Pittsburgh Steelers called me after the draft to see if I was interested in signing a free agent contract with them. Other teams reached out to my agent.

Most teams projected me to play safety, which I fully understood given my size. During my training for the draft, I prepared for the position switch by slimming down to 210 pounds from my college playing weight of 215 to 218. The weight loss would help my speed.

The Indianapolis Colts' head scout called me to say they wanted me to play outside linebacker. They were really thin at the position. On all of these calls I stayed stoic and noncommittal, but the linebacker opportunity was an intriguing option for me. After checking their roster, and their draft class, and comparing their situation to that of the other interested teams, my agent and I elected to go with the Colts. They offered me a whopping $5,000 signing bonus, which was more money than I had ever seen. I remember thinking *Well, if I don't make it in the NFL, I can travel the world for years!*

I immediately spent a lot more time in the WSU weight room, to put on more muscle, so at least I would be a little closer to legitimate linebacker weight. I reported to Indianapolis a month later at 214 pounds.

Going to Indiana was an exciting and scary time. My mom always encouraged me to explore the world, but I had never lived beyond a seventy-mile radius of Spokane. I was lonely and missed my friends and family in Washington.

The Colts kept all the rookies in the same hotel. I went back there one day after a morning workout feeling a tenuous separateness from a world in which I wasn't sure I belonged. Feeling like I was in a foreign country, I would lie on the couch looking out the window, staring into the parking lot of a massive strip mall.

My downtime was spent studying my playbook and listening to music.

I was comforted with the newly released album from my favorite band, Pearl Jam—*Binaural*. The lyrics of one song, "Insignificance," seemed to perfectly reflect my circumstance.

> *The plates begin to shift*
> *Perfect lefts come rolling in*
> *I was alone and far away*
> *When I heard the band start playing.*

As had been the case since Pearl Jam's debut record exploded on the scene my freshman year of high school, Eddie Vedder, the band's lead singer, seemed to know exactly what I was going through. Instead of sending me deeper into feelings of loneliness and insignificance, I felt as if I had a companion with me. As it has for most of my life, music helped me grieve, heal, and move forward.

As always, the plates continued to shift. The day before the rookie offseason training program began that May, the Colts put me through some defensive back drills in front of all their defensive coaches and promptly moved me to safety. *Thanks, guys. Glad I bulked up to 214!*

Trying to make an NFL roster as an undrafted rookie is almost impossible. The odds are stacked against you. You're at the bottom of the pecking order in everything: salary, playing time, amenities, coaches' attention. And the Colts were loaded with talent, including future Hall of Famers Peyton Manning and Edgerrin James. I was assigned jersey No. 45.

"*I'm pretty frustrated right now,*" I wrote in my journal on July 26, 2000. "*My coach reduced my reps today. I don't make any more mistakes than the guy behind me. I'm a better football player. I'm tougher. I don't know if Coach has given up on me or what, but it has made me*

irritable. . . . I knew it was going to be tough. I knew that from the begin-
ning. I know I can compete. God has a plan for me. I need to talk to my
parents. It's quite lonely. They can't break my will. I will fight and kick
and scream."

I played well on special teams during the preseason games and
started to gain some confidence. While I wasn't really sure if I had
the skills, I embraced the idea that if I put in greater effort and
had better understanding and mindset than my opponent, I had a
better chance of succeeding and of playing in the NFL. That was
something I knew I could control.

In week 4 of the exhibition season, we played the Pittsburgh
Steelers in Mexico City, of all places. I had to get a passport, and we
were told that we might be short of breath in the game because the
city is well over a mile above sea level. I loved this type of adversity.
It was one of the later preseason games, so teams usually play low-
profile guys like me for a lot of minutes because they don't want to
risk getting any of their stars injured in a meaningless exhibition
game. Right before the game started, the skies over Mexico City
opened up and there was one of the most powerful thunderstorms
I'd ever witnessed. The officials kept the teams in the tunnels, and
the crowd of fans ran for cover as lightning and thunder exploded
brilliantly right above the stadium. In the midst of the bedlam
and anticipation for the game, I felt a profound quietness. *Man,*
this is awesome! This is my kind of game. Enjoy this, Steve-O. Take it
all in.

I played every down on special teams and maybe three-quarters
of the game at safety. I had a couple of special teams tackles and
recovered a fumble on a punt return that led to our first touchdown. I was all over the field at safety. I remember walking off
the field after the game and looking down at my uniform, so full
of grass stains I could barely see my number. I was so tired and
satisfied. I felt like a kid, or a soldier. I'd just fully and completely
exhausted myself in my mission to play in the NFL.

I made it to the final roster cut on August 27. Then, I was sum-
moned to meet Colts head coach Jim Mora in his office, where he
briefly and quite dispassionately cut me.

"Steve," he said, "I just don't believe you can play safety in the NFL."

The news was devastating, a crushing failure to process. Up to that point in my young life, I had mostly experienced personal success on the football field. I was overwhelmed by frustration and a feeling of failure. I had worked so hard and given everything I had to come so close to . . . *nothing*. I wasn't sure I would ever be able to shake the disappointment. It was like when someone you love breaks your heart.

I sat in the van on the way back to the Indianapolis airport, replaying in my mind each preseason game, each play. One play in particular stood out. In the second preseason game, we traveled to Seattle to play the Seahawks, my hometown team. Tons of my friends and family were at the game. On the opening kickoff, I flew down the field with wild abandon. The speed and ferocity of an NFL kickoff is truly incomprehensible if you have never experienced it firsthand. I blew past the guy trying to block me and was well positioned to absolutely blindside the kick returner on about the 10-yard line. The angle was really tight. I adjusted my trajectory slightly, had the returner in my crosshairs, drew closer and closer to my target, fired away, and missed—by about two inches. Millimeters were all that separated me from making that tackle.

As I jogged to the sidelines, Chad Cota, a veteran safety and one of my mentors during my time with the Colts, came up to me, slammed my shoulder pads with his fists, and said enthusiastically, "Dude, you were so close to demolishing that guy! If you make a tackle like that, I guarantee that you'll make this team."

As I traveled home, I was frustrated that a couple of inches might have been the difference between making an NFL team and moving back to my mom's house and the bedroom I'd slept in since I was twelve years old.

I was listless once I returned to Spokane. Although I had no direct exposure to, or formal training in, what it meant to be resilient, I was still fairly confident that I had the skills to play in the

NFL. My plan was to stay prepared for the next opportunity. I worked to be ready to have someone in my crosshairs.

My dad hounded me to call every team's general manager and tell them I was training and ready to play for them. This was not my style—at all. My nature, for better or worse, is to be patient and prepared, and if the opportunity doesn't come then perhaps this wasn't the path for me.

The opportunity did come.

In late October, the New Orleans Saints called and said they were going to sign me to their practice squad. We had played the Saints in our third preseason game, and I made a couple of tackles on special teams. In doing so, I caught the eye of Saints special teams coach Al Everest. I signed with them on November 21, 2000.

As luck would have it, after just one week on the practice squad, I was watching my new team play the Rams in St. Louis on TV, and two backup linebackers, guys who primarily played special teams, were injured. One of the team's personnel staffers called me after the game and told me that I'd be playing special teams the next Sunday: "So, be ready, Steve."

I went in early the next day to study film with Al. We studied extra film together after practice that entire week. He told me that he loved my style of play and that he had told Saints head coach Jim Haslett and Saints management that if the chance came up, he was 100 percent behind me becoming a Saint. This gave me a huge confidence boost.

That week with Al, I learned more about special teams technique, strategy, and how to prepare for a game than I'd learned the previous eight years in high school and college. Little did I know, this was just the tip of the iceberg of practical wisdom I would gain from Al.

On December 3, 2000, I made my official NFL debut, and on the opening kickoff of the second half, I made my first official NFL tackle. Flying down the field, I blew past the guy trying to block me and was pretty well positioned to blindside the kick returner, Deltha O'Neal. I adjusted my trajectory slightly, had the returner in my crosshairs, closer and closer to my target, and I fired away. Boom! I dropped him. After the play, as I was jogging toward the sidelines, I heard the public address announcer in the Superdome say, "Tackle by No. 37, Steve Gleason."

I went on to play the rest of that season on special teams. We made the playoffs, and I was able to help the Saints win the very first playoff game in franchise history, a 31–28 win over the St. Louis Rams, the defending Super Bowl champions, on December 30, 2000. We were rudely eliminated the next week by the Minnesota Vikings 34–16.

My resilience had paid off. I was playing in the NFL. After the season ended, I met with Saints management and they told me I would be playing in NFL Europe, with the Rhein Fire in Germany. This was something like a spring developmental league. So I would play ten extra games and get some experience at safety.

Before I went to Europe, I planned to meet my brother in Nicaragua to surf, so I would get some adventurous use out of my passport. My trip to Nicaragua opened me up to a style of exploration that would become part of the foundation for the rest of my life. Kyle introduced me to yoga and Hindu stories like the Ramayana, and suggested that he and I commit to spending less than $1,000 while we roamed the beaches of the country for a month. We met people and ended up staying with them or in hostels or in our tent. The generosity of people who had a fraction of the money of most of the people living in the United States astounded me.

Of the many glorious memories from that trip, one stands out. We decided to travel up the coast to Popollo. We hailed a bus that was actually an American school bus, but there wasn't any room in the passenger area. Kyle, who had been in Peru for the past year, was pretty fluent in Spanish and negotiated with the driver. He struck a deal where we would ride on the top of the bus over the dirt roads for a couple of hours. The driver cautioned us to watch out for power lines. On the drive, Kyle started singing "Peaceful Easy Feeling," by the Eagles. I joined in. Here we were, thousands of miles from home, in a foreign land, loving life, singing at the top of our lungs on the roof of a school bus.

And I got a peaceful easy feelin'
And I know you won't let me down
'Cause I'm already standin'
On the ground

When we got dropped off, the landscape was surprisingly barren and uninhabited, a coastal wilderness. Kyle asked for directions, and the driver just said to walk west and we'd run into the beach. We carried our backpacks and surfboards through the sandy terrain in an all-out windstorm for a few hours. We were exhausted and there were no waves, so we set up the tent on the beach and made some dinner. Hundreds of miles from civilization, we lay on the deserted beach. As dusk quickly turned to darkness, our favorite constellation, Orion, appeared as brilliant and bright as we'd ever seen it. We were struck with a profound sense of awe at the vastness of this scene. I felt so tiny and minuscule in the grandeur of the galaxy and the universe. My smallness was a beautiful gift. An immediate closeness and unity with the perfection of creation.

The trip changed my life. We traveled on a tight budget, but it's no exaggeration to say it was immeasurably priceless. The intimate connection with people and nature satisfied something within me that was the best and truest aspect of me.

AS I RETURNED TO FOOTBALL, it would be nice to say that the rest is history, but as we wrapped up training camp that fall, the Saints called me in and, briefly and with the same dispassionate tone, told me they didn't need me on the team. I was released on September 2, 2001.

Back to square one.

The day after I returned to the home and room I'd lived in since the seventh grade, I noticed that $5,000 was missing from my bank account. I texted my mom from my flip phone, asking her if she knew anything about it. She said no. I called my dad and asked the same thing with the same reply.

When I got home, I walked into the dining room that overlooked the neighborhood. My mom was sitting at the table with a letter in her hand. "Stephen, I'm sorry," she said as she handed over the letter with tears in her eyes. It was a lengthy explanation of how she was in some pretty serious financial trouble, and yes, she had taken the money. I was in absolute shock. My mom had been my rock. I would fall asleep on her lap while she read me stories as a toddler. I remember her offering me courage and strength when I was young and afraid to do things like climb a tall tree, or swim in the waves of the Pacific Ocean. When I experienced pain and embarrassment, all the mistakes I'd made in high school, she was there, without judgment. She was steadfast.

It was clear that Mom was twisted up inside, as I watched her break down in tears. I'd rarely seen her do this, other than in the rage-filled fights she had with my dad before their divorce. It was easy to forgive her, but I switched my bank accounts. Over the next twelve months, I gave her another $20,000, but had to finally stop. I also made the decision to move to my dad's house, a difficult decision that I still question to this day. I love Mom so much and I know this must have hurt her.

I DIDN'T KNOW HOW MUCH MORE of this football life I wanted to endure. I'd played an extra ten games in Europe, and my body and mind were weary. Despite this fatigue, I stuck with my training routine each morning and continued to stay prepared. Two months later, the Saints called again. One of the defensive backs on the team had accidentally shot himself in the knee; they needed me on special teams. Who knows what would have happened to my NFL career if that guy hadn't had such misfortune?

Once again I was lucky.

It has been said that luck is the residue of design, but I'm not sure that philosophical outlook rings true. Where we're born. Our DNA. Even the genetics and conditions that determine work ethic, self-control, or discipline. Are those the product of design? If one believes in some divine plan, it can be difficult to reconcile phenomena like infant deaths, or why approximately a dozen children die of starvation every minute. During my career, I had scores of people tell me, "God put you here for a reason." While I may have agreed with that, in the past, I had to chuckle at comments like that. Would they insist that was true if they knew the reason I returned to the Saints in 2001? It seems that in my NFL career there was very little design, if any. I think it was in large part due to luck.

In my second game back against the Atlanta Falcons, I recovered a fumble on a kickoff return that set up a touchdown and helped us to a 28–10 win. I played well enough down the stretch of the 2001 season that the Saints signed me to a three-year contract. That probably sounds comforting, but the NFL doesn't have guaranteed contracts, so since there was no signing bonus, the contract could be terminated at any point if I wasn't performing up to the organization's expectations.

During the 2002 season, I made the team, and we had the top special teams unit in the NFL. This was anchored by Coach Everest's teaching and wisdom, and highlighted by our star return man, Michael Lewis, or as I liked to call him, the "pocket rocket." Michael was known as the Beer Man because he worked as a Budweiser truck driver before he decided to give pro football a try in the Arena Football League. He eventually earned a tryout with the Saints and blossomed into one of the best return specialists— and stories!—in the league. Mike and I joined the Saints at nearly the exact same time and played in NFL Europe on the Rhein Fire together. In 2002, he returned two kickoffs and a punt for touchdowns and made the Pro Bowl and All-Pro team. I finished the season with a team-high 27 special teams tackles and also blocked a punt. Freddie McAfee was our veteran leader on special teams, but he pulled his hamstring and missed some games midway through the season. A popular phrase in sports, and especially football, is "When a man goes down, someone else has to step up." I quietly stepped up.

I certainly didn't see myself as a leader. I was merely working to do my job within the scheme and philosophy, and using the techniques Al Everest taught us. I led the special teams unit in nearly every category that year and enjoyed one of the best years of my career. I was named the NFL's Special Teams Player of the Week after I blocked a punt in a 34–24 win against the Carolina Panthers in week 10. It was the Saints' first blocked punt in five seasons. I was voted an alternate to the Pro Bowl, and ESPN named me to their Pro Bowl team. Freddie Mac was actually voted to the Pro Bowl that year as the special teams specialist, even though I had a better season statistically. But "Fast" Freddie certainly deserved to go, simply on the merit of his incredible seventeen-year career. He had taken me under his wing, and I was so stoked to be his teammate. I was happy with how things had turned out after two chaotic seasons.

I felt immense gratitude for this journey I was on. I also knew I owed nearly all my on-field success to Al Everest, the guy who noticed me two years earlier during the preseason and insisted that the head coach Jim Haslett and Saints management hire me. Al was my guru, as well as my friend.

One of his mantras was "A jackass works hard all day long, but at the end of the day, guess what?? It's still a jackass."

Al Everest taught me how to "work smart" in the NFL. He reinforced the concept that human power doesn't lie in height, strength, or speed. Our power resides in our mind. Al called everyone "stud." I remember one saying he dropped on me and others: "Hey, stud, great players develop great systems to create great habits. Mediocre players are lazy with their habits and routines. Do you want to be great or mediocre?" This insight resonated with me. I liked the idea of creating systems; habits and routines I didn't even think about, once they were developed. Al would repeatedly emphasize that games were merely a product of how I worked, trained, and studied *outside* the game. He worked to instill ways to enjoy the process of training, rather than just the games or objectives. He and I would sit in his office every day, studying opponents' patterns, habits, and style, going back and forth to help me create meticulous pre-practice and practice habits along with a strong pregame routine. I'm extremely lucky our paths merged. Similar to my experience with Coach Doba at WSU, Al's philosophy and approach to the game allowed me to flourish in the league.

The transition from an everyday starter in high school and college to strictly a special teams player was surprisingly easy. I just wanted to play, and I willingly embraced my role as the blue-collar, counterculture athlete. I'm not really sure why I was successful on special teams, but I suppose it's partly because I listened to and absorbed everything Al offered me. Over the next few years, through Al's coaching and a lot of hard work and practice, I established myself as one of the top special teams players in the NFL. I led the team in special teams tackles during those years and blocked a punt in each of the 2002, 2003, and 2004 seasons. Only future Hall of Famer Ed Reed blocked as many punts during that span. My teammates voted me the captain of the special teams units, and our opponents compiled their game plans around me on coverage and return units. Many teams would double-team me or target me with their best player.

During game weeks, I prepared meticulously so I would be able to execute my assignments. When the games rolled around, I played with creativity, intelligence, and intensity. Although I felt fear almost every time I stepped between the white lines, I was confident in my preparation and was usually able to maintain poise, but I had my moments. During the 2004 season, we were getting dominated by the Carolina Panthers. On a kickoff, I got trucked by Kemp Rasmussen. I was on my knees trying to digest the play, and he walked over and stood over me, subtly taunting me. How did I respond? I punched him right in the nuts. I quickly turned and started sprinting to the sideline, but I almost ran into a ref who was throwing a flag. Busted. I was ejected and got fined $10,000.

The violence of the game and the kamikaze nature of my special teams role took a physical toll on my body. I endured and played through numerous injuries, including getting knocked out cold twice on kickoffs and multiple knee injuries that required arthroscopic surgeries. I also broke my thumb, hyperextended my elbow, bruised my lung, pulled a hamstring, strained my neck, and suffered an abdominal injury that felt like I had swallowed a Chinese throwing star.

During the crazy dramatic ups and downs of those first two seasons of my NFL career, I encountered a lot of discontent, loneliness, and fear of my own insignificance. Looking back, I realize these were early glimpses of learning the wisdom of acceptance, patience, and trust. This acceptance, in my view, is the essential foundation of resilience. When I can accept reality *as it is*, then I have the opportunity to explore solutions, or transform myself to move forward in the midst of uncertainty and chaos. On a more tangible level, I learned the power of developing systems and habits to develop character, and to enjoy the process of bringing some order from chaos.

I would lean on my NFL experience during what would come later.

6

Michel

So brown eyes, I hold you near.
'Cause you're the only song I want to hear
A melody softly soaring through my atmosphere.
Where soul meets body.
— BEN GIBBARD, "Soul Meets Body"

In 2004, on the Thursday afternoon of the New Orleans Jazz and Heritage Festival in the main food vendor area, somewhere near the cochon de lait stand, amongst the joyfully sweaty music lovers and Native American war drums thrumming nearby, my world collided with the world of Michel Varisco.

That encounter changed the course of both of our lives.

Michel went to the University of Colorado in Boulder with Bart Morse. Bart and I knew each other through some of my good friends from Gonzaga Prep—Dave Stewart, Ed Bruya, Ryan Malone, and Todd Edmonds—who were in the same fraternity at the University of Washington as some of Bart's buddies.

Bart and I were, and still are, interested in seeking knowledge and truth. Also, we have fun together. I like to think of myself as creative, but Bart is much more creative than I am. And his creative ideas almost always resonated with me.

In 2004, Bart called me and said he was thinking about coming to New Orleans for Jazz Fest, as it is known by locals. I had discovered Jazz Fest a few years earlier, so I thought this was a stellar idea. It is one of the preeminent events on the New Orleans social calendar. The title really doesn't do it justice. First of all, the musical lineup for the two-week festival features acts from nearly every genre out there—rock, rap, blues, country, zydeco, even gospel—so it's not just a "jazz" festival. The shows are simultaneously held on thirteen stages strategically located around the infield of the Fair Grounds Race Course, so you can roam the grounds and see various acts at different times throughout each day. But Jazz Fest is about so much more than just the music. There are interview sessions with musicians, kids' shows, art and crafts stands, roving dance troops, and incredible food and drink stands from local and regional vendors. It's really one giant, communal party, with music as the backdrop. Like Mardi Gras, Jazz Fest is one of the unique and unifying events in New Orleans. Many New Orleanians plan their lives and calendars around the last weekend of every April and the first weekend of May.

For a music lover like me, Jazz Fest is one of the highlights of the year. I've been a regular since 2001, when I attended the Fest by myself during spring workouts before my second season with the Saints. I was so impressed by the community and culture, I vowed to attend every year if I was fortunate enough to make the team.

On the call, Bart mentioned that his friend from college, Michel Varisco, lived in New Orleans; he thought we should try to hang out with her at some point.

Bart's exact words were "Michel is a really cool chick, Steve-O."

I had moved into an apartment in Uptown New Orleans. Most of my teammates either lived in the gated communities of the surrounding suburbs or in high-end condos downtown, but I wanted to get a taste of the real culture and texture of the city. I was one of the few players, if not the *only* player, living in Uptown at the time.

The apartment was located in a large, old, oddly designed house owned by the Patterson family and located on the northeast corner of Coliseum Street and Louisiana Avenue. The two-story structure was L-shaped, with the main house (the short side of the L) facing Louisiana Avenue, one of the main boulevards in antebellum Uptown. The rest of the house (the long side of the L) extended behind the main building and featured two levels of small studio-style apartments. I'm guessing these were servants' quarters back in the day.

I lived in one of the first-floor rooms in the back portion of the complex, which made it feel like a quaint boutique motel. Outside of this back portion was a fully fenced-in yard that essentially served as a courtyard for the tenants. It had a barbecue grill and plenty of space to lounge and just hang.

My apartment was maybe 500 square feet, with high ceilings and lots of windows. Two sections were split by a tall brick fireplace and a partial wall. For being so small, the apartment had a very open feel to it. To the left of the entrance was a small daybed that went unused during my time there. This side of the apartment also had a nice bathroom and a tiny kitchen. The cooking space was so small, I could reach my arms out and touch both walls of the kitchen. On the opposite side of the apartment, farthest from the door, was the "living area," with a really cool loft.

Outside the front door there was a small pool. Above the pool, the owner had built a giant trellis, which held grapevines for his homemade wine.

I made countless meals in that tiny kitchen, then I'd sit on the stoop outside the front door, eating with just a pair of board shorts on. When I finished my meal, I'd just jump in the pool right from my stoop. Sometimes, I'd eat the hottest habanero pepper I could find from Whole Foods Market, sit and absorb the juices, and after the heat completely consumed my mouth, fall slowly into the pool.

Writing about it now conjures beautiful images and strong feelings of nostalgia. This is the place where I grew to love New Orleans, and one of its daughters.

Bart flew into New Orleans a day or two before the Thursday of Jazz Fest and stayed at my place. My brother, Kyle, was also staying with me, as he often did. The three of us spent our days hanging out, playing guitar, barbecuing, swimming, and talking about our various life philosophies.

On the Wednesday before Jazz Fest's second weekend, Bart called Michel to see what she was up to. She told him that the next day—"Locals' Thursday," as New Orleanians called it—was a special one because of the annual Jazz Fest Triathlon, known as the JFT.

Bart, Kyle, and I were curious: "A triathlon during Jazz Fest?!" We all assumed it was a serious, competitive event.

Michel explained that the JFT is essentially drunken revelry, structured around an informal, made-up "triathlon." A bunch of her brothers' friends from Jesuit High School in New Orleans had started the tradition. The group would gather at the New Orleans Museum of Art in City Park and bike 1.5 miles to the festival, which is held in the infield at the Fair Grounds Race Course. Around 5 p.m. that afternoon, they'd compete in the second leg of the JFT, a run around the Fair Grounds' one-mile dirt racetrack. Finally, there would be a swim in Bayou St. John, where according to Michel, guys would wear women's swimsuits and other home-made costumes. Each leg of the triathlon would feature a "shotgun start," where every participant was required to "shotgun" a beer before going past the starting line.

Bart got off the phone and explained everything to me and Kyle. We all agreed that it sounded awesome. Stoked, we headed off to Walgreens to buy swim caps for the bayou swim.

I don't remember having any expectations about Michel before meeting her. If anything, my expectations were low. The women I'd met in New Orleans were, how should I put it, ordinary, compared to my past. Fairly superficial, materialistic, and not interested in any type of exploration. During my first four years in New Orleans, I hadn't had any significant relationships.

Girls weren't really a top priority for me early in my career. I was focused on playing football and exploring the world. In the offseasons, Kyle and I traveled to places like Nicaragua, Ecuador, the Galápagos Islands, New Zealand, and the Lost Coast in northern California. We surfed as often as we could. I was also busy exploring my inner world. Guided by Kyle, my cousin Brendan, and my own calling, I practiced yoga and read books like *Awareness, People's History of the United States, Ishmael, My Ishmael,* and *Living Buddha, Living Christ.*

So I had no expectations when Bart, Kyle, and I showed up at Locals' Thursday. It was a typically humid New Orleans spring day, with the sun peeking through the clouds, baking the tens of thousands of locals in the crowd. Four years into my New Orleans tenure, I felt I could lay claim to being one of them. I mean, I was standing there eating boudin balls in a swim cap—that's as *New Orleans* as it gets, right? Then out of nowhere Michel appeared, a small, tan girl, with her thick mane of brown hair up in two buns on each side of her head. She was wearing a weathered red shirt proclaiming "Everyone Loves an Italian Girl." She kissed Bart on the cheek, walked over, and stood in front of me quite boldly. She looked down at my flip-flops, then looked at my shirt, then her huge brown eyes stared fiercely into my eyes.

She paused, a slightly puzzled look on her face. Four heartbeats later, she quipped, "Steve, you're a lot cuter than you look."

Half of me was confused with that intro, and the other half was pleasantly amused. I responded, "Uh . . . Hi, I'm Steve." And I thought, hmm, maybe this cute, bold Italian was not an ordinary girl after all. Michel's disarming, Yogi Berra logic put a smile on my face. She smiled, too, and came in with a kiss on the cheek.

I wouldn't call this a love-at-first-sight moment. I'm not a love-at-first-sight guy. I don't think that even exists.

But I was intrigued.

Kyle went off to the ATM while we munched on some Jazz Fest grub. Michel excitedly told us it was time for the watermelon sacrifice.

Watermelon sacrifice?! She failed to mention that on the phone the night before.

Among the many New Orleans traditions Michel and her family have exposed me to over the years, the JFT, and specifically this watermelon sacrifice ritual, rank as my favorites. I've loved it since Day One.

As Michel, Bart, Kyle, and I arrived at the Fais Do Do stage, some obscure afternoon musical act was wrapping up its set. The JFT participants were a mash-up of ragamuffin artists, bankers, bartenders, and slightly less ragamuffin stock traders, lawyers,

Marines, teachers, and since my initial 2004 participation, NFL football players. Like a rising tide, this beautiful flock of JFT urchins gravitated together, orbiting around an older, sun-drenched man who was dressed in a jumbled mishmash of legitimate running gear, equally legitimate voodoo garb, and a not-quite-legitimate ballerina tutu—this was the Watermelon Man.

Out of nowhere, a watermelon appeared in the trampled, muddy grass. Immediately people started piously chanting some droning mantra and satirically dancing, while swirling around the sacred fruit, like planets orbiting a star. After hearing the chant a couple of times, I was able to make out the words as I clomped and gyrated around the melon on its grass and mud altar.

> *Watermelon, watermelon, red to the rind,*
> *If you don't believe me, pull down your blind*

As I danced and sang with the hodgepodge congregation, I realized this was less satire than a truly reverential celebration of life in New Orleans—with all its sultry imperfections and sideways beauty. I was willingly and knowingly consumed, filled with the spirit of the tradition, chanting in my loudest voice.

> *Sell it to the rich, sell it to the poor . . .*
> *Sell it to the woman standing in that doooOOOOooor.*

After an uncomfortably, mesmerizingly long time, the Watermelon Man threw the melon high in the sky. It touched the sun. As it fell, I looked around at the faces of the parishioners and saw anticipation, eagerness, and salivation.

The watermelon crashed to the earth, exploded, and everyone pounced. Rabidly, they snagged pieces of the sacrifice off the sloppy turf and shoved them into their mouths, their faces dripping with red juice.

I joined right in. Basking in pure, unbridled joy.

After this watermelon sacrament, Michel introduced us to her brothers, Pauly and Vinnie, and her boyfriend, Hunter, who was the founder of the JFT. We told Hunter, and his JFT co-founder, a perpetually grinning, long-haired dude named Spitz, we were overwhelmingly impressed with the event so far.

The next event was the one-mile (8 furlongs) run around the Fair Grounds horse track. Then it was on to the final leg of the triathlon.

While the watermelon sacrifice was transformative, the finale sealed the JFT inauguration for me.

When Jazz Fest concluded at dusk, we left the Fair Grounds and walked with thousands of other sunbaked locals to the heavenly intersection of Mystery Street and Esplanade Avenue, a timeless triangular block of old, colorful, crooked houses. Esplanade also has a handful of tiny local, European-style restaurants with names like Lola's, Cafe Degas, and Santa Fe. Across Esplanade is a tiny triangular park with fountains and flowers, and benches and tables with chessboards carved into the tops. Adjacent to the park sits Terranova's, a tiny, equally triangular local grocery run by three generations of the Terranova family. Michel and I later made our first New Orleans home a block away from this magical, sacred place.

This wasn't the first time I'd been exposed to the nostalgic tranquility of the intersection of Mystery and Esplanade, but it was revealed in a new light—and life—for me on this Thursday evening as we made our way to the epic finale of the JFT.

On the north edge of this little slice of heaven is Our Lady of the Rosary Catholic Church, a small, ancient domed church adjacent to Cabrini High School, the all-girls Catholic school founded in 1905. The JFT group gathered in the parking lot of the Cabrini campus, which sits just across Moss Street from Bayou St. John.

The "triathletes" were dressed in various costumes, ranging from full-bodied, papier-mâché sharks to women's swimsuits worn by grown men. Some guys had water wings. I felt right at home, though slightly under-costumed in my swim cap. I was in my element, Peter Pan in Neverland.

In the parking lot where everyone was gathered, the Cabrini Dads' Club had set up a burger, beer, and hot dog stand for anyone and everyone leaving Mystery Street. After a time, the competitors began to prepare for the swim. I saw people taking shoes off, donning swimsuits and swim caps, and grabbing beers. I followed suit, then walked over to the rock wall on the border of the parking lot, amidst the bikes, helmets, and discarded clothes and looked out toward Bayou St. John, one of the most picturesque and popular vistas in the city. It is a serpentine waterway that flows serenely from Lake Pontchartrain along the eastern perimeter of City Park to the city's historic Mid-City neighborhood. New Orleanians flock to its dark, shallow waters to kayak, fish, picnic, and lounge along its banks. At its widest, the bayou is a couple of hundred yards across, but at the spot near the Magnolia Bridge where the swimming leg of the JFT took place, it narrows and is only about fifty yards wide.

I had never swam in Bayou St. John, nor in any of the warm, murky waters of the South. Standing next to Vinnie, I wondered, "Should I keep my shoes on? What the hell is on the bottom of that water?"

I'd heard ominous tales of cars, refrigerators, and assorted cast-off junk down there, rusting in the mucky bottom.

"You should be fine," Vinnie said, as he pressed his hand against the wall, leaned over, and untied his shoes.

Okey dokey . . .

I took off my shoes, and we all found the imaginary starting line for the shotgun start. Beers downed, our disheveled crew of costumed warriors stampeded through the Cabrini parking lot toward the bayou, took a right turn on to Moss Street, then found our way to the banks of the bayou just past the Magnolia Bridge. Several people started diving into the murky brown water. I didn't know how deep the bayou was, so I just did a swimmer's dive, skimming through the surface of the water. I was raised in the mountains of the Northwest. I'd only known natural water to be cold and clear. But this water was astonishingly warm. It felt like a mud bath—so foreign.

We swam through the chocolate, papier-mâché-melting waters, right next to the chrome-silver Magnolia Bridge. After crossing the bayou, I was climbing out of the sweaty water and heard Vinnie scream out in pain amid the mass of sloshing bodies behind me.

He'd cut his foot! The guy who had assured me that I would be fine barefoot in the bayou had a gash on his foot so gnarly it would later require a visit to the local emergency room for a tetanus shot.

Meanwhile, on the grass bank just above the bayou, the group started in on push-ups. Twenty of them, counted aloud in a military cadence. Then we migrated back to the Cabrini parking lot, where Hunter christened the day by bestowing spoof awards on a few people. We all collapsed in a pile of joyful exhaustion.

We ended up hanging out with this group later that night at a place in the Marigny neighborhood, a small white stucco-sided restaurant with a neon red-and-green sign, just east of the French Quarter. Bart, Kyle, Michel, and I gathered around a wobbly wood café table with a few others until the wee hours of the morning.

Over the weekend, Bart, Kyle, and I hung out some more with Michel, her brothers, and their crew. Michel even invited us to her parents' house in Lakeview for red beans and rice, the traditional Monday New Orleans meal. Michel's entire family was there: her father, Paul; her mother, Jill; and Pauly and Vinnie and their girlfriends. Michel's ninety-three-year-old grandfather, Big Lew, walked over as well from his house across the street. This was something I had never experienced before. Most families separate through the generations. College graduates leave to pursue careers. Children seek their independence. But the Variscos were different. Not only did they all stay in New Orleans over the generations, all of them lived within one mile of one another. One mile! Unbelievable. I learned through these early months of my friendship with Michel that it was the norm for families to stay together in New Orleans.

Michel's mom, Jill, was inviting and full of joy. She kept asking us, "Y'all need anything, baby?" And Jilly could cook! Red beans and rice was a meal I'd never had or even heard of before. And she kept inviting us to eat more. *Yes, ma'am!* Michel's dad, Paul, as I grew to learn over the years, is amazing. He is the best of us. He is a music lover and remains the lead singer of his still-popular, onetime high school band, Paul Varisco and the Milestones. We started spinning some of his massive record collection. It covered an entire wall in the living room. At some point, I asked him if he had a Led Zeppelin album, my favorite classic rock band. Not only did he have it, but he regaled us with the story of going to their 1973 concert in New Orleans. The Variscos were this totally functional, flourishing family unit. The type of family unit I'd longed for growing up. When it was time to go, Kyle, Bart, and I walked Big Lew home with Michel and he entertained us with some spectacular one-liners: "Don't get old," "I'm still kickin', but not that high," "Take your time and hurry up," and "Tough titties make strong babies," then as he struggled to unlock his door with his key he said, "Put a little hair over it, this'd be a lot easier."

A few days later, Michel came over to my apartment to hang with me, Kyle, and Brendan. I loved her transparency and realness. Michel had and still has this unique ability to say things that are borderline offensive, but people love her more for it. Like her remark to me the first time we met: "You're a lot cuter than you look!" It was like a Zen koan.

I'd grown to appreciate the unique underbelly of New Orleans, but this was the first time I'd been so close to it and experienced it through a group of such remarkable people. In Michel, her family, and her friends, I had found kindred spirits, people who shared my love of life.

Kyle and Brendan lived with me on and off during the 2004 season and we'd grown exceptionally close. We traveled together during the Saints offseasons. This upcoming offseason, Kyle, who I call "Bruzzie," and Brendan, who I call "Nerb," were planning a survival trip to the Lost Coast in northern California. I was exploring the idea of a five-week self-tour in New Zealand. We were a tough threesome to break into. But Michel had come over frequently throughout that year, and almost immediately we became a foursome. Kyle, Brendan, and I really had a love for Michel and her bright, honest spirit. She wore blue jeans, trucker hats, T-shirts, and Converse All-Stars. She was so much like us. She was really cute *and* one of the boys, too, this tiny, sprite-like bundle of energy, who would sit outside on the little concrete stoop that led to the courtyard at my apartment and captivate our group with stories. She could get us belly-laughing. Michel could definitely "hold the room." During that time she and Hunter broke up. They had dated off and on for a few years so this wasn't unusual. Michel would bring guys on dates to hang out with us, and we'd always tease her: "Ah, that guy is a tool!"

One night, the three of us were sitting on the floor, under the bedroom loft. Michel had just left, and I told Kyle and Brendan, "Damn, that girl is awesome. If one of us doesn't marry her, we're a bunch of dummies."

I'm no dummy.

Over the next few months, we hung out every day, as best friends. We went to the movies, read books aloud to each other, heard live music with her brothers, had dinner with her parents, and took Big Lew to lunch.

A few nights after the season ended, we were out at Cosimo's, a historic dive bar on Burgundy Street in the French Quarter, with our homie and my guitar teacher, Benny, and some women he'd picked up. We sat at a small square table, zoned in only to each other. After a couple of martinis, with some nervous energy Michel said, "Steve, I had a dream that you were dating my friend Ainslie but that we snuck on the other side of the levee and I kissed you anyway." After a moment's pause she said, "Usually it takes a day to stop feeling the feelings of my dreams, but this one won't go away even though I've tried to make it go away." And then, with her eyes looking at her feet, she said, "I think I like you." This was the silly, strange, and seductive part of Michel. She is so spontaneously open. I never know what she'll say next. She never knows what she'll say next!

I think I also knew at the time that we liked each other, but I was hesitant to go there. At least not just yet. We got to my house that night at 4:30 a.m. so I asked her to stay over. She did, but I didn't make a move.

A couple nights later I went out to dinner with Michel and her brother Pauly at Rock-n-Sake, a sushi restaurant in the Warehouse

District of New Orleans. Our conversation turned to adventure. I told them about the upcoming trip to New Zealand I had planned during the offseason.

"Man," Michel said, restlessly. "I need some adventure in my life."

"Well, this isn't super-adventurous, but I'm driving across the country in a couple days," I said.

I paused for a moment, as we all looked at one another, then I added, "You should come!"

She waffled. She mumbled something about having to work and that she would need to get her parents' approval. Yes, at twenty-seven, Michel, being the good Italian girl that she was, needed to run the idea past her mom. But Pauly endorsed the idea.

It was not easy to get a yes from Michel, but after getting her whole family's approval, she decided to come with me on the four-day journey from New Orleans to Spokane. We took my bio-diesel pickup truck, which Michel thought smelled like Popeyes chicken because it ran on vegetable oil instead of gasoline.

Midway through Texas we began talking about our past relationships and rebellious days. I'd already heard about some of her ex relationships and wild past, but we hadn't talked much about mine. I told her about the one girl I'd dated for three years in high school, Jen Austin.

She asked me how many people I'd slept with, and I told her none. After I dated Jen, I told myself that I wasn't going to have sex with someone until I have a similar connection, a true friendship with a girl. She was as surprised as I'm sure everyone reading this book is. She'd playfully brought with her a shiny red copy of the Kama Sutra, and very carefully put it back in her bag.

On the second night, we stopped at a hot spring in Winter Park, Colorado. We were alone, under the stars, looking at the perfectly lit snow-capped mountains. It was that scene where the new couple kisses for the first time. This was the moment. I was hesitant. Michel clearly noticed, confused.

"You're such a good friend of mine," I told her. "I don't want to mess this up."

I knew this was going to go one of two ways. Either we were going to date for a while, and then we'd eventually break up, which would be one of the worst things I could imagine. Or . . . we were going to get married and be together forever. Period. Those were the only two options. Was I ready for this? Both options were scary.

The next night, after a long day of driving, a guy with bare feet and a shirt that said "Holy Shit" checked us into a hostel. We lay there and hugged and Michel asked, "So . . . We still can't kiss?" This time, I relented. But before we kissed, I laid down a ground rule: "We have such a good friendship, if this is awkward for you or for me, I think we should stop and make it so we can still be friends."

She took the "awkward" line to mean that she needed to be a really good kisser. And she was. It wasn't awkward. It was best friends ascending to love. It was beautiful. And perfect. We fit well together and it was not weird at all.

Our relationship gradually developed into something that I think only a few people ever discover. Soul meets body stuff.

7

NOLA

You can live in any city in America, but New Orleans is the
only city that lives in you.

—CHRIS ROSE

The first few years of my NFL career were a crazy, chaotic
time. A dance of failure and flourishing, loneliness and connection, joy and sorrow. While I knew I was still a player
who could get cut at any time, the 2002, 2003, and 2004 seasons,
and blocking three punts, allowed my mind to rest a little easier.
These last couple years had gone far beyond any expectations I had.
I felt so ridiculously grateful for Al Everest. He is the *only* reason I
learned to block any punts.

I didn't want football to define me. It was what I did, not who I
was. My annual base salaries during my early years in the league
were $225,000 to $300,000, but I earned only a percentage of those
during years 1 and 2 because I wasn't on the team for the full season. My job security was precarious, so I lived as simply as possible.
If I could establish myself on a roster for a reasonable period of
time, the sport could provide me the resources to enjoy a quality
life beyond football.

While I never really felt totally secure on the Saints roster, I was
able to dig in, set down roots in New Orleans, and really get to
know the city. It truly became my second home.

I spent a lot of that time exploring, riding my beach cruiser bike around the city's historic neighborhoods. I talked Saints' longtime equipment manager, Dan "Chief" Simmons, into taking the face-mask off an old Saints helmet, and I used that as my bike helmet. I quickly felt part of New Orleans's distinct culture and vibe. The city attracted artsy, eccentric, resilient people, and I identified with them. The city and I were a perfect fit. New Orleans was different, and I guess I was, too.

New Orleans is one of those cities that if you just go to the tourist spots like Bourbon Street, you miss the real story. There's a secondary, underlying part that once you discover it is magical.

I found this magic in the city's legendary musical venues like Tipitina's, Maple Leaf Bar, and Donna's, where great acts like Theresa Andersson, Troy "Trombone Shorty" Andrews, John Boutté, World Leader Pretend, and John Gros and his band, Papa Grows Funk, performed. There seemed to be no limit to the restaurant scene, and there was something for everyone, from low-budget po-boy shops to five-star white-tablecloth culinary institutions: Antoine's, Galatoire's, and Commander's Palace. Whatever you were in the mood for, New Orleans had it. When cities get big, they often get corporate and national. They tend to have the same chain restaurants and lose their intimacy. New Orleans has long resisted this commercialization. The stores on Magazine Street are mostly locally owned. They're not franchised out. The city's fiercely provincial neighborhood associations have steadfastly fought fast-food restaurants from opening franchises in the city. You can still find a McDonald's or a Popeyes, but they're scarce and you have to go out of your way to reach them.

New Orleans, with all its faults, has always had this sense to know we need to hang on to that family, that intimacy. To the past.

The part I most love about New Orleans is its people. New Orleanians have fun. In fact, they go to great lengths to have fun and know how to do it better than the residents of any other city I've ever visited.

You can be a highly paid, tremendously successful oil and gas trader during the week, then transform into a ballistic party animal and dress up in costumes for Saints games on the weekends. In a lot of cities, you have to be one or the other. In New Orleans, you can be both.

There are ritualistic, black-tie Krewe of Rex debutante balls during Mardi Gras. But the same people that attend those formal balls are also the ones dressed in giant foam fleur-de-lis costumes when they're running the Crescent City Classic. This ethos is what makes New Orleans so cool. There's a grit and grunginess to it that isn't so prim or proper.

Michel's brothers, Pauly and Vinnie, and some of their friends epitomized this New Orleans spirit. In their regular, 9-to-5 lives, they were super-professional. But they had this other side to them that was totally crazy and fun.

As Michel and I started to hang out together more often, her cool New Orleans friends and family took me in as one of their own.

I wasn't your typical professional football player so I fit in immediately with this group. I never wanted to be known as just a "meat neck." I enjoyed having varied interests outside of the sport. I wrote poetry and was a voracious reader. I learned to play guitar, practice yoga, and study Eastern philosophy. I grew my hair long so I could donate to Locks of Love, a nonprofit charity that provides custom-made hair prosthetics to disadvantaged children.

Michel's family learned that I wasn't a buttoned-down type of guy when she brought me to their big family Christmas dinner at Galatoire's in 2004. Galatoire's is a New Orleans institution, one of the most famous and revered white-tablecloth restaurants in the city. It was founded in 1905 and sticks out like a sore thumb amid the touristy T-shirt shops, "big-ass beer" bars, and strip clubs along Bourbon Street. Friday lunches at Galatoire's are so popular that people wait in line for hours to score a table. Some well-heeled New Orleanians actually pay squatters to stand in line for them. It's not uncommon for Friday lunch parties to stay at their tables and socialize all the way through to dinner. Eating at Galatoire's is what dining in 1960s Paris must have felt like.

Michel's family started the annual Christmas dinner party tradition there several years earlier with friends Rookie Leopold and Rodney Salvaggio and their families. The reservation is always on a night close to Christmas, and everyone in the party of twenty or so gets dressed in their best formal holiday wear. Since the restaurant had a dress code, I showed up in Goodwill secondhand velvet pants, a plaid sport coat, and a Captain America T-shirt, but no one batted an eye, as long as I wore a coat.

The night started with a traditional dinner but as the wine and cocktails flowed it transformed into something different, unique, and wonderful. About an hour into the meal, Michel's dad, Paul, stood up in the middle of the noisy room and started whistling and clinking his wineglass with a spoon to command everyone's attention. He was a natural showman.

"Ladies and gentlemen," Paul said above the din. "We would like to welcome you to Galatoire's with a Christmas song!"

He then launched into "We Wish You a Merry Christmas." While Paul crooned, he worked his way around the white-tile floor and passed out copies of the lyrics to nearby tables. The patrons were initially puzzled and hesitant. You could tell they weren't sure what to make of this middle-aged man, interrupting their otherwise peaceful holiday meal, with an unsolicited Christmas carol.

But as friends and family at the Varisco table gradually started to chime in, a few sheepishly joined the sing-along, which ended with a smattering of applause.

Then, Paul started into "Jingle Bells." More people lowered their inhibitions and joined in. By the third carol, everyone in the restaurant, including the black-tied waitstaff, was enthusiastically belting out "Deck the Halls" at the top of their lungs. After an hour of spirited caroling, we eventually settled the bill and headed out of the restaurant, serenading all with a repeat of "We Wish You a Merry Christmas" as we went out the door.

New Orleans wasn't just all fun and games, though. A deeper connective tissue runs through the city. The Variscos—Paul and Jill, Vinnie, Pauly, and, of course, Michel—taught me about the importance of family and community here.

It seems normal now, but when I first moved to New Orleans I was astonished by the closeness of the families I met.

My rookie year, Mark Hughes, a friend of mine who worked

in the Saints' public relations department, invited me to his parents' house for a Christmas Eve get-together. Mark was a young single guy like me, and he knew I didn't have many friends in New Orleans since I'd only been in town for about a month, so he wanted to make sure I wasn't alone during the holidays. When I arrived at the Hugheses' house in Metairie, there must have been a hundred people there, and they were all family members. I made a remark about how amazed I was that so many of them had flown there for Christmas. Mark promptly replied that no one had flown in, and, not only that, everyone lived within ten minutes of the house.

During my time there, I have been overwhelmed by the way that the concept of family has been so integrated into the city. It was not something I was accustomed to. I always tell people that the sense of family and community is this city's strongest asset. I absolutely love going into a locally owned restaurant and feeling like I just stumbled into a neighbor's house as they are setting the table for dinner. That experience can be found all over the city.

One of the first and coolest New Orleans traditions Michel and I experienced together was the New Year's Eve bonfire. On the surface, it didn't sound like much of an event: On December 31, Mid-City residents haul their old Christmas trees to the neutral ground near the intersection of Orleans and Carrollton Avenues, then light them on fire just before midnight. But I should have known better. This, after all, is New Orleans.

Early on the day of the bonfire, some friends and I used my truck to take my tree to the site. I was astonished by the immense pile of trees already there. Later that night, a block away from the bonfire site, two huge ladder fire trucks were overseeing the barely controlled chaos. There were maybe five hundred people spread through the neutral ground and the streets. It seemed that everybody had firecrackers or bottle rockets with them. The streets were thick with sulfurous smoke and there was debris everywhere. As me, Michel, and our friends Chris and Madeline walked through the chaos, with explosions erupting all around us, it felt like we were in a war zone during a riot or protest.

When the clock approached midnight, we made our way to the discarded Christmas trees, where the crowd and mayhem intensified. Gradually, we slinked and elbowed our way through the mass of humanity toward the pile in the center. Suddenly I was blinded as they lit the pile. Thirty-foot flames shot up and soared into the air and the crowd roared its approval. The atmosphere was exhilarating. I didn't anticipate the grandeur or intensity of this event. In fact, I remember yelling to a friend, "In any other city, this would have been stopped before it ever started!!" We eventually made it to the front of the crowd. Absolute jubilation. People yelling and singing. Flags waving. Several people were running around the fire naked. Celebratory jubilation.

Eventually, the roaring flames began to slowly die down, the smoke began to clear, but the party rolled on. It remains one of my all-time favorite New Year's Eve memories. Sadly, two years later the city clamped down on the party. They put the fire department in charge of the operations and mandated that only three or four trees could be burned at one time.

BY THE SPRING OF 2005, Michel and I had fallen madly in love.

Actually, I'm joking. Love at first sight? Madly in love? We both agreed phrases like this are for airbrushed fairy tales. We also cringed at the word "lover." We weren't interested in being madly in love. We were interested in a real, full love, not a mad love. We didn't want to be lovers, we wanted to be whole. We decided that we wanted to *move* each other and grow. After a workout one morning at the Saints facility, Mic came over to make lunch and hang with me. She was relaxing in the pool in the courtyard while I was cooking kimchi omelets, one of my favorite meals. We were playfully making fun of the term "lover," and in the courtyard on Coliseum Street under the grapevine, it clicked. We said we weren't lovers, we were movers.

Besides, the term "lovers" would have been patently inaccurate. As I said before, I was a virgin when Michel and I met. As you can imagine, this came as a surprise to Michel at first. It was even more astonishing to her close friends, who quickly became fascinated by the fact that Michel's new twenty-eight-year-old, Saints-player boyfriend was a virgin.

One night I drove Michel and two friends to see the movie *The 40-Year-Old Virgin.* Throughout the show, I could hear whispers and giggles from her friends, Suzanne and Ainslie, like they were ten-year-old girls forbidden to talk in church. And I could sense Michel giving them the eye. I knew my virginity was intriguing to them, which made *me* laugh, but I'd had awkward encounters in the past.

During the 2002 Saints training camp at Nicholls State University in Thibodaux, Louisiana, in the locker room after morning practice, one of my teammates, Joe Horn, and I were talking. Joe was a Pro Bowl wide receiver and one of the most popular, outgoing, and high-profile players on the team. His nickname was "Hollywood." He was the man, as they say. Meanwhile, I was a nobody at that point in my career. I'd been cut the previous two seasons.

"Gleason, I bet the ladies *love* you, your style," he said. Then, in his unique "Hollywood" locker-room-style talk, he asked, "What kind of girls you fuckin'?"

Hmm, how to respond to this? Here I was in the middle of a half-full NFL locker room with probably fifteen players in earshot. Joe was the most outspoken and popular dude on the team. Over the previous two seasons, I'm not sure how much we'd actually spoken with each other. What the hell was he going to say if I told him the truth?! I figured I'd buy a little time. "Joe . . . ," I replied, "that's not really my style, man."

He figured that I meant that I wasn't going to kiss and tell, or I guess this would be a fuck and tell.

"Come on, Gleas!" he said with a smile. "This is the locker room. We cool here! What kind of ladies you fuckin'?"

I took a breath and said, "Joe, I like the ladies, but I'm a virgin." Silence.

Joe was stunned. And based on the expressions on the faces of the handful of half-dressed guys around us, he wasn't the only one.

I stood in a towel, looking at Joe, blushing. I was uncomfortable, but there was also some weird sense of contentment and maybe even a feeling of confidence.

Joe said something very cool: "Daaaamn, bro. You got my respect," with his trademark enthusiasm. "Even though, you one crazy dude."

Hollywood and I talk and have a great respect for each other to this day.

By that point in our relationship, Michel and I spent most of our free time together: reading out loud, playing cards, taking road trips, doing yoga, and seeing movies. I introduced her to my two favorite Hindu myths, the Bhagavad Gita and the Ramayana, as well as the *Kill Bill* films, and she fell "madly in love" with them.

During her Friday night bartending shift at the Bridge Lounge, I dressed up in all black and stealthily snuck beneath the bar. I stood up, shocked her, and said, "Hi, Mover." Then I presented her with an actual katana samurai sword, straight from the Kill Bill series.

She carried it around with her everywhere, except for places Mama Jill told her she couldn't. I taught her how to play the guitar and also bought her a used drum set after she impressed me by jumping up on the stage during a wedding and playing "Hard to Handle" to a perfect drum beat.

Later that summer, I sent an email to Michel before leaving on a trip home to Spokane:

MRV,

I have liked you from the day we met because of your inherent strength of character. I can't spar with anyone the way we do. Strength of character mixed with just the right amount of tenderness and vulnerability. My mom is "strong" only because she has built a wall around herself. You are strong AND loving. It is exactly what makes you so special. I am not overusing the word when I say it is unbelievable that you are the way you are. New Orleans and your environment seem unconducive to your development. I think having two older brothers helped. Or maybe it is simply a case of finding a gem in a gravel pit.

The bottom line is we are good together. Sweet.

Sparks don't keep a fire going, it's the coals that keep it hot, fed by the logs from the woodpile, that came from the growing green tree, that drink from the cool river. I don't want to be the spark, I want to be the river for your fire.

Goodbye for now.

SG

Michel emailed me back the next day.

Dear Steve-O,

I wish I could tell you this in person so I could hug you and smell you and touch you and kiss you like crazy and lay in bed naked with you and fall asleep next to you and wake up in the middle of the night and look at you sleeping and smile, because I know how happy we make each other.

Steve, I love you. I love your body, your muscles, your arms and butt and back in particular. I love the way your arms feel when they are wrapped around me. I love your hair, the way it looks and feels in my fingers and the way it smells. I love your face. I honestly could stare at a picture of you for a long time and not look away. I love to look at you. I love your ears—and your mouth. I love kissing you and losing myself into dreamlike states. I love getting naked with you. I love touching and exploring all of your sensual parts and hearing your noises. I love being touched by you and sweating and fitting so perfectly together with you. I love thinking about things we've done together when I am missing you, which is a lot for sure.

I love talking to you, mostly because I love our honesty with one another. I love that we talk about most everything. It's amazing after some nights of talking to you how satisfied I feel, like I almost don't even need you next to me. I love that we make each other belly laugh and love that we are goofy a lot of the time. I love the words you use to describe me. I love that you wrote a song for me and I love the song. I love to hear you sing and play the guitar. I love reading with you and hearing you talk about your life and goals for the future. I love how smart you are and how disciplined you are in everything that you do. I love to watch you play football. Besides making me want to rip your clothes off, it amazes me that you go out there and are good at blocking and tackling the shit out of big men.

All of these things add up to making you the most attractive person I have ever met. And the best part about it is that you love me too, that I am totally myself around you and you love me for it. It's been pretty sweet for me to watch you grow into your love for me, if that makes sense to you. I have had a hard time dealing with the intensity of my emotions for you, as I think you know, but I am finally at a place where I am comfortable with my feelings, and it rocks.

Luv,
Michel

LATER THAT FALL, I reported to training camp in New Orleans in Michel's Volkswagen convertible bug for the start of my sixth NFL season. On Thursday, August 25, as we prepared to play the third exhibition game of the preseason against the Baltimore Ravens, Tropical Storm Katrina started to make its way toward the Florida peninsula. The storm gained strength over the open ocean and grew into a Category 1 hurricane as it swept across the southern tip of Florida. It entered the Gulf of Mexico the next day. New Orleans residents and local meteorologists cautiously monitored the storm's progress as we headed to the Superdome for our game against the Ravens. By the time the game ended, Katrina had started to gain strength and was charting a path over the warm Gulf waters north toward the Louisiana boot. Saints officials gave us twenty-four hours to gather our belongings and make arrangements for our families. The team evacuated to the San Francisco Bay area on the afternoon of Sunday, August 28. Our plane was the final flight out of New Orleans before officials shut down Louis Armstrong Airport. Michel and her brothers checked into the Hyatt Regency hotel next to the Superdome as we left, but after much frantic urging by me and her brothers' pregnant wives, they thought better of the idea and evacuated to Baton Rouge on an arduous eight-hour drive on I-10—one that usually lasts an hour.

The whole Saints team was put up in a hotel in San Jose, California, near Oakland, where we were scheduled to play another preseason game later that week. The morning after the storm hit, we were in the hotel getting taped up for practice and had the TVs on. I came down the hotel stairs to hear that the levees had broken in New Orleans. Everyone was trying to contact their families and figure out what the status of their houses were. It was heavy and totally chaotic. And the chaos continued for months.

After the game, we flew directly to San Antonio, Texas, which served as our base of operations for the rest of that season. We lived downtown in a hotel near the Alamo and the River Walk. Michel came to stay with me after a few weeks and she filled me in on the devastation in the city. By that time, most of her family members had relocated to different cities in eastern Texas.

At the time, I had doubts about the Saints ever returning to the city. Saints management initially told us not to talk about moving back. We'd all heard that owner Tom Benson was thinking about moving the team to Texas. It was a strange time. The NFL was forced to make unprecedented changes to our schedule because of the damage to the Superdome. We played our "home opener" against the New York Giants at their home field in East Rutherford, New Jersey. We played the rest of our "home" games at Tiger Stadium in Baton Rouge and the Alamodome in San Antonio. Our weight room was a makeshift setup at a local university. The nomadic experience took its toll. We finished with a 3–13 record and head coach Jim Haslett was fired at the end of the season, along with all of his assistants, including Al Everest.

Of course, we did actually return to New Orleans. I didn't go back to New Orleans until a month or so after the 2005 season. Things had been cleaned up to a small degree, but much of the city was destroyed, riddled with FEMA trailers and vacant, flooded houses.

It was in complete shambles. The most shocking part for me was experiencing the wreckage through Michel and her family. Her parents, brother Pauly, and grandfather had houses in Lakeview; they had eight feet of water in their homes and lost everything. They were forced to buy an overpriced house in Uptown not far from my apartment and they shared it with Pauly and his family. They lived there for three years while their Lakeview homes were rebuilt. Their experience was replicated countless times across the city and region.

It was a horrendous, overwhelming time in the city. But I also saw many people who lost everything who were willing to comfort others, help them to shed their losses and take small steps to recover. It was inspiring and it lifted my heart. To do our part, my mom and I partnered with a friend I had made through the Saints, Josselyn Timko, and started a nonprofit called "Backpacks for Hope," to provide school supplies to kids going back to school.

People like to say that the Saints gave hope to the residents of the city by returning. I see it differently. New Orleans is a city with a history that spans centuries. That history is anchored by people who are resilient, persistent, and tenacious. Many of the people that chose to return did so long before the Saints committed to coming back. So, in that sense, the people of New Orleans were the catalysts for the city's rebirth. Much of what I've learned about resilience has come from the people of New Orleans.

8

Rebirth

When the night watchman lets in the thief
What's wrong now
The Saints are coming, the Saints are coming
—STUART ADAMSON & RICHARD JOBSON

September 25, 2006, was a day that will not be forgotten in this region.

The reopening of the Superdome was one of the most anticipated events in the city's long, rich history. When it was torn asunder by Hurricane Katrina, the stadium had suffered hundreds of millions of dollars in water and wind damage. The damage was so great many feared the stadium would have to be demolished. But Louisiana governor Kathleen Blanco thought otherwise. She knew the importance of the Superdome to citizens of the city and state—both economically and symbolically. She fast-tracked funds to renovate the iconic stadium during the first nine months of 2006.

For New Orleanians, the Superdome is much more than a football stadium. It is a civic treasure, revered in the same way Chicagoans love Wrigley Field and Bostonians feel about Fenway Park. And over the years it has served this region well, as a storm shelter during hurricanes and as a communal gathering spot for countless games, concerts, Mardi Gras parades, and parties.

In times of joy and sorrow, the Superdome has been here for the people of New Orleans. And on Monday, September 25, 2006, it was back from the brink of destruction.

Governor Blanco understood that we needed to rebuild the Superdome to send a message to the entire world that the city wasn't simply going to survive the worst disaster in American history. The people who have lived in this community for generations were returning in triumph.

The anticipation for our home opener had been building for months. A massive banner announcing the kickoff date— "REOPENING 9-25-2006"—had hung on the side of the building since the construction project began in January. Every commuter on I-10 coming and going through New Orleans could read it.

To allow time for workers to complete the $195 million renovation, the NFL scheduled all of our preseason games and first two regular-season games on the road. Normally, such an extensive renovation would require twice as long to complete. But the NFL knew it needed to get the Saints back to New Orleans as soon as possible to spark the city's recovery process. Doug Thornton, the manager of the Superdome for the state of Louisiana, oversaw the Herculean construction efforts and worked around the clock to ensure a refurbished, NFL-ready stadium was delivered on time.

SEAN PAYTON WAS the perfect coach to lead the Saints' rebuilding project. General manager Mickey Loomis's decision to hire Coach Payton in 2006 was one of the most visionary moves in franchise history. He became the face of an organization that for years had had a poor reputation. The Saints had won just one playoff game in their first four decades, and after Katrina, a here-we-go-again attitude permeated the organization. And the city.

Coach Payton was a disciple of Hall of Fame coach Bill Parcells and a strict disciplinarian. He immediately created a sense of urgency for every player, coach, and staff member in the building by holding everyone accountable on a daily basis. In training camp, he sent a message to every player by trading star receiver Donté

Stallworth to the Philadelphia Eagles. He gained credibility with players by confronting management over the poor quality of our hotel in Jackson, Mississippi, before our first preseason game.

He set goals and established a vision to create a first-class football organization by investing in well-rounded coaches and players who were sufficiently talented but, more importantly, were passionate, caring, accountable, and poised.

I was refreshed by Coach Payton's confidence, communication skills, and teaching ability, but we didn't exactly take the league by storm. We lost all four of our preseason games, and in our first regular-season game, we allowed a 74-yard touchdown pass on the first play of the game. Fortunately, the play was nullified by a penalty. We went on to win the game in the final minutes, then won our next game in Green Bay against the Packers, who had beaten us 52–3 the previous season. We were 2–0 and one of the biggest surprises in the NFL.

By game week of the home opener, the passion and energy around town were felt by everyone in New Orleans. Thirteen months earlier, houses and lives had been destroyed. Within the homes, pictures and memorabilia, jewelry, art, everything valuable to the lifeblood of these people had been ripped away when the levees gave way. Thousands of people had died. There had been endless emotional pain and suffering.

Leading up to the Monday night game, if people recognized me, they would tell me how proud they were to be from this city, and how they needed us to win this game. The Saints, in many ways, represented the city's return to glory, and its residents' return to normalcy. A victory would be redeeming. A loss would be crushing.

Our archrival, the Atlanta Falcons, and star quarterback Michael Vick were the opponents. Both teams were unbeaten. It was the biggest game in the nation and it was being broadcast on the NFL's grandest stage: *Monday Night Football*.

Our practice on the Friday night before the game was vividly memorable for me. We conducted it at the Superdome. It was our first chance to be inside the stadium since the massive renovation.

The paint was still drying from the frantic last-minute construction work. For half the players and coaches on the team, it was their first opportunity to actually see the Dome and get a feel for the playing conditions and atmosphere inside it. This practice was mostly about processing emotions rather than Xs and Os.

At the end of practice, Coach Payton called the team together and everyone took a knee around him. He said, "My job as a football coach is to get you ready to play football. And the only way I know to do that is to simulate the conditions that you're going to have here on Monday night."

With that, the house lights in the Dome went out and they piped in the intro music to *Monday Night Football* over the stadium public address system: *Dun-Dun-Dun-Dah! Welcome to New Orleans, Monday Night Football.*

A video popped up on the Jumbotron in the end zone. A car was driving through the neighborhoods and people were clapping and cheering and speaking directly into the camera: "Great to have you back." "Go Saints!" "Bless you, boys." The five-minute video then documented the history of Hurricane Katrina and the previous thirteen months in New Orleans. It allowed the guys who had lived through the last year, including me, to vent some of their feelings. Several of us were crying. It also allowed the new guys to appreciate the magnitude and significance of the return. When the video finished, they brought the house lights back up, and Coach Payton addressed the team a final time. "Now you see those people on the screen, those are the fans of New Orleans. They're going to be here Monday night, and we can't let them down. We're playing for them. The only way to make this a special night is to win this football game." It was a passionate and emotional moment.

During our preparation for the game, special teams coaches John Bonamego and Greg McMahon noticed weaknesses in the Falcons' punt protection scheme; they showed a tendency in their blocking technique that we wanted to try to exploit. Specifically, the center and the personal protector, the player positioned halfway between the center and the punter, always blocked opposite each other. When the personal protector lined up to our left side, we felt confident that the center was going to go to our right. So the coaches schemed up a play to try to block one of their punts.

Of the eight players in our punt rush package, six were going to remain unchanged. But the two inside players, me and Aaron Stecker, had to focus on the alignment of the personal protector. Our plan was to run a stunt at the line of scrimmage to create havoc with their blocking scheme. I had blocked a punt against the Arizona Cardinals two years earlier using a similar scheme, so I was familiar with the techniques involved.

I learned how to block punts during the 2002 preseason, after I nearly blocked a punt in an exhibition game and Al Everest told me the next day that I could get there if I understood better technique. He told me I was running through the gap at the line of scrimmage with my shoulders square, allowing opponents too much of my body to block. Instead, he instructed me to turn my shoulders sideways, as if I were trying to squeeze into a closing elevator. I had never blocked a punt in high school or college, but I became skilled at the technique in the NFL.

On game day, the team set up something unique to my experience: every player was supposed to use this weird red carpet valet service where we dropped our cars with attendants in front of the stadium and entered the Dome on a roped-off red carpet through the middle of the screaming crowd gathered outside. I wanted no part of that. I believe in, and had relied upon, systematic routine, and my pregame routine had been destroyed the past season, so I drove in the back entrance as I had always done, parked in my spot, and walked to the locker room amidst familiar silence.

The NFL understood the significance of the game and had lined up a Super Bowl–worthy lineup of musical entertainment. The Goo Goo Dolls played an hour-long set outside the Dome before the game. Two of the biggest bands in the world, U2 and Green Day, performed a three-song pregame set at midfield, backed by the Rebirth Brass Band and the New Birth Brass Band. Spike Lee, Snoop Dogg, and former president George H. W. Bush were on the sidelines, along with a bunch of other celebrities and dignitaries.

There was so much emotion and passion throughout the Dome that night, you could feel the pulsating energy on the field.

The stadium was still buzzing from the U2/Green Day performance when we kicked off to start the game. Atlanta failed to get a first down on their first series, so the punt team lined up on the sidelines to go on the field at the Atlanta 29-yard line. I saw Coach John Bonamego walk over to Coach Payton on the sideline.

Bonamego: "I want to come after it and block it."

Payton: "Now?"

Bonamego: "Yeah."

Payton: "OK. Go for it!"

I was shocked to hear the block called right after that very first series, especially in that field position, which usually calls for the unit to set up a punt return. But that was the maverick style that made Coach Payton the most successful coach in Saints history.

Our play involved an interior stunt where I cross from the right A gap—the lane just to the right of the center—and loop around to the left A gap. Sure enough, the Falcons had some confusion on their assignments. Their deep snapper, Boone Stutz, slid to his left to take Stecker, and their personal protector, Kevin Mathis, slid to the right to block our outside rusher, Curtis Deloatch. It was a bizarre scheme, one I hadn't seen before in my NFL career. I didn't hit the A gap like it was drawn up, but because they used this slide technique, I actually ended up unblocked and the B cap opened wide for me. I had a straight, unimpeded path to Michael Koenen, their punter. As I raced toward him, I felt like I was too wide with my angle, and I was unsure if I'd make *it.*

Then . . . as I saw the ball come into focus, I realized *I've got this!! Ahhhh yeah baby.*

The timing was perfect. I blocked the punt with my left hand just as it rocketed off Koenen's right foot. The ball ricocheted toward the Falcons' end zone, where Curtis fell on it for a touchdown.

The Superdome nearly exploded. The sudden, unexpected nature of the play shocked everyone—the crowd, the fans, the ESPN broadcast crew.

Quarterback Drew Brees later said the percussion of the ball hitting my hand sounded like a shotgun blast on the sideline. Michael Vick said the roar at impact was the loudest he'd ever heard in a football stadium. A friend said I was single-handedly responsible for the most beer ever spilled at one time in history.

The entire stadium detonated into chaos, a roiling sea of euphoria. But my mind was quiet. I mostly felt a sense of relief. I knew precisely the power, impact, and significance of this moment. Sprinting through the end zone, arms extended from my sides, I was flying. I looked back to see Curtis dunking the ball over the goalpost, then dropped to my knees at the 10-yard line and let the waves of energy wash over me.

On the broadcast of the game, the ESPN production team allowed the emotional scene to play without comment for thirty-four seconds, a lifetime in network television.

I could have jumped out of my own skin. I felt like I was in every inch of the Superdome, up in the crowd, so happy that I could do this for the people. I wanted to sprint up into the aisles and thank every last person. Our New Orleans family. It was pure, infinite joy. People were in that stadium cutting loose all of their frustrations, their anger, their emotion from the past year. And I thought *This is it. We're back.*

The Falcons never recovered. We went on to crush them 23–3, our third win without a loss on the season. We were the talk of the NFL, the biggest story in sports. And my play immediately became the stuff of legend.

A pack of reporters swarmed my locker afterward. One of them told me the blocked punt—my fourth in seven seasons—made me the team's all-time leader in the category. The record still remains today.

Because I had been in New Orleans for the previous six seasons, I understood the culture and mentality of the city, at least to some degree. I was dating a member of and would later marry into a New Orleans family. I also had endured the chaos of the previous thirteen months. The significance of the block, even in the moments immediately after the play, was not lost on me.

"I've been here for seven years, and I think sometimes people think the future of New Orleans is in doubt, and we're here to do everything we can to help people create a bright future," I said to reporters afterward. "Fifty years from now, New Orleans might be under the Gulf [of Mexico]. But we'll all remember tonight.

"Any of the guys that were here last year understand how big this is for the city of New Orleans, because we were right in the middle of all of it. To go 3–13 a year ago, it was agony. I've been here for a long time. I've got a lot of connections here. I've got people here that I know and love. Our goal was to come out and provide joy for those people and that's exactly what we did. That feeling of relief and basically just providing happiness for someone else. That's what you do. It can't get any better than that. I'm just grateful that I could be a part of it."

After I finished postgame interviews, I met Michel and we drove down St. Charles Avenue and ran into a crowd of friends celebrating outside Igor's Lounge. People poured out of the bar and piled onto my truck and yelled and danced and toasted me with their drinks. We never got out of the truck. Legend says that I head-butted our friend Spitz and that Michel jumped out of the truck and yelled, "I am going to suck his dick for the whole city tonight!" and we drove off into the night. Neither Michel nor I remember that part exactly but the tale still lives among our friends.

After Igor's, we headed further Uptown to catch the Papa Grows Funk show at the Maple Leaf on Oak Street. The bar was packed. Band leader John "Papa" Gros saw me in the crowd, called me up on the tiny stage at the front of the dance floor, and handed me a tambourine; I played as the crowd went nuts. We left in the early morning hours of Tuesday.

The blocked punt was the highlight of my career and of our storybook 2006 season. We went on to finish 10–6 and win the NFC South Division. We advanced to the NFC championship game for the first time in franchise history but lost to the Chicago Bears 39–14 in a driving snowstorm at frigid, windy Soldier Field. Late in the third quarter, we were forced to punt after a safety and I tackled Devin Hester after a short 5-yard return. It would prove to be the final tackle of my NFL career. Considering Hester is widely thought to be the best return specialist in NFL history and a future Hall of Famer, it wasn't a bad way to end it.

I missed the entire 2007 season because of a meniscus injury in my left knee. It required arthroscopic surgery, one of several surgeries I underwent in my career to repair torn meniscus, the cartilage that sits in the middle of our knees.

When I signed a three-year contract with the Saints in 2005, I remember telling my brother and parents that if I made it to the end of this contract, "I'm out." I wasn't interested in completely wearing out my body.

In the spring of 2008, I visited Coach Payton in his office at the Saints' training facility, and told him I wanted to thank him for everything he'd done for me and that I'd had a great career. "But I'm going to retire," I said.

We stood and hugged each other. Tears filled my eyes, and I was overcome with gratitude. I was happy with what I had done in the NFL, and that there was so much life ahead of me. Still, the decision wasn't easy.

I had grown very close with Coach. In one of my favorite interviews, he said, "When I got here in 2006, Steve was one of the first guys I saw. He was coming out of the weight room and I thought Steve was one of the equipment guys. He looked like a Shetland pony. But we weren't looking to keep mascots. They had to help, and he did. Pretty soon we were like, 'Well, we can't cut him now.'" Later he said, "Steve has that toughness and spirit. He has this grit. He's so New Orleans." To hear my head coach connect me to this community in such a positive way is the clearest evidence showing that my career was a true success.

Coach Payton, and the friendships, not just with players, but with coaches, trainers, groundskeepers, and management, made it tough to walk away. This city and this football team had brought me into the light.

Everyone sees the spectacular touchdown catches, blocked punts, and pick sixes, but the league is built on discipline. Gap discipline. Route discipline. Lane discipline. Coverage discipline. My definition of discipline is *Do what you're supposed to do, when you're supposed to do it.* I had enough ability and enough discipline to last eight seasons in a profession where the average career lasts 3.6 years. I watched more athletic guys come and go, because coaches couldn't rely on them to be smart and stay disciplined. Blocking four punts in my final five years didn't hurt either. In 2002, Al told me, "Listen stud, if you block a punt, your team has a ninety percent chance of winning the game." I took that to heart. I understood that if I could block a punt, someone's gonna keep me.

I was walking away while I still had decent health. I'd accomplished far more than I could have dreamed possible eight years earlier. I rode the wave of, and even played a small part in, the organization's rise from being the Aints to being the best team in the league. I was on the first Saints team to win a playoff game and make it to the NFC championship game. I was ESPN All-Pro in 2002, and I made one of the most iconic plays in NFL history and retired as the club's all-time leader in blocked punts.

The post-Katrina blocked punt was the kind of moment you dream about your entire life: Being in front of tens of thousands of fans in the stadium and millions of fans on TV and doing something of great consequence. I did it, and I love that I did it. That's why we watch sports and why we play sports—for a moment like that. I love the people of New Orleans, and for me to get a chance to give them that much joy was extraordinarily special. For many people, it's the only thing in my playing career that they remember me for, and that's cool with me. I'm the little kid who dreamed of playing in the NFL and doing something great. And that night, I did.

9

165 Days

The sea is awful and its storms terrible, but these obstacles
have never been sufficient reason to remain ashore.
—FERDINAND MAGELLAN

Three years after we met at the Jazz Fest Triathlon, Michel and I sat cross-legged on the Magnolia Bridge, eating dinner as two high-pitched squealing nutria mated in the dark, still water below us. I pulled Michel's grandmother's ring, given to Michel by Mama Jill upon Yvonne's passing, from my pocket and asked her to marry me. It belonged to her great-grandmother, Viola Michel. I said, "Our life will never be perfect, but I promise to do my best to make you happy until the day I die." Joyously, she hopped into my lap and said, "Yes!" then quickly reminded me of the commitment we had made a few years earlier. We had gone on a monthlong trip to explore the coast of Chile, as well as Easter Island. There, while at a hostel with colorful walls, exactly one year after we kissed for the first time, I was no longer a virgin. There, we made a pact that I had to die after her, so she wouldn't feel the sadness or grief of my death. I responded by reminding her of my commitment to live until 109.

Our decision to get married on the same bridge was an easy one. It had become the heart of the city for us, a sacred place. It was where we first met so it seemed the perfect spot to officially begin our life together. The picturesque bayou winding through the Mid-

City neighborhood reminded me of my roots in the Northwest. We rented a small yellow shotgun house a block from the water. Our first home.

The rain was relentless on May 16, 2008. Our wedding ceremony was scheduled to begin at 6 p.m. Michel and Mama Jill watched the radar anxiously all day, praying the weather would not demolish our plan. At exactly 5:48 p.m., as the last drops fell, Michel and Jill practically floated down the aisle, a perfect embodiment of chaotic joy.

At the wedding party that night at the Pitot House, along the shores of Bayou St. John, I stood on a chair in my New Orleans–style linen suit and thanked our family and friends for their love and support: "We are living a wonderful life. Michel and I were instant friends, and now we are best friends. Inevitably, life brings all of us challenges and pain, and we are not immune. That day may come for us, but Michel and I are stronger together, and I'm confident that with the friends and family surrounding us here tonight, we can get through any situation."

I had no idea how prescient those words would be for us.

Michel and I were in love with life, and we were like "beans and rice," as we say. One of the reasons we clicked so well is our mutual unconventionality. We would show up to Saints events looking like hippies in T-shirts and flip-flops. My mom once remarked at a Saints team event, "You two sure don't look like the other people here." A teammate's wife actually told Michel that she reminded her of a cute "little orphan." We weren't your typical NFL couple.

Our honeymoon plans certainly weren't conventional, either.

I've always been an ambitious traveler. I took a five-week solo trip to New Zealand in 2004 and loved every minute of the experience.

New Zealand is a spectacular country. It's the size of California, with a majestic landscape, spectacular surfing, alpine mountains, clear, cold rivers, and best of all, only four million people! There are places where you can snowboard and surf on the same day.

On that trip I had no set plans other than to surf and explore. I did, however, need a car.

Even though I made decent money at the time as an NFL player,

I was a frugal traveler. So the first night I got into Auckland, I walked around from bar to bar, asking people if anyone was trying to sell a van. Finally, this girl in a hotel bar told me she had a station wagon she was trying to sell. I told her that wouldn't work because I had a surfboard, and she said her station wagon had surf racks on it. "It's a good car," she said. "I've had it for a year now and no problems." I test-drove it with her the next day—it was painted green and had a manual transmission with a stick shift—and bought it on the spot for $600 U.S. I had to adjust to driving on the left side of the road, but otherwise it was nearly perfect.

I drove all over the two islands and usually slept in the back of the "Green Hornet" or outside under the stars. At the end of the trip, I resold the wagon and vowed to return to this enchanting country as soon as I could. I loved New Zealand and the people so much, I even scouted real estate and contemplated moving there after my NFL career ended.

Taking a solo trip to New Zealand in my late twenties was one thing. Going on an around-the-world honeymoon adventure with my new wife and only backpacks on our shoulders was another experience altogether. Michel, though, was into it, once Mama Jill approved the idea. Michel, at thirty-one, still needed that approval. Once she had it, we started planning.

We picked the countries we wanted to explore and bought tickets taking us to Athens, then to Kathmandu, on to Bangkok, Bali, Perth, Auckland, Honolulu, and finally back to New Orleans. We left on July 10 and planned to return December 21, 183 days total. We strategically packed our backpacks and showed up to the airport. Except for two nights in a hotel in Athens—and scheduled stops in the port cities of each country—we had no solid plans.

I've always tended to push my limits, but on this adventure I pushed Michel's as well. I don't think she truly understood what she'd signed up for until the minute we checked out of our hotel. She looked at me, wide-eyed, and said, "Steve. I have to go number 2. What am I supposed to do?" I told her she'd have to go to a store or a restaurant. She said, "Wait, what? No! I don't do that in public places." I said, "Well, Mic, you do now."

We spent the rest of the trip living in tents and camper vans. In Australia, we rented a white minivan with a picture of a Cat Woman painted on the side that said, "Come and make me Purr." I'm not a big fan of campgrounds. On the first night in Cat Woman, we parked in a national forest and were awakened by a hard knock to the window by an officer with a bright flashlight, demanding we get out of the vehicle and then leave the site. From then on, every night while I searched for a spot to park and sleep, Michel would lie terrified, her sleeping bag completely zipped over her head, not wanting to get into more trouble.

When we bathed, it was in rivers, glacier lakes, and truck-stop bathrooms. We cliff-dove and did hot-cold plunges from the Mediterranean Sea to topless hot springs in Greece. One night, we befriended some Sufi Muslims and ended up at an all-night retreat five hours' drive from our tent in Turkey. We'd joined them shirtless from the beach and Michel was freaked out the entire time about hiding the cross tattoo on my upper back. In the Gulf of Thailand, we got shipwrecked in a single leaking kayak, and had to swim to a gnarly, jagged rock a half mile from shore, where we eventually got rescued by a boat taxi. We were served roasted dog for dinner in a village in Sumba where the nearest running water was three miles away. We learned that to pluralize words in Indonesian you'd say a word two times. In Australia, we discovered Aborigines do not have a word for yesterday or today, because they only live in the present.

One night we lay awake, staring at the ceiling of a stale Indonesian hut. I'd talked us into eating raw pig intestines and heart for dinner. Mosquitos were feasting on the bloody cuts on our arms and legs from a long day of surfing in a spot slightly dangerous for Michel's skill level. Roosters were crowing though the sun was not yet rising. I said quietly, "Hey Mic . . . Do you think we should have taken this trip before we got married, just to see if we *should* get married?" She did not reply.

For Thanksgiving in New Zealand, I surprised Michel with a visit to the Hobbiton from *The Lord of the Rings*, then later that afternoon, a bungee jump experience off a massive cliff. Terrified of heights, Michel let me choose the option where our heads would plunge into the water on the initial drop. Despite her initial exhilaration, the next day she woke up with a fever blister and ended the day with strep throat. She'd had the same response after I'd urged her to jump off the seven-mile bridge in Idaho and out of a plane in Mississippi. We both realized that mental stress can manifest physical illness. But in the end, she agreed that the jump was worth it.

Most of the time, Michel appreciated my love for adventure and exploration. And though she usually resisted at first, she enjoyed it when I pushed her limits as well. There were times, though, when she didn't. In the Greek islands, she got upset when I dove off of cliffs she deemed dangerous. In New Zealand, during a hike up Cape Reinga, a spectacular spot on the Aupouri Peninsula, I jumped over a "do not cross" sign to take photos of a lighthouse. It annoyed her, a devoted rule follower.

"Why do you always have to cross the rope?" she asked exasperatedly.

"Because crossing the rope is the only way to live," I replied.

Remarkably, though, we never seemed to tire of each other, despite being together 24/7. Except for our argument at a retreat hostel in Pokhara, Nepal.

We had just finished a digestive cleanse. The process involved drinking two cups of saltwater (without puking!), doing yoga poses like Happy Baby, standing in a linebacker stance, hands on our knees, and violently pushing our bellies out as far as possible, and then quickly sucking in. Then, pooping in the Nepali toilets, which were oval holes in the tile floors. The goal was to poop enough until it turned into perfectly clear water. It took us three hours to cleanse our systems. We showered, and we both ate four full plates of mashed rice, lentils, and garlic. Afterward, we were told not to fall asleep because we had to be awake for our organs to learn to work again.

Our only fight on the trip occurred after the cleanse, as we were getting dressed to take a night walk. I'd been flipping through a book about New Zealand I'd brought, pining about my love of the landscape, indirectly demeaning Louisiana, which upset Michel. An argument ensued, magnifying the one thing Michel and I could not agree upon in our relationship: where we were going to live.

Michel, pulling out a jacket from her backpack, asked, self-effacingly, "Who the hell brings a white raincoat on a six-month trip around the world??"

To which I replied, "Spoiled southern girls."

I intended to live sustainably on a piece of land in the Northwest, but Michel, as much as she tried to share this interest, wanted to be home with her family in New Orleans.

Life soon had a way of figuring this out for us.

For the last leg of our trip, we traveled back in time, literally, to Hawaii. Michel couldn't quite get over the fact that we left the Fiji airport at 8 p.m. on December 7 and arrived in Hawaii at 5 a.m. on the same day.

When we landed in Honolulu, we used our iPhones for the first time in six months—calling and connecting with family and friends—and watched the Saints beat the Falcons at a sports bar. We started to plan our final two weeks of the trip in Hawaii but found it strangely foreign, even though we were back in our own country. Perhaps it was *too* civilized.

We realized how much we missed our families and friends. Add to that, Michel desperately wanted a hot shower. So, we cut our trip short and flew home, 165 days after departing New Orleans, excited at the idea of sleeping undisturbed in our own bed.

In Hawaii, we had easy WiFi access for the first time in ages, so Michel and I scrolled through our inboxes. I read an email from a fund manager I'd started working with a year earlier. Some of my investments were not looking good. On the flight home, I felt a sense of restless anxiety rather than relief. After we landed in New Orleans, that stress only grew.

10

Failure

Take me to your darkest hours, and I'll never desert you.
—NATALIE TAYLOR

In early 2007, I got involved with a group that did alternative real estate investments. One of my best friends, a former Washington State teammate, convinced me that these investments were a can't-miss.

I bought in, going against the advice of my regular financial advisor and my accountant. Michel's family thought it was a poor decision as well.

I also spoke with my dad, who said, "Stephen, it sounds too good to be true. I don't like this."

Michel, always by my side, supported me, but she was also losing sleep; the feeling of financial dread kept her up at night.

As the global recession took hold at the end of 2008 and into the spring of 2009, it became clear that my investment was a disaster. After a few months spent hoping things would correct, I was sitting in my truck outside of our house, and my phone rang. The fund manager said, "We're going to close the fund."

That fund had nearly $1 million of my money.

Money that had just evaporated.

Sitting in the truck, I couldn't talk—I couldn't yell—I couldn't even cry. I was numb. My heart pounded. Blood and adrenaline raced. That money represented nearly all the energy and all the hard work I'd expended on the football field. Now it had vanished.

It was a chilly New Orleans day, but there were beads of sweat on my forehead and arms. Over the next couple of weeks, the painful circumstance intensified exponentially. In addition to losing the many hundreds of thousands of dollars I had in this real estate fund, I'd also agreed to take on over $10 million in mortgages that were tied to it. It looked as if bankruptcy was imminent.

All my life, I had been the disciplined one. And the minimalist, financially conservative one. I'd learned that there were *no* short-cuts in life. Now I'd become the reckless fool. I kept asking myself, *Dude, what the fuck were you thinking?! Why did you do this?*

It was pretty simple—and craven. I had allowed myself to be enticed by greed.

The anguish I felt was enormous. I'd made a couple of million dollars over the course of my career; not a huge sum but I was planning to go off and live an almost modern monkish lifestyle. I had envisioned myself with Michel, quietly and simply living a sustainable life on land somewhere in the Pacific Northwest. We'd grow our food and tend our land.

I had worked hard to accumulate the resources so I wouldn't *have* to do something unless I was truly passionate about it. And my passion was living sustainably, buying land on a mountain river, building something simple but nice, capturing the sun, wind, water, and other natural forces that enabled us to live that way. After eight years in the NFL, that freedom had been right in my grasp. But now it had dissolved. I felt immense shame and regret.

During the next few months I scrambled to find a bankruptcy attorney. I also felt pressure and an urgency—from Michel and from surrounding cultural and societal norms—to find some kind of *normal* career. I did not want to get a real job, but I'd fucked up so badly that I felt I had to. But what should I get into? At this point, bankruptcy hadn't occurred, so I still had some money and didn't have to jump at the first opportunity. What else was I passionate about? In this period of anguish, dreaming about what I might do was fun and provided a respite from my mental torment. I thought about teaching. Maybe coaching. I even looked into becoming a firefighter.

As Michel and I were exploring ideas and options, my NFL mentor and guru Al Everest offered me a job on the staff of the San Francisco 49ers as the assistant special teams coach. Al was my all-time favorite coach.

Oh, man, a huge part of me was ready for this! An NFL job on the West Coast. And I loved special teams. I knew that, learning from the master himself, I'd be a good coach. This would be a lucrative gig, but even more, I now dreamed of one day mentoring a young kid fighting for an NFL career, just like Al had done for me.

Ultimately as Michel and I discussed how this might work, we decided the cons outweighed the pros. NFL coaches work extraordinarily long hours, frequently switch jobs, and often have to relocate to new cities, especially if they climb the coaching ladder. They have to go where the work is. That wasn't going to mesh with my plan to be an active, present father and husband for my family. It takes a special—and slightly obsessed—human being to be an NFL coach. It's a great career for a lot of people. But I realized I wasn't that person. I declined the offer.

Michel and I decided our best route was to take advantage of an NFL program that paid for vested players to go back to school and earn their degrees—in my case, a postgraduate degree. For the past five years, I had been passionate about sustainability. Starting in 2004, I drove cars and trucks that ran on either biodiesel or recycled vegetable oil. Perhaps I could make a career out of sustainability? If I could get my MBA, I figured I could work in a clean energy consultant firm, and then possibly start my own firm. A career in sustainability and clean energy became my focus.

I took the GMAT and applied to various business schools. Tulane proved to be the best fit. I could stay in New Orleans, and I was close friends with their athletic director, Rick Dickson. Since I didn't need a job right away, I thought an MBA would be ideal. I could go to school for two or three years and figure out what to do next.

A professional opportunity came quicker than I imagined. At a holiday party at Michel's brother Vinnie's house, I met Jeff Jenkins. He asked me what I planned to do now that I was retired. I enthusiastically launched into my MBA/sustainability/help-people-who-wanted-to-go-green plan. After several minutes of listening to my environmental evangelism, Jeff said, "Steve, I'm the president of the sustainability department at Shaw Group. I'd love to have you be part of our team." This party turned out to be a job interview.

I had no idea what the Shaw Group was, but I soon learned it was a Fortune 500 company based in Baton Rouge, with the sustainability department headquartered in Chicago. Over the next week or two, Jeff, Michel, and I worked out the details. I switched from the full-time MBA to the executive MBA program, and took a full-time position at Shaw, getting paid nearly $100,000 a year. While I wasn't really interested in a corporate career, this was an opportunity to learn the ropes in a field I loved, while working my way through school. I also spoke with the Saints about being an alumni ambassador, a part-time gig where I would visit the Superdome suites every home game as well as occasionally speak at schools throughout the 2009 season. In the midst of this financial failure, Michel and I thought we were making courageous and intelligent choices, and things seemed to be unfolding well.

But this adjustment turned into a mental struggle. I was grateful to Jeff Jenkins, who took me under his wing. I learned so much about the world of sustainability on my trips to Chicago, and I got to watch the Cubs, my favorite Major League Baseball team, every trip. But the *real world* felt foreign to me, so difficult compared to my NFL routine. I had to wear a suit every day. While I was doing the laundry, I said to Michel, "With the Saints I could go to work in pajamas if I wanted. They washed my clothes for me, and they fed me breakfast and lunch every day! At Shaw, I have to get approval for fucking pencils, and I have to wash my own clothes after I work out."

I was kind of joking, but it was one of those jokes that reflected the truth. I was really wrestling with my existence outside the NFL bubble, where I'd been pampered and lived on a different plane.

Also, I still felt regret and a bit of self-loathing for my investment mistakes. One of the life philosophies I loved came from Hermann Hesse's *Siddhartha:* "Praise and blame, gain and loss, pleasure and sorrow come and go like the wind. To be happy, rest like a giant tree in the midst of them all."

But rather than following this wisdom, I violently resisted the winds of my new reality. I had a great time at Tulane, and we met a close group of fun, caring friends there. I enjoyed the work I was passionate about, and Mic and I were living an active, social life in the heart of New Orleans. But there was still a self-created underlying stress. I was clinging to the future I had once envisioned. I was not living within the here and now. I was struggling to accept the boundaries within which I was now required to live.

There were nights I would lie awake in bed next to Michel and cry out and pound my fist on the bed. I wanted to live the life I *should* have had. The life I had dreamed about and had been so close to achieving. I wasn't willing to accept this new reality. I'd been able to forgive my dad countless times growing up. I'd been able to forgive my mom when she stole thousands of dollars from me. But, in this situation, I wasn't able to forgive myself. Michel was supportive, but she also urged me to focus on what to do now. I felt so defeated.

Instead of feeling uplifted by the Saints' epic championship run during the 2009 season, I felt inadequate and isolated because of it. While I was playing ambassador with the suite holders, the team won their first thirteen games and made the first Super Bowl appearance in franchise history—without me.

This was a very humbling time as I painfully wrestled with my ego and embarrassment. I'd had no problem with my retirement at the time I made that decision, but the combined events of the past year were torturous. I loved the feeling of contributing to a team. Yes, I had a sustainability team, but that paled in comparison to what I had experienced in my football career. As the Saints continued to set fire to the league in that magical 2009 season, a sense of insignificance and isolation emerged full force in me.

Super Bowl XLIV was a low point in my career and life. And the fact that I felt that way depressed me even more. I went to the game with Jeff Jenkins, who had invited me to join him and some Shaw executives. We flew to Miami on the CEO's private jet. I called a couple of Saints coaches and front office folks to see if I could stand on the sidelines during the game. Understandably, people were crazy busy and getting ready for the game. No one called me back. Instead, I watched the game in the stands with my friend Steve Rehage. The most lonely aspect came after the Saints' 31–17 win. I walked alone to meet up with Jeff and the Shaw Group executives. Pulling the hood of my sweatshirt firmly over my head. Comparing myself to the team, I felt painfully envious of my former teammates. I felt as if I were insignificant. Separate from everyone and everything.

I was alone. I wanted to feel that I somehow contributed to this. At the same time, I was criticizing myself for my envious reaction. *Dude, this team is packed with amazing people, and many of them have helped you become the player and person you are today.* Feeling lonely and then judging myself was an awful combination.

I don't remember much from the trip home, but I know I didn't share what I was feeling. I tried to be brave and enjoy the celebration with the guys who had so generously invited me. I did the same thing with my friends, family, and the people of New Orleans. I was trying to be happy and grateful for what I had, but there seemed to be an underlying, dull ache. This was by far the lowest and most stressful point in my life.

The suffering was so raw. I only shared my embarrassment with my brother, and my friends Jim Salters and Tony. I didn't have any people in New Orleans to work with to process this, other than Michel.

Michel, as always, was with me. She understood my suffering and felt my pain. She, like me, had to hide her angst about the Saints' winning season from everyone close to her, because it obviously did not make sense that either of us would be anything but thrilled. She'd been a Saints fan her whole life.

But still, all I could feel was my insignificance, my loss of status, along with regret and financial humiliation.

I was still commuting to Shaw Group global headquarters in Baton Rouge a few times a week. On one of the trips, I pulled my car over on I-10 and called Mickey Loomis, the general manager for the Saints. He was one of a handful of front office executives who had been with the Saints from the time my career started. He was from Oregon, and we had a good relationship. On the call, in a fit of despair, I asked Mickey if I could have a Super Bowl ring since I had been a team ambassador the whole season. Mickey told me that rings were only for the team and full-time employees.

After all my parading about living simply, and my claims of abandoning worldly materialism, here I was, begging for a ring, a shiny hunk of metal to feel better. I felt I'd become a total hypocrite.

I was not alone in my suffering, although I certainly assumed I was. Studies show that the transition to the real world for NFL players when their playing days are over is a difficult and often painful one. There is a plethora of emotional problems, depression, feelings of failure, and even a surprising number of bankruptcies. I had become the statistic I had worked so hard my whole life to avoid.

One of my favorite books, *From Strength to Strength* by Arthur C. Brooks, refers to this post-playing career struggle as "the principle of psychoprofessional gravitation."

"The idea," Brooks writes, "that the agony of decline is directly related to prestige previously achieved, and to one's emotional attachment to that prestige. If you have low expectations and never do much (or do a lot but maintain a Buddha-like level of non-attachment to your professional prestige), you probably won't suffer much when you decline. But if you attain excellence and are deeply invested in it, you can feel pretty irrelevant when you inevitably fall from those heights. And that is agony."

I was certainly no Buddha. My mind was like a wild animal tethered to a tree, racing around and around. In sports, I was trained to defeat my opponents by outsmarting and outmaneuvering them. But with this financial embarrassment and the collapse of our intended lifestyle freedom, there was no opponent. This was no one's fault but mine. I was fighting this, like I would an opponent, but that just amplified the pain and frustration.

Additionally, we had started trying to have a baby in New Zealand and naively believed it would happen there. We were actually surprised a month later when Michel got her period. Getting pregnant was much more difficult than we thought. She got her period every month for the next year, and each time it was more difficult for the both of us to accept and deal with. Michel started a strict fertility diet and did acupuncture. We sourced bee pollen from local bee farmers, tracked her daily basal temperatures, and read 300-page pregnancy books together. After a year of unsuccessful natural remedies, we met with Dr. Belinda Sartor, a fertility specialist. After Michel underwent a couple of surgical procedures to remove polyps and provide other therapies, we took a test and found that both of our reproductive systems worked separately, but not in unison. Michel's cervical fluid killed my sperm. In order for us to get pregnant, we'd have to try in vitro fertilization. We laughed at Michel being a "sperm killer," but this was a huge emotional struggle for her.

Meanwhile, we were still dealing with the question of where to live our future lives.

In the spring of 2010, Michel and I took Mama Jill to one of our favorite neighborhood Greek restaurants, Mona's. In a corner booth, overwhelmed with despair, I broke down.

"I feel miserable, and stressed," I said through tears. "I'm really scared. I want to be honest, because honesty's been our strength over the years. I feel stuck in a place I do not want to be. I feel like part of me is being lost. I want to take off and search for something. I want adventure. And I don't think I'm ready to have kids."

Michel knew most of what I was feeling. She was relieved to have her mom with her to share the heavy burden. But Mic had *not* known about my fears of having kids. That confession rattled her. She had put so much effort into getting her body ready for pregnancy. Honest, transparent communication had been the cornerstone of our relationship. This connection is why we were so good together. From the beginning, we committed to being open and vulnerable with each other, even if it was painful. *Especially* when it was painful. This acknowledgment *hurt*. It hurt to say, and it tore Michel up to hear this.

"Have you *ever* really loved me?" Michel asked.

I pulled her close. "It's hard enough loving myself recently . . . but I love you!"

Neither of us slept that night.

On the eve of our two-year anniversary on May 15, 2010, she wrote me a letter:

Dear, Steve-O,

So I'm sitting on our couch, listening to our latest genius mix, looking at pictures of our life on the Apple TV, watching the rain fall outside our screen porch, gazing at the bridge over the bayou and thinking about you. I love you is the bottom line. I love you more than ever and miss you when you're not with me. And even if I'm feeling irritated by you, I would still rather be with you than anyone else. And I swear I want you to be happy. It kills me when you're not. And it kills me that I know I'm part of the reason—because I don't want what you want. On another note, I'm proud of you every day, because I know how hard it is for you to do what you've done. I'm amazed, really. To leave football and have to make some hard decisions like you did. I know you went against lots of "anti-NOLA" and "anti-corporation" instincts to end where you have. And I know that being where you are today is the last place you wanted to end up, but I'm so proud of it. To do what you're doing in school and to see how much you've accomplished at the Shaw Group in less than one year impresses me every single day. You battle adversity so well, and I think you are one of the best people I know, already with lots of success in a business that you are totally "green" in.

Bottom line, as I said before, I love you, Steve-O. And I thank you for all you do for me—for loving me and supporting me and being patient with me and making me laugh and doing things that make me proud of you. Everyone has issues, and we'll always have issues but we love each other and we have fun together as well. And I believe that as long as we have the amazing open communication that we've always had, that we're gonna be OK. That we're gonna be great, like we always have been. We may not know what we're doing as much as I thought we did back then, but we do a pretty dang good job. And we have a lot more to do in the future!

Happy second anniversary, Steve-O. I love you. Mic.

It was the perfect gift from my best friend. My mover. At that moment, Michel's letter gave me strength. It resurrected the strength of my character I'd always believed was a crucial part of me. I thought, *Mic is right. What if I stop fighting this? We've made some courageous decisions in the midst of real pain. Life is good. It's time to recognize that, and trust that you can be OK, no matter what.*

About a month later, I started to notice strange twitches in my upper arms and shoulders.

11

Disbelief

Truth will always be truth, regardless of lack of understanding, disbelief or ignorance.

—W. CLEMENT STONE

On Labor Day weekend in the summer of 2010, Michel and I decided to take a trip with her brothers and their families to the Grand Hotel Resort in Point Clear, Alabama. Built in 1847, "the Grand" is a sprawling hotel overlooking Mobile Bay. When we arrived, I went out to explore the vast, spacious grounds and immediately connected with the place. We needed a break, but the trip was also to help me and Michel rediscover a bit of the peaceful, joyful, goofy freedom that we so treasured. It wasn't the epic adventure I craved, but I was starting to be open to this version of our life.

On our third afternoon there, the kids were running around, dancing by the bonfire, and people were cheering at the TVs, watching Louisiana State play North Carolina. There was a sturdy oak tree outside our rooms, so we decided to do a pull-up contest on one of its low-hanging branches. Vinnie went first and did six pull-ups. Pauly, one-armed, did four. I did three.

Three pull-ups.

What. The. Fuck?!

I dropped off the branch and looked out over the hotel grounds toward the sunlight shimmering off the bay.

Michel, slightly embarrassed for me, said, "Well, looks like we need to buy a pull-up bar for the house."

I had stopped lifting weights after retiring from the NFL, but I maintained my muscular strength through cycling, swimming, and yoga. Ten pull-ups should have been nothing for me. Routine. I had taken a sixty-five-mile charity bike ride earlier that day, so I dismissed the weakness as the by-product of the exhausting ride.

After our friends and family left, Michel and I had the final day of the weekend to ourselves. We spent it chilling in the pool and walking near the bay. We felt that natural ease together we had known since we met six years earlier. We were united again. We were us. Beans and Rice. I was happy with my *mover*.

Earlier in the summer, I had started to experience involuntary twitches in the muscles of my upper arms and shoulders. They weren't painful at all, so I initially brushed them off. I actually thought they were kind of cool. As young as third grade, my buddy and I would try to test what we could do with our bodies. The more ridiculous the better: burps, armpit farts—he could touch his nose with his tongue. I could wiggle my ears and move my eyebrows in an alternating dance. A few times, I noticed random twitches in my quadriceps right above my knees. We would laugh hysterically if we saw these. As an athlete who found exhilaration in exhausting myself, I'd noticed similar sensations in my legs after a long practice. So initially I thought nothing of those involuntary twitches.

But they persisted. Nonstop. And they were starting to spread to my lower back, chest, and upper quads. It was like a special effects scene from a sci-fi movie. The spasms were visible nearly everywhere on my body.

I went to see the team doctor at the Saints training facility. He confidently said it wasn't anything to be concerned about. I wasn't fully convinced by his conviction, though. I knew my body.

On the way home, I stopped at the lakefront, sat on one of the benches overlooking Lake Pontchartrain, and called my naturopath, Patrick Donovan, who was based in Seattle. He'd helped me solve the ulcerative colitis I was diagnosed with in 2005, as well as helping with other aspects of my life. I gazed north across the lake and saw the sun descend to my left in the late afternoon sky as I told him about my symptoms. He listened and laid out a few possibilities.

"It could be a molecular imbalance in your body chemistry," he said, "or a mechanical issue with your spine."

"OK," I said, "that makes sense."

He added, "But it could also be a neurological pathology."

"Neurological pathology?"

"You know," he said, "diseases like multiple sclerosis or Parkinson's."

He paused and added, "While it's a microscopic possibility, I'd say the worst-case scenario is ALS."

"ALS?" I asked. It was the first time I'd ever heard the acronym.

"Lou Gehrig's disease," he told me.

I quickly interrupted the muggy New Orleans silence: "Ah, gotcha."

"Yeah, again," he said, "it's not something we need to be concerned with at this point, Steve."

I stood up and walked to the water. I knew the odds were minuscule, but the conversation stayed with me. I had no clue about the details of ALS, but I knew it had killed Lou.

Per my naturopath's suggestion, we first checked to see if I had a molecular or metabolic issue. Over the next several weeks, my body was pumped full of amino acids and supplements. One by one, dozens of body chemistry misalignments were dismissed.

Once these were ruled out, we scheduled an MRI at a local hospital in mid-October. Michel and I were hoping the symptoms were related to a football spinal injury. It made sense to us that this could be an injury that a neurosurgeon could fix.

After the MRI, we met our friend Steve Rehage for lunch at Mr. John's Steakhouse on St. Charles Avenue. Midway through the meal, we got word that the MRI showed no signs of mechanical damage. Uncomfortable silence. Tightness in my chest. *Microscopic possibility . . . Worst-case scenario.* After an eternal instant of paralysis, I woke up from the catastrophizing in my mind. I looked at Mic. Our eyes met. She looked stunned. Stoic. But tears streamed involuntarily down her cheeks. Rehage brushed it off. *Now what?*

Later that night, there was a subtle heaviness between us as we recapped the events of the day. *Was something seriously wrong with me?*

A week after the MRI in late October, Michel and I went to see Dr. John England, one of the top neurologists in New Orleans, at his downtown office. I spent four arduous hours taking a battery of tests: a muscle strength test, a brutally painful shock treatment test, electrodiagnostic tests including nerve conduction study and electromyography (EMG). The tests concluded that I definitely was showing signs of lower motor neuron damage. After finding physical evidence of exaggerated reflexes, he concluded there was possibly upper neuron disease as well. Now it was just a question of what was causing the nerves to kill the muscles. And to hope that whatever it was, was treatable.

After the extensive testing, we sat down with Dr. England. I asked if he thought what I had was "bad." After months of spreading symptoms, increasing muscle weakness, and all of these tests, the answer was pretty obvious to me.

Dr. England said there was not enough evidence to know definitively yes or no. "It usually is better to do it a step at a time," he said. "I don't want to tell you something now that is incorrect."

He mentioned that he had med students visit him all the time, thinking they had ALS. "They're all stressed out because their muscles are twitching and they just learned about ALS so they think they have it. Instead they're just stressed," he said.

Hmm, I thought. *I've definitely experienced plenty of stressful moments recently.*

We left the hospital in a state of exhausted shock. Michel drove me to Tulane to take an exam. I had become great friends with my MBA classmates. I spent more time with them than anyone other than Michel. Mic loved the group, too. We went out to dinner with them regularly. It was special for me to have a group of friends that Michel loved who were not initially connected to her or her family.

I had kept my close friends updated on this situation over the past few months. After Mic dropped me off, I walked through the Tulane campus and looked around at the students who were laughing, reading, and planning their future. I wondered about my future—our future.

I saw my friend Kyle Brechtel, and we walked together to our classroom in the Freeman School of Business. While we walked, I thought back to a recent night with Michel at our little yellow New Orleans–style shotgun house near Bayou St. John. We were sitting at the desk in our office, which we planned to one day turn into a baby's room. Mic sat on my lap and typed, "What is ALS?" into Google Search on her laptop. We read the description silently together: "ALS is a rare, progressive neurodegenerative disease. It affects control of the voluntary muscles needed to move, speak, eat and breathe. ALS normally affects people in their 70s. ALS is always fatal. There is no cure." *Affects people over 70? I'm 33 years old. What. The. Fuck?! This can't be right. Can it?*

As we got to class that day, my mind continued to race. The visit with Dr. England. The prospect of having an "always fatal" disease. Once a "microscopic possibility," ALS now was starting to seem like a reasonable plausibility. Fear and all sorts of complicated emotions welled inside me.

On the floor of the small amphitheater, our professor started his lecture. I had to stand up and lean on the wall, trying to compose myself. A few people looked up at me. I put my face in my hands and started silently crying. Finally, I said, "I'm sorry. I don't know what to do." Everyone stopped and looked at me.

"A lot of you know, but I had a visit to the doctor earlier today. And . . . we don't know for sure, but things . . . aren't looking good."

I put my head down. I wept. A couple of friends came and comforted me as I whimpered against the wall. They walked me into a nearby study room, where I eventually composed myself. Then, we returned to the class.

A week later we scheduled a spinal tap to see if there were any inconsistencies there. After I nearly passed out from being poked in the bone by mistake, trying to get to the thecal sac, the tap was performed. Everything seemed normal, but the protein levels were slightly elevated, which we would learn is not consistent with an ALS diagnosis.

That gave us an ounce of hope we could cling to. But . . . after weeks of constantly praying and hoping that life would go our way, I was growing dubious that praying and hoping was the right approach.

I hadn't spoken about any of these issues with my team at Shaw, so I thought it was time that I brought them into the loop. In the Baton Rouge headquarters, I told my boss, Jeff Jenkins, I had something to discuss with him. We had become good friends after working together for a year or so. We went to his office and sat down. I loosened my tie, and told him about the recent developments and the tests I'd just undergone. Some strange combination of emotions danced within me. That twirled with the fear of what lay ahead. I had intended to stay composed, but the intensity of the dance compelled me to take the armor off. "I'm not sure what to do, Jeff. I'm grateful for what you've done for me, but . . ." Tears filled my eyes. Jeff looked at me and said, "Steve, we got you, my friend. Go find the best doctors and figure this thing out. And keep me updated." I stood up, we hugged, and I walked out of his office.

ASTOUNDINGLY, we were faced with the possibility of a terminal diagnosis. If stress played a role in it, this was the time to drop any and all stress. There was no place better to let go and breathe than the rivers, mountains, and lakes of my youth. So, I headed to the Northwest, the place I felt most at peace, to clear my head.

While I was there, I made some crucial decisions. After much mental and emotional back and forth, I withdrew from MBA classes at Tulane and took a leave of absence from my executive position at Shaw Group.

In mid-December, Michel and I met again with Dr. England. After a couple of months of bouncing from test to doctor to test to doctor, we realized why ALS is referred to as a "rule-out disease." There is no single, definitive test to ultimately establish its diagnosis. Instead, it's a process of elimination; you take tests to rule out other possible conditions. And by this time, we had ruled out just about all of them.

"Steve," Dr. England said solemnly, "all signs point to ALS."

Michel and I weren't surprised. I stood up, shook his hand, thanked him for his help, and asked him who he recommended for a second opinion.

We made an appointment for January 5 with Dr. Robert Miller, the medical director at the Forbes Norris MDA/ALS Research Center in San Francisco.

While we were both pretty sure by now that I had a disease that was *always fatal*, there was something within both of us, maybe contempt or maybe stubbornness, or maybe just plain ignorance, that felt that there had to be a path of healing. And if anyone could discover that path it was me. It was us.

I headed to the West Coast the day after Christmas. I left a letter for Michel. This was something I did routinely when I traveled and was away from her. I called them InWilyBipow notes: It's Not Why I Love You, but It's Part of Why.

Michel:

If you're reading this . . . It means that I am about to leave for the West Coast. I guess there is no actual beginning of the healing process, but this trip is "part of why" I believe I will someday soon be in better health. Before I leave I thought I would tell you a few things. Mostly just the things that emerge in my thoughts.

Michel, once I wrote that you are the river for the fire in my soul. You nourish the ground that feeds the plants that grow into the trees which eventually die and become the fuel for my fire. So today, as I look at the fire I realize it has now become Our Fire. Not my fire here or your fire there, but Our Fire together. We both look in on our fire and either add fuel to our fire or pull fuel and dampen Our Fire.

I have, in the past, overdramatized my letters to pour emotion to the moment in focus. It was almost "fun" to imagine the emotionally onerous life. I suppose that is a product of the good life. Now, there is no need for the overdramatic. We face tremendous struggle and challenge today. It is quite possible that I will die much sooner than my planned age of 109. And we have not been able to get pregnant for 2 years. That is heavy stuff. I almost can't fathom what those two challenges mean.

Strangely enough, I know that we have been stronger than ever in the past month or so. That is important. These challenges could have exposed an unconscious weakness in our relationship but instead our finish has been forged and polished. Maybe we really do know what we are doing!!

Some fuel for Our Fire . . . Michel, I want to have children with you and I want to raise them together. If we are diligent and determined, I believe we can have children together. It may be that Life's grace is needed more than diligence or determination to overcome my health issues and raise our children together, but I remain steadfast. So, I am pledging my commitment to our family fire. I want it and I know it can come to pass.

So, if you're still reading, know this. You will not be across the country for the next few weeks, you will not be by my side either. You will be part of me, more than you have ever been. And I, you. There is no distance. I am You.

Stephen Gleason

I DROVE OUR Jetta SportWagen cross-country to Los Angeles. I stayed with Rehage, who had a place a block from Venice Beach.

A few days later, Michel flew out to meet me, and after spending New Year's with Rehage, Bart Morse, and some of his and Michel's college friends, we drove up Highway 1 the day before our appointment. On the way, much to Michel's delight, we saw thousands of elephant seals and spouting whales. We stopped for dinner at a restaurant called Nepenthe in Big Sur, overlooking the mountains and ocean. It was possibly one of the coolest places we'd been together. As the sun began to fall, we were told that if you stare at the sun just as it hits the horizon you would see a flash of green light. We saw it. Considering the circumstance life was presenting us, I would have found an ordinary sunset extraordinary. So this moment with Mic was simple perfection. I felt the light of us.

That night, we stayed at one of our favorite boutiques in San Rafael, the Panama Hotel. We'd spent many carefree nights here while visiting my brother, Kyle.

As amazing as the day had been, the reality of our situation—the likelihood of my death in a few years—utterly engulfed me. How was this possible?! In the darkness of the hotel room, which had been such a safe and cozy sanctuary in years past, I crawled onto Michel in bed and wept. What did the future hold? Through sobs, I pleaded weakly, "Michel, I love you. I'm sorry. I don't want this. I don't want this! I don't want to die. I don't want to die. *I don't want to die!! I don't . . . want to . . .*"

Despite the stressful morning ahead, I slept through the night. The next morning, we met up with my mom, and the three of us headed to the Forbes Norris ALS/MDA Research and Treatment Center in downtown San Francisco.

We first met with Nurse Bob to conduct an ALS Functional Rating Scale test, which provides an assessment of a patient's body movement functionality, speech, breathing, swallowing, dexterity, and fine motor skills. I scored 44 out of 48, which provided Michel with a bit of something like hope. A couple of hours later we met with a second nurse for more exams and questions. Hours later, mouths dry and too drained to even attempt conversation, we waited for Dr. Miller in an impersonal office that looked no different from any other office. He walked in, wearing a red bow tie and white lab coat. He wasted no time: "Steve, I've diagnosed thousands of patients over the years, and after reviewing your records and your blood work, it's my opinion that you have ALS."

Michel looked wide-eyed and stone cold. She seemed more mad than anything. My mom quietly cried.

I had already abandoned hope by this time, but hearing those words was still shocking. *Always fatal . . .*

After a pause, I asked, "How many times have you been wrong?"

"Well, I've been wrong," he said. "Not many times. But it has happened a few times."

He told us about three people he diagnosed with the disease, including one lady who worked as a tugboat captain in San Francisco Bay and lived to be 102.

"Steve, there are some people that want to make their own story out of this," Dr. Miller said.

"I am committed to be one of those people," I said defiantly, and naively.

"Anything's possible," he said. "You're so early. You never know."

We were at the hospital for six hours to receive news that, eerily, we already knew.

Michel and I had done some research on ALS. But reading black-and-white pages of explanations and data did not adequately prepare us for what life would be like with the disease. We were still innocent and ignorant of what lay ahead. We walked out of the stale exam room and passed several people gathered in a large clinical room. It was like a freak show. But these weren't freaks. These were warm-blooded, living human beings with hearts and minds, all sitting silently in large wheelchairs facing in random directions. Some staring at the walls, some staring at us. They weren't moving or talking. Most of them were twisted and contorted in strange ways, different somehow from ordinary humans. Knees together, knees too far apart, hips way to the side of the seat, with crooked spines. Their heads leaning to the side, or hanging straight down, or leaning to the side *and* hanging down, or tilted and leaning against some bar. But their eyes. So warm, present, and available. Looking at me. Looking through my eyes, within me. Silent stillness. The incongruity of the inhumanity and the warmth, the preciousness of these beings annihilated me. Was this what I was to become?

It was nice to step outside the hospital; I felt like I hadn't taken a breath in hours. I stretched my arms up and touched the sky. I felt a moment of relief. After months of questions and concerns about what this was, finally, we had the answer.

The next day, I hiked to the top of Twin Peaks in San Francisco with two of my former New Orleans Saints teammates and probably my two closest friends from my time in the NFL, Scott Fujita and Eric Johnson. Eric also brought his Zen guru, Master

Ming Yi Wang. Eric had driven up the coast from his home in Los Angeles, picked up Scott in Carmel. We combined the hike with a Pu-erh tea cleansing, which is basically chugging tea like a frat boy chugs beer. We each had these gigantic thermoses full of the stuff. We reached the top of the hill, watched the sun rise, and started drinking more tea. Scott must have had an overactive bladder that morning because he kept having to go pee off the side of the cliffs. When Master Wang serenely said, in broken English, "Oh, Scott in trouble. He have weak dick," we erupted in laughter. The four of us held hands and looked off into the foggy sunrise.

I told them, "On the sidelines before games, coaches used to try to pump me up and yell, 'You ready, Gleas?!,' which I always thought was funny. Five minutes before a game seemed like the perfectly wrong time to ask that question. I'd reply, 'No choice.' In the NFL, we get ready for games *before* we're on the field. I guess there is no *getting ready* for this journey. I have no choice but to get in the game. The future is unknown and no one knows what life will bring us, but with the support of my friends like you, I'm in, ready or not. No choice."

"Steve, I will follow you to the ends of the earth, if that's what it takes," Scott said.

Michel flew back to New Orleans that night. She worked in the office for a restaurant group, Juan's Flying Burrito, and had to get back to work. But more importantly, she needed the support of her mom and dad. We had to deal with this together, but we also had to deal with it individually and separately. I composed an email to forty friends and family members in my inner circle:

Well.

Let's get to it. Yesterday I met with one of the best Amyotrophic Lateral Sclerosis (ALS) physicians in the world and he diagnosed me with ALS.

I have spoken with everyone on this email chain in the last few weeks so I think most know the deal. The deal is that nearly all diagnoses are terminal (our doctor mentioned 3 cases of conditions stabilizing), the average lifespan is 2–5 years post diagnosis. Which puts a slight detour in my plan to live to 109.

I intended to write some inspiring piece about staying optimistic and beating this diagnosis with the same determination and persistence that kept me in the NFL. People like hearing that. Deep down inside myself, I believe that is true. But . . . I want to be honest with you. . . . I am very scared and frustrated. I don't feel like beating anything. I don't feel like doing anything or keeping my chin up or calling more doctors or taking prescription drugs or joining a support group or figuring out health insurance or revising my will or going to church or being blessed by the pope (or the pipe) or wearing magnets or eating bird food or clearing chakras.

I feel like being depressed. And I feel like crying. And I feel like kicking someone's teeth in or having my own teeth kicked in. I feel like pinching myself and waking up. I feel like screaming. I feel like flipping God the finger. I feel like feeling sorry for myself. I feel like running away to the moon.

You see, in reality, our bodies are saucy meat sacks that break down and die. Fighting and persevering, and persisting and determining and optimistic-ing, and chin up-ing doesn't work for everyone. But . . .

At least 3 times it has worked.

So, feeling better about being honest with the few of you who are on this email, I promise to fight and believe and expect the extraordinary and smile and laugh and cry and love our lives for every breath that remains. Please, please help me do that . . . until I'm 109.

Gratefully,
Steve Gleason

12

Into the Unknown

Man can learn nothing except by going from the known to
the unknown.

—CLAUDE BERNARD

The majority of people diagnosed with ALS die two to five
years later."
Let me tell you, hearing that sentence can *really* fuck
with your head.

Dr. Miller was simply being straightforward, objective, and real-
istic. After the onset of symptoms, 90 percent of people diagnosed
with ALS die within that time frame. ALS *is* a death sentence. So I
interpreted his words as "I need to prepare to die."

I'd had minimal exposure to death in my life. But I had contemplated my death a fair amount over the years. I didn't consider this
gory or macabre. It was healthy, considering my lifestyle. Starting
in seventh grade, I started skiing and snowboarding. My friends
and I pushed the limits, especially during our teenage years, jumping off giant cornices and racing through forests. My rookie year in
the NFL, I started surfing, and I had some near misses with death
on the slopes and in the water. Paradoxically perhaps, these were
two of the places my spirit was most free. Sacred places. My cousin
Brendan and I had a motto: *Choose death.*

In the NFL, kickoffs were something of my *death practice.* Lots
of aspects of life cause fear. I had this fear of simply walking onto

the football field. I would tell myself, "Hey, if I die today, or on this play, then I'm OK. I've had a good life. And I feel good about accepting death."

This outlook—this philosophy, if you will—inspired me to appreciate the precious beauty of life.

But now, with death right in front of me, that perspective felt naive and childlike. Death—my death—was now very real. It took everything I'd previously considered and understood to the ultimate level. I was wandering through this strange, foggy world of ALS without a guide. And, surprisingly, the fear I felt from such imminent death was accompanied by a slight sense of wonder. These philosophical explorations had energized and invigorated me since I first began looking into them in high school. Was I truly ready to "choose death"? Did I have any other options? What would I do with the time I had left? What was worth living for in the face of death? These were the questions I began to sit with.

Mic and I spent many nights searching and scratching for possibilities, for alternatives. We knew nothing about what to expect. One night, we searched "Does Stephen Hawking have ALS?" on the Internet. He was a hero of mine, but I had never actually known the specifics of his condition. When I learned he did have ALS, or MND (motor neuron disease), it instantly encouraged me. While he was obviously a unique and incredible human being, the fact that he had lived a long, purposeful life opened a possibility for me, albeit a microscopic one.

In a very concrete and tangible way, this ALS diagnosis brought my mind and life into clear focus. Two years after my disastrous real estate investments, our economic situation was still pretty dire, and bankruptcy was still a possibility. But my bankruptcy attorney told me the chances were lower each day. My terminal diagnosis dissolved my lingering regret about all that. I was now committed to live and love in the here and now, with every breath that remained. It was liberating.

The diagnosis also unified me with Michel more than ever. We truly believed I could be cured. We knew it.

We walked to the Magnolia Bridge a few days after the diagnosis. I said, "Mic, if you're still in, I still want to have a baby with you."

The sun was high in the cool winter sky. My back was against the rail of the bridge; I could see the bayou and City Park behind her. "Obviously, my future, our future, is a mystery, and"—I hesitated, worried she had changed her mind—"and I know we've been unsuccessful for over two years, but I know this can happen."

Michel did *not* hesitate. "I'm in. All the way in. There's nothing I want more than to have a baby. Your baby." I pulled her close. "Our baby," she finished. "Our family, Steve-O."

We walked home hand in hand. That night, energized and motivated by our commitment to have a family, Michel wrapped her arms around me, and said, "Steve-O, they don't know anything about you. I really believe you can be healed."

I agreed.

"In the unknown," I said, "anything is possible."

We had genetic tests done. They showed that my ALS was sporadic rather than familial. This meant I wouldn't pass it on to our children. We decided to move forward and have a baby through IVF.

In our commitment to heal, we turned to our family and friends first. Our friend Steve Rehage recommended I stay at his place by Venice Beach and work with Master Bruce Sun, a Chinese acupressure therapist in LA. This was perfect because I'd be closer to San Francisco, where I would be getting regular checkups at the Forbes Norris institute. I figured that was good mental therapy as well, so I headed to California for a few weeks.

On February 9, 2011, exactly twenty-seven days after my diagnosis, Michel called me during my morning walk on Venice Beach.

Before I could say hello, she cried, "Steve-O, WE'RE GOING TO HAVE A BABY!"

In her joy, I could tell she had so much more to say, and I was happy to listen.

She then told me her mom had driven her to the fertility clinic. Mic took an HCG blood test, then went to a restaurant to await the results. She said she was so nervous she was shaking; she couldn't make out the words on the menu. After thirty minutes or so she got a text from the clinic saying to come back as quickly as she could.

"I read the text over and over and over and over," she said. "I was breathing so heavily. I said, 'Mom, does this sound like it actually worked??'"

She was so detailed and transparent in her delight, I was right there with her. She said they walked back into the clinic and saw Dr. Sartor and Ashley Bono, the woman who had texted her, amidst a room full of smiling people.

"I immediately dropped to my knees and started bawling," she said. She told me she wouldn't stop talking, that she told everyone that she had just had a dream where Dr. Sartor solemnly told her it hadn't worked. And after an awkward pause, everyone just started laughing.

"I feel so relieved," she added. "Steve, I feel like I can breathe again. I can't ever remember feeling such joy! I didn't think of ALS once this morning. I just thought of us. It was just us! I'm so happy for us!"

We spoke for a few more minutes, doing nothing but enjoying each other and the moment of weightless joy.

As I walked along the beach, I just kept thinking what a beautiful life it was. All of it.

Speaking of the unknown: I didn't know much more about being a daddy than I did about ALS. That intensified my focus. *Was it a girl? A boy? What would we name it? How could I pass on the best of myself, while also sharing my weaknesses, and mistakes? If I was going to be dead soon, how could I best partake and participate in this kid's life? How can I best love you, my child?*

A couple of years earlier, I'd watched the movie *My Life*, with Michael Keaton. Keaton's character is diagnosed with terminal cancer, and knowing he might not be alive when his son is born, he begins to make video recordings to share who he is with his baby. This now became my mission. My purpose—*my ultimate purpose*—would be to share as much of myself as I possibly could with our child. I decided to record video journals, which I called "300 Seconds," five-minute snapshots of memories and what I'd learned in my life. The radiant, creative fire within me was ablaze again.

I recorded my first "300 Seconds" on March 11, 2011, in the office of our little yellow shotgun house on Grand Route St. John:

> It's my intention to present what I think is the best gift that I can possibly give to my child. The gift is intended to be a story, a compilation of my life, what I've done, where I'm from, who I am. I want to present that in a way that is somehow meaningful, that I can pass on as much of who I am to you, my child. This is for you. I know it's not going to be perfect. It's going to be honest, and real. There's gonna be some screw-ups at some points, which there already have been. I think the most important thing is that I have really loved my life, and I've worked really hard to be what I think is a good person. As a result of that I have attracted some really exceptional people into my life, the most important of whom is your mother, Michel. I love her very much. I hope you enjoy this project I'm embarking on. I know there will be parts that are frustrating and that's OK. I really love doing this. It's a fun project for me, so I'm excited to continue with it. I love you, and I am out.

A week later, Michel and I returned to the Forbes Norris ALS/ MDA Research Center to register in a clinical trial for a drug called Dexpramipexole. It was certainly not a cure, but we were told it could possibly be more effective than Riluzole, the one drug on the market at the time. Also called Rilutek, that drug was proven to prolong life expectancy for up to three months in *some* individuals. During the visit, I underwent respiratory testing with a couple of nurses gently holding a tube in my mouth, urging me to blow. "Now blow, Steve. Blow. Blow. Blow harder! Yes! Yes! Blow harder! Harder!" Michel erupted with laughter. As did I.

One of the weirdest early symptoms of ALS is uncontrollable laughter. I could not stop howling, and I had to take a few breaks before I was able to finish the test. Turns out I was still a good blower. If I was going to be dead in a few years, I was committed to laughing and smiling while I cried and died.

We met with one of the clinic's top neurologists, Dr. Jonathan Katz, whom I liked very much. Not only was he one of the top ALS experts in the world, he'd received his medical degree from Tulane, so he knew my story. I really enjoyed our time with him. He was also a smart-ass, in the best way.

I mentioned the research we'd done, and learning a bit about Stephen Hawking, and asked how I might be able to live beyond this three-year expiration date. One key, he said, was to find a purpose or passion, especially something that didn't require using your body.

I also asked about using a ventilator to live. I had no idea what this meant for me. He told us that some ALS patients live long, productive lives with the assistance of a ventilator. He told us ALS eventually takes away your ability to breathe on your own, but the ventilator mechanically breathes for you.

We were so confused about so many aspects of how I should be living my life. I bombarded him with questions: What diet should I follow? Should I try the keto diet? Should I be exercising? Was it bad for my muscles to ride my bike? Would my muscles last longer if I followed a certain lifestyle?

"Trust your instincts," he told me. "Second-guess nothing."

Dr. Katz also said he thought I'd be on my feet and able to walk for the next eighteen months, which was truly joyous news for me and Michel.

The visit cleared some of the dense fog covering this uncharted world. We left his office feeling uplifted, even excited, and leaving the hospital I was cradled by the sun. I reached out and held Mic's hand tight. I whispered, partly to her, partly to myself, "Trust your instincts. Trust your instincts, Steve-O."

THAT AFTERNOON on a flight back to New Orleans, I tried to figure out exactly what my instincts were: what had shaped my life to that point, and what was important to me right then. I had already decided to make the video journal library for our child. I knew that was the right instinct. Dr. Katz motivated me to create a list of what I considered my instinctual commitments. This list has been a rough road map through the unknown since I created it in 2011:

- Healing—I intend to heal. I know this is possible. To fully recover physically. Cured. Let's explore all possibilities.
- Family—I want to be a husband and a father. This is my motivation to live, and my ultimate purpose.
- Exploration & Adventure—I may be dead in a few years but I'm going to fully live while dying. *Shit, we're all dying, right? We're all on a timeline.*
- Serving Others—In high school I learned "If you want to serve yourself, seek to serve others." I had experienced the joy of practicing this throughout my life.

As I shared this list with Michel, we began to explore active steps to take to make the list a reality. We had already embarked on the healing and family aspects.

IT WAS A WINTRY cold day in February, and I had just finished a cold plunge in Michel's parents' pool, holding my breath as long as I could underwater. Everyone thought I was crazy for getting in the pool when it was so cold, but I knew the power of pushing my limits. This was a practice I had employed throughout my life. It was invigorating and inspired creativity. Still wet, I told Michel about an adventure idea: What if we buy a custom 4-by-4 van, drive it across the country into Canada, through the Yukon Territory, then on to Alaska? Admittedly, it was an ambitious plan, and probably a bit crazy—I had a terminal disease, and Michel was pregnant. But Mama Jill approved; she had long since grown accustomed to our off-the-wall ideas. "Y'all go enjoy yourselves, while you still can," she said.

I had a vague idea of what we could do to fulfill my final point—serving others—but for now, that would have to wait.

Steve and one of his lifelong best friends, Jim Salters, with some of their Gonzaga Prep football teammates. © Gleason Family Collection

Steve as a boy, age five, on the annual summer road trip to California with his mom and brother. © Gleason Family Collection

Steve playing in a Saints game versus the Tampa Bay Buccaneers in 2002. Photographer: Jamie Squire © Getty Images

Steve's punt block during the first Saints game after Hurricane Katrina on September 25, 2006. © Bill Feig

Michel and Steve after he blocked the punt versus
the Atlanta Falcons on September 25, 2006.
© Gleason Family Collection

Reality: Steve decided to wear Michel's shorts
at Lake Coeur d'Alene in summer 2006,
six weeks before the punt block vs. Atlanta.
© Gleason Family Collection

Steve on a rock in Lake Tekapo, New Zealand, during his and Michel's six-month
honeymoon. © Gleason Family Collection

Michel and Steve at Nepenthe in Big Sur, California, the night before his ALS diagnosis on January 5, 2011. © Gleason Family Collection

Upon his return from New Zealand in 2004, Steve met up with his brother, Kyle, on the "Lost Coast" in California. © Gleason Family Collection

Steve; his brother, Kyle; and their cousin Brendan in Alaska, the summer after Steve's ALS diagnosis. © Gleason Family Collection

From left: Rosie Varisco (Niece), Julie Varisco (sister-in-law), Clare Durrett (PR Team Gleason), Pauly Varisco (Michel's brother), Lily (niece), Leah Varisco (niece), Charlie Varisco (nephew), Michel, Paul Varisco (Michel's dad), Steve, Rivers, Jilly (Michel's mom), Vinnie Varisco (Michel's brother), Hilary Varisco (sister-in-law), PJ Varisco (nephew), Coco Varisco (niece), Blair Casey (caregiver). Gail Gleason (Steve's mom) in front of the Rebirth statue outside the Superdome, 2012.
© Michael Hebert

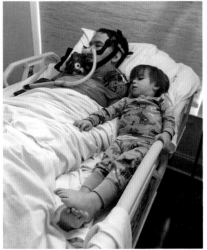

Steve and Rivers in his hospital bed with face masks, pre-trache, 2013.
© Gleason Family Collection

Steve, Michel, and Rivers in Machu Picchu, 2013.
© Suzanne Alford

Steve onstage with Mike McCready and Pearl Jam at Voodoo Fest in NOLA in 2013. Steve is wearing a shirt given to him by Eddie Vedder, and Mike is wearing a Team Gleason shirt. © Alex Restrepo

Saints former quarterback Drew Brees giving Steve "Fo to Fo." © David Grunfeld

Steve's dad, Mike; Steve; and Steve's son, Rivers. Three generations of Gleason boys, going skins, on their annual trip to Idaho in 2023. © Gleason Family Collection

Steve's wall of inspiration from his perspective from his bed. Keep shining Steve-O. © Jenni Doiron

Caregiver Beau Baker pushing Steve's gut to promote a bowel movement during the morning workout. © Ted Jackson

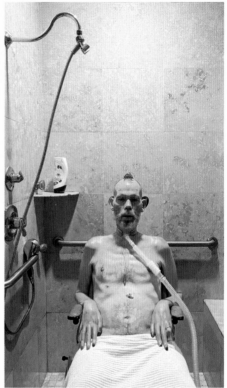

Reality: Steve in the shower, seventeen years after the punt block vs Atlanta.
© Beau Baker

Gray sleeping with Steve. She asked if she could could draw even though it was past bedtime. Yes yes yes! A moment to live for. © Gleason Family Collection

Rivers and Gray Gleason. Discover the truth! © Gleason Family Collection

Steve, Michel, and Rivers being presented the Congressional Gold Medal in January 2020. From left to right: U.S. Director of Public Engagement Cedric Richmond, Rivers Gleason (below), Senator Bill Cassidy, Steve Gleason (seated below), Representative Steve Scalise, former Speaker of the House Nancy Pelosi, Senator Chuck Schumer (back row), Michel Varisco Gleason. Image is from the Congressional Gold Medal Ceremony January 15, 2020, in the U.S. Capitol Statuary Hall.
© AP Photo/Manuel Balce Ceneta

Rivers throwing the first pitch for a Cubs game in 2022 at Wrigley Field, celebrating Lou Gehrig Day. Steve, Gray, and Kyle Olasin are in the background. © Clubs Organization

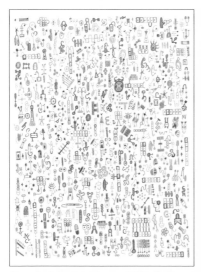

Steve's favorite piece of Michel's art, titled *Logistics*. © Michel Varisco

Steve and Gray under an oak tree in their Lake Vista neighborhood. © Frank Relle

The Gleason family's 2022 Christmas card, doing blindfolded meditation and yoga. © Gleason Family Collection

Shortly after I had the video journal idea, Michel and I met with a filmmaker who was interested in documenting our journey. From that point on, our lives started being recorded. Friends and family joined in on the filming.

I still had no idea what awaited. I just knew there was no choice other than to proceed. The future was terrifying, but, at this point, I was able to acknowledge the fear, and my instinctual commitment list provided some stability. My attitude was, I have this diagnosis and even if it does crush my body, it's not going to crush my mind and spirit. It's not going to define my life. This is my opportunity to be an example to other people, and to my family—an example of resilience.

Mic and I decided to keep my condition private for the time being. Going widely public didn't fit on my "instincts" list. My initial priority was healing, and I didn't want anything to complicate that mission. The right time to announce this diagnosis would arrive.

I began to explore all avenues—both conventional and alternative—in an attempt to heal.

We both agreed that one of the first places I should visit was the shrine of Father Francis Xavier Seelos, the legendary Redemptorist priest who lived in New Orleans in the mid-1800s; part of his legend is that he was blessed with mystical healing powers, the result of his intense life of prayer. The previous fall, Michel had submitted a petition prayer to become pregnant, and that had eventually happened for us. So I was open to the idea of a miracle, and drove to St. Mary's Assumption Church in the Irish Channel neighborhood where the shrine was located. I wasn't raised Catholic, and I remembered my dad discrediting the Catholic Church because they created rituals not based upon scripture. But the communities of my Jesuit high school, Gonzaga Prep, in Spokane and Jesuit High School in New Orleans had been the most loving, nurturing "families" in my life. Healing wasn't about conceptual dogma for me. It was about openness, trust, and love. I was open to healing from God through Father Seelos's reputed powers.

I spent the next few weeks crisscrossing the country, seeking and exploring alternative healing methods. I visited a Chinese Wu Tang monk. I traveled to Atlanta a few times to do weight training with Vladmir Chubinsky, a Ukrainian wrestler turned massage therapist. I flew Master Bruce, the acupressure therapist, in from California for regular sessions.

At the obsessive insistence of my dad, and as a continuation of my willingness to explore any avenue of potential healing, I purchased thousands of dollars' worth of Nikken Magnet Therapy products. I slept under a heavy magnet blanket, wore magnet soles in my shoes, drank from a magnet water bottle, and used a magnet air purifier. The products disappeared one by one from the house. Michel, an avid minimalist, thought these things fit much better in her parents' attic.

I saw Dr. Michael LeBlanc, a dentist in Thibodaux, who removed the fillings in my teeth because some people believed the mercury contamination might be a cause of ALS.

I met with one of the most popular psychiatrists in the United States at that time, Dr. Daniel Amen, at his clinic in Marina Del Rey, California. Dr. Amen was an expert on sports-related brain injuries and had served as a consultant for the NFL. My dad did a lot of legwork to arrange the visit, and when I finally got to see Dr. Amen, I told him about my diagnosis and explained my symptoms to him one by one in great detail. At the end of our $500 session, all he said to me was "I'm sorry, man. There's nothing I can do for you."

I wasn't too surprised by his response (my dad was, but at least he was able to see firsthand what I experienced after each of these efforts). We were spending tons of money, and more importantly, tons of time on these efforts. And time wasn't on my side. This is what happens when searching for miracles, I suppose. The chances for success are microscopic and there is a lot of disappointment. But I committed to staying the course, to staying faithful and continuing the mission.

And that mission wasn't the only thing that was continuing. . . .

The disease was progressing. While it wasn't yet noticeable to other people, ALS was slowly and steadily killing my muscles. I could feel them weakening almost daily.

In early February 2011 while I was staying in LA, my brother, Kyle, and I went for a walk on Venice Beach. I was very aware that my symptoms were progressing, and I knew it wasn't healthy to ignore or deny this. As we walked along the shore in our hoodies and yoga pants, I said, "Dude, let's race! You'll probably beat me, but let's see if some of this healing practice is working."

During my playing days, I could run a 40-yard dash in 4.46 seconds, which was above average for players at my position and exceptional for most people. On the beach that day, I told Kyle, "Let's go all out, as fast as we can." We removed our flip-flops and took our positions in the sand.

In my prime, my legs—my burst in the first 10 yards—were my strength. In football, that burst is everything, especially for defensive players. Feeling that power propel me like a rocket on liftoff was one of the greatest feelings of pure freedom in my life. This day on the beach, that freedom was lost. It was like I was running in water. The muscles in my legs simply wouldn't fire. Kyle did not beat me. He absolutely torched me. And then he turned around and raced me backward—and outran me while he was backpedaling.

This was an especially brutal moment. I *loved* to run. Not only that, I had been really, really good at it. So good that I made an entire career out of it. Running was a major part of how I found meaning in my life. It was part of my identity. I dreaded the thought of not being able to run. And that was no longer just a thought—it was now the undeniable reality.

How did I respond to this reality? With all-out, uncensored, and uncontrollable laughter. As I was walking in the sand after our "race," even before I could fully digest what had just happened, Kyle started relentlessly tickling me. I'd always been the faster brother, but he was a state finalist in high school wrestling. Once he got to sixteen, I knew not to fuck with him. And I sure couldn't mess with him now as he continued to tickle me and took me down in the sand.

"Not only am I faster than you, I'm also stronger than you, Bruzzie," he said. We were both hysterically laughing. Like a slithering, sinister villain in a horror movie, Kyle whispered in my ear, "This is revenge for twelve years of older brother torture!"

In my weakened state, I was utterly powerless, and yet somehow, at that moment, being tickled in the arms of my little brother, the brother I had nurtured as well as tortured over the past thirty years, my powerlessness was entirely welcomed. And I just kept laughing. I think that laughter was the relief of truly accepting what was happening to me.

Afterward, as I walked along the beach on my own, the same sand where Michel had told me we were going to have a baby, I contemplated this new reality: Was that the last time I would ever try to run? Did my acceptance of this reality mean I now failed to believe? Had I lost faith? And perhaps most important: What was next?

The plain truth to this new reality was that there was absolutely nothing I could now do about the way the ALS was progressing, certainly not in the moment. And if this progression continued, I understood this was just the beginning. As much as I loved to run, as meaningful as running had been in my life, I would have to let it go. And I knew I COULD let it go. I still had so much to be thankful for in life.

But that loss was a bleak reminder of my impending future. Walking. Talking. Typing. Showering. Eating. Dressing. Wiping my ass.

It *was* just the beginning . . .

LATER THAT SPRING, I took a trip to Austin, Texas. Austin is my kind of town, but the purpose for the visit was to look at a Sports-Mobile, a customized van we were looking to buy for our potential cross-continent adventure. It was just an overnight trip so Michel stayed back in New Orleans.

In Austin, I thought it would be fun to stop at the original Whole Foods to grab a late lunch. While I was getting my MBA at Tulane, the professor who most inspired me was John Elstrott. He taught entrepreneurship, had many successful ventures, and was the chairman of the board at Whole Foods.

I ate outside under an awning as the sun was setting. The muscles in my right hand were starting to weaken, making it difficult to grip the utensils. Fortunately, I was a southpaw so I was able to eat with my left hand. My right leg had also started to weaken, so I walked with a very subtle limp. When I finished eating, I slung my backpack over my left shoulder and headed to the rental car, I stepped off the curb awkwardly and tumbled to the pavement. My arms and legs were too weak to catch me and cushion my fall, and I crashed chin first into the concrete. As I was falling, I released this goofy, awful scream: *Arrgghhhbblleooof!*

There were dozens of people in the parking lot; a handful of them saw what happened and rushed over to see if I was OK. Normally, when people fall, they immediately get back up and announce, "Yeah, I'm OK. I'm OK." I didn't do that because I didn't have the strength to pick myself back up. I just kneeled there for a moment and collected myself. I finally managed to say, "Yeah, I'm all right." After a few seconds, I got to my feet. A couple of guys were concerned and hung close by.

"Hey, man, you sure you're OK?" they asked.

I nodded yes, then slowly made my way to the car. Once inside, I buried my head in my hands and this time I did not laugh. I was alone, hundreds of miles from anyone I knew, getting picked up off the asphalt of a fucking parking lot by strangers. How was this even happening?! How was this *real?!?!*

I wept.

Then I called Michel, briefly explained what had happened, and wept again, openly.

A week later, Michel and I were visiting the Whole Foods store near our house, and my legs gave out again. I fell awkwardly as we were crossing Esplanade Avenue. It was the first time Michel had seen my body fail like this. Up to this point, it had been easier for her to be optimistic and believe that my symptoms weren't real. I could see the distress in her eyes as she struggled to help me to my feet before the oncoming traffic reached us. I didn't weep this time, but I sure felt like it.

In mid-April, I attended a tai chi class instructed by our friend Michael Francis. Tai chi is an ancient Chinese martial arts discipline, specializing in defense training and meditation. I thought the classes would help my balance. Rather than peaceful and liberating, the session was apocalyptic for me. My muscles were too weak to hold many of the poses. Frustration took hold of my mind and wouldn't let go.

When I came home that afternoon, Michel was hastily getting dressed. Our good friend Thais's wedding was that night and she got on me for being late.

I told her about my experience at the class. "Michel," I said, "this is really happening to me!"

She tried to rationalize the whole thing away. "But you've never even tried tai chi. Maybe it was just because it was your first time."

"Why are you always trying to make things better than they really are?!" I shot back.

"Because I don't know what else to do!" Michel said, and now she melted into a wave of tears.

I calmed down and took a long breath. "I'm trying to be positive," I told her. "I really am."

"Well," she said, "try harder."

JAZZ FEST ARRIVED a few weeks later. One of my best friends, Dave Stewart, flew in from Spokane, and we took him to his first-ever Jazz Fest Triathlon. We met up with the crew at the Fais Do Do stage for the second leg of the event. JFT co-founders Hunter Higgins and Bryan Spitzfaden (Spitz) make a commemorative T-shirt every year for the occasion, and this year they put an action shot of me blocking the punt against the Falcons on the shirt. It was a silent nod to my situation, even though only a few people knew about my diagnosis at that point. While I was very much aware that my body was changing, my condition was still not outwardly noticeable to most people. If you paid close attention, you could notice the slight limp when I walked and that my right bicep was smaller than my left one. But otherwise, I looked normal, and I was speaking well.

When the tutu man performed the watermelon sacrifice that day, I enthusiastically joined the ceremony and gobbled down a couple of slices of the sweet, juicy red melon. We then walked to the racetrack for the one-mile run around the dirt oval. Hall of Fame musician Allen Toussaint had been recruited to conduct the ceremonial shotgun start to the race and he dutifully performed the duties during the mayhem, even while beer sprayed all over him.

Michel and I briefly tried to join the run, but I realized after a few wobbly, awkward steps that my legs wouldn't fire. We walked the rest of the way, listening to Lucinda Williams sing in the distance as we met the runners at the finish line. We closed down the Fest by watching Cyndi Lauper perform on the main stage. She sang the *Goonies* song "Good Enough" for her encore, and we all danced joyfully during the beautiful sunset.

We then walked to Cabrini High School for the JFT's final leg, the swim across Bayou St. John. In the school parking lot, I happily took off my shirt and donned my green Crocs and swim cap. Michel was three months pregnant and forbidden by Mama Jill to participate in the swim. Instead, she enthusiastically performed the shotgun start, and we half walked, half jogged to the bayou. Dave helped me down the steep bank and we dove into the dark, still water. As I started to swim, I could see my friend Spitz bobbing ahead of me in his traditional shark head costume. But I struggled to keep up with him. As I half swam, half dog-paddled across, I lost one of my Crocs, and a friend, unaware of my condition, innocently chanted, "Glea-son's dying! Glea-son's dying!" as he watched from the Magnolia Bridge. Pauly, one of the few in the know, saw my struggles, dove back into the bayou, and swam with me and Dave for the final few yards. I made it to the other side, but I was so weak and exhausted that I needed the two of them to lift me out of the water. I couldn't hold their hands or bend my arms or legs, so as they pulled me out of the bayou, my body was perfectly straight, like a corpse, and my stomach scraped all along the concrete flood wall. It was painful, but I'd had a lifetime of training in how to embrace physical pain.

The greater challenge, as I was losing my physical strength, was learning about how to befriend emotions like embarrassment and shame. After my previous falls, I'd become fairly stoic in similar moments. And I remained stoic when I was out of the water. I also had a crowd of people around me, and feeling the love of the JFT tribe was soothing.

This experience was much more difficult for Michel. She witnessed this entire drama play out from the banks of the bayou. The boy she loved, the boy who had pushed her to adventure, the boy who had been her safest place was withering right in front of her. While everyone gathered around me, she stood alone, tears falling down her cheeks. And she too was finally thinking, *This is really happening.*

I CONTINUED TO seek out different ways of healing.

At the recommendation of Tony Hazel, one of my best friends from high school, I visited a Native American healer in California. We spent two days in sweat lodges—it reminded me of my test of strength in the gold Buick sauna of my childhood. We made bonfires, while he advised me to avoid cemeteries or anything to do with the dead. I enjoyed my time here until, at the end of the retreat, we returned to his suburban home. He sat me down in a La-Z-Boy recliner, turned on loud TV sitcoms, and served me a dinner of SpaghettiOs on a plastic TV tray. *What the hell was I doing here?!*

But I continued my quest. I refused to close my mind to any possibilities. And I guess I was refusing to open my mind to the ultimate reality.

During a visit to Spokane, my dad asked me and Michel to see a faith healer named Kevin Dedmon. There's no question that my very fundamentalist religious family had had a strong influence on me. In high school, I taped a white cross on the face mask of my helmet; in college, I designed my own tattoo, a cross with a crown of thorns around the top that spelled Jesus. I had remained a virgin until I met Michel, partially because of this religious influence.

I was always drawn to the deeper, mysterious questions about living well and doing good. After college, I began to explore other belief systems. I figured that following one's curiosity to explore truth was the furthest thing from heresy. And more and more, I questioned everything. I wondered why the omniscient, all-loving creator of the universe supported absurdities and atrocities like slavery, child sacrifices, or public stonings of unmarried girls who were not virgins. It became clear to me that the Bible had a good amount of metaphorical, perennial wisdom and truth, for all humans to live a better life, but it was not an indisputable source for historical, objective truth.

In a "300 Seconds" video journal, I told our as-yet-unborn child how I prayed.

This will go in as our first "Great Creator" journal. I think I'll just say my own prayer, and maybe this will be helpful. But I pray this multiple times a day.

One—I say the Our Father and I say the Hail Mary . . .

And then I have my own prayer. The first part goes like this: I am united with the infinite source of all healing, God the essence of all that is. I pray, God, that essence heal my brain, my mind, and my body. Thank you for the grace that comes with that healing. If I have moments of emotional fear, understand these feelings and digest them with honesty and forgiveness. I see my physical body in perfect health. I am well.

The second part of my prayer is: I am clear of my purpose for this earthly life. I was born in the mountains and wandering rivers, yet I am aware of this life's sacredness no matter where I sit. With every breath that I give I am free. I am spiritual, artistic, inspiring, and different. I am happy to be this way. Amen.

So I went to my dad's faith healer. I figured that this was my opportunity to show that I had the faith to be healed. In our church school, we were very familiar with the story portrayed by the author of Mark. A woman who had been suffering for years, and had spent all her money seeking help, but continued to worsen, was in a crowd around Jesus. She thought, "If I just touch his clothes, I will be healed." Jesus felt her touch his cloak and ultimately says, "Your faith has healed you." Whether the story was historically accurate or not, I thought it was a good guide, showing me I can continue to be open-minded and believe it was possible to heal.

Dedmon was a big deal in the healer community. He was the author of several books on Evangelical theology and had taught healing at the Bethel School of Supernatural Ministry, which claimed to have graduated more than 13,000 revivalists in more than a hundred countries. Michel was skeptical, to say the least, but at that point, I was willing to give it everything I had.

Inside the Healing Rooms Ministries Church, several rows of chairs had been arranged in a semicircle on the carpeted floor. At the front of the room a mic stand, musical equipment, speakers, and amplifiers were set up on a riser. About fifty people were in the crowd, mostly elderly and middle-aged White people in conservative attire. Other than a very subtle limp, I appeared to be in normal health. My dad, Michel, and I found seats in the middle of the fifth row toward the back of the audience. It didn't take long to realize Dedmon was a polished speaker. He went on and on about his faith-healing skills: curing paralysis, healing broken arms on the spot, and bringing people back from the dead. He talked for more than an hour about healing people through faith and he stoked the crowd into a frenzy. I thought, *Is this what Jesus did?!* At one point, he had us stand and sing in unison "It's the end of my pain as I know it" to R.E.M.'s "It's the End of the World as We Know It." People were getting riled up. You could tell some of them really believed what he was preaching.

I tried to remain open but I grew restless. I kept raising my hand to get his attention, but he ignored me. I finally interjected, "Look, man, you've been talking for a while now. You keep talking about getting creative. I say we all get creative here, and we start the healing."

He politely said, "OK," but went back to playing the crowd into a compulsive hysteria.

A few more minutes passed. I told Michel, "I'm going up there." And I did. I walked slowly down the aisle and made my way to the head of the room, where I informed the pastor, "I'm gonna run." He seemed surprised and hesitant at first. But he quickly bought in: "Go for it!"

I turned to the crowd and motioned for them to support this. They responded by clapping and cheering me on. The pastor sensed the moment and said, *"Look at this. This is God doing this! This is awesome! Go ahead. Check it out. Try to make it hurt right now."*

I crouched into a starter's stance like a track sprinter, stretching my left hand to the floor with my fingertips touching the carpet and my right hand pointed behind me, horizontal to the ground. I then rose up and tried to sprint as hard and as fast as I could. I felt the energy and the burst. But instead of streaking across the carpet, I lurched into a series of awkward, choppy steps before my legs gave out and I collapsed face-first onto the floor.

The crowd gasped and fell silent.

"That's OK," the pastor said, sheepishly. He walked over to my crumpled body on the floor. "Good try . . . This was a break-through. That was . . . four steps!"

The crowd responded with a smattering of applause and cheers of encouragement as I wobbled to my knees and unsteadily rose to my feet. The pastor asked for some "big guys" in the audience to assist me toward the back of the church. In a helpless, confused, and desperate fit, I tried to run one more time with each of them holding me by my arms. But I fell again after a few steps.

"That's OK," the preacher repeated. "The healing might not happen right away. Just keep believing. And keep praying."

That was the last time I would run.

The big guys walked me to the back of the church, while Dedmon continued to preach to the rest of the congregation. My dad found me and hugged me from behind.

"If you trust in Him every day, Stephen, I believe you are going to be healed," he said as he rubbed my shoulders. "I truly believe that. The battle is going to be staying focused on healing every day. We're not going to knock the shit out of anybody right now. And you're not going to run a hundred miles an hour just yet. The first place the healing takes place is in your heart and in the mind."

"Yeah," I said. "My heart feels good, and my mind feels good, but my body is not working. You know that, right?"

"I know that," Dad said.

Michel joined the group. She was irate with Dedmon and furious at the people who didn't realize he was a fraud. She was mad at my dad for believing in him and putting me in this situation.

"This is bullshit!" she said.

I hugged her to my chest. Pulling Michel tight, feeling her heartbeat against me, I felt annihilated emotionally, but somehow I also found some understanding and compassion.

"My dad," I said, "like everyone who loves me, is hurting and just trying to find a solution."

A few nights later, still feeling baffled and defeated, I wrote this journal entry.

I am most lonely at night. Which, I suppose, is normal. We are distracted by day. Tasks and errands and food and people.

I am extremely frustrated right now. Progression continues . . . I'm 34. How can this be? My rising was 34 years ago. The return is calling. But why?!

The guilt of the fundamentalist church has instilled a fear in me that I should not question or falter in my faith. But, as my favorite writer, David James Duncan, says, "Only the admission of ignorance can open us to fresh knowing."

So today, in my ignorance, perhaps, I put forth that God is absent. "Seek and you will find." I have knocked. Called. Prayed. Texted. Listened. These are honest emotions which come and go. Passing. Writing them down does not further harm me. They are in my mind. And doesn't God know our mind?

There are a couple of initial conclusions:

1. God is present and active in the physical universe but is, for some reason, not responding to my questions of why this is happening and how I can heal.

2. Or is God absent? Or how about something more positive— God is neutral. Like gravity or light. These forces act according to the cosmic laws and never alter their characteristics. The man falling from a building may ask gravity to release its grip. Or he may ask why gravity is pulling him down. But gravity will not answer or alter.

This is an objective, empirical truth discovered through open investigation. The truth is . . . Beautiful. Perfect. Holy.

Can I leave my guilt and fear behind? If so, I think this is progress; fresh knowing.

The experience with the faith healer curbed my pursuit of alternative healing. I was reminded of a story a doctor told me about a family where the dad was diagnosed with ALS, and the children said that he spent four years chasing his tail trying to find a cure, but he never woke up to watch the sun rise.

So, what would I do with the time I had left?

I planned to fully live—and watch the sun rise.

13

Resolve

Resolve: Leading from discord into concord during the
   course of harmonic change.
Resolve: To cause (a symptom or condition) to disperse,
   subside, or heal.
Resolve: To decide firmly on a course of action.

I had never witnessed anyone die.

The closest I'd come was in eighth grade. A pack of my friends and I decided to walk the back way to my house, rather than take the streets. I loved the location of our house on the steep ridge leading up to the top of Five Mile Prairie. Our school, Assumption Catholic, was situated on the same steep ridge, but it was about a mile west. That day, we went behind the school and hiked along the dry, sagebrush-ridden basalt ridge, looking for ways to scale it and get to the top of Five Mile Prairie. We planned then to walk along that barren, desolate top overlooking the city of Spokane, then drop down the ridge and go to my house. On this hike, we discovered a cylindrical cliff that led to the top of the prairie. The cliff was probably between fifteen and twenty feet high, with plenty of craggy nooks to place our hands and feet to climb up.

I was one of the last to begin. Looking up, I watched our buddy Tim Aguilar climb. I'm not sure what happened, but as he was almost to the top, he fell. Straight back, and even in the air he looked as if he were lying peacefully in bed. In my mind, it happened in slow motion. When he landed, perfectly flat, he didn't move, other than his head limply bouncing once off a flat black lava rock. I raced over to him. Blood rushed from his nose and the corner of one eye. My mind was frozen, my body numb. "Get an ambulance!" someone yelled from the top of the prairie. I immediately thawed out and raced to our school. A couple of guys were running with me. We got to the office and gasped "Call 911! There's been an accident!" I don't remember much in the chaos of the next several minutes, but firemen and paramedics followed us up to the scene, secured Tim's body on a stretcher, and took him to the hospital. He ended up recovering fully, but when I saw him land on that rock, saw the blood, I was sure that I was witnessing what it looked like to die.

Two decades later, I was certain I was witnessing my own death—not as part of a slow decline from ALS, but as something immediate, as instantaneous as Tim's fall.

We spent a weekend during Easter Break with the Varisco family in Orange Beach, Alabama. We shared a condo with Vinnie and Julie and their kids; Paul and Jilly were next door with Pauly and Hilary and their family.

Michel and I went swimming in the shallow water of the Gulf of Mexico to get in some light exercise without putting too much strain on my body. I waded along the shoreline in chest-high water so I could still touch the sand with my feet. Then, very gradually, a subtle undertow pulled me into deeper water. Unlike twenty years earlier, when my mind froze and my body went numb after Tim's fall, my mind was clearly aware of what was happening, but my body was in a bizarre, dreamlike slow motion. In astonishment and with raw, primal fear, all I could do was look at Michel, and do my best to cry "Help."

From my time surfing, I knew the ocean was *infinitely* powerful, but my mind was still baffled at my weakness. I had always been a strong swimmer, but now I was seeing—and comprehending—in stark detail just how much my body had withered. My eyes fixed on Michel, and although she couldn't hear my quiet pleas, she saw my face and instantly recognized the fear within me. I heard her yell desperately to her parents. My breathing quickened and my heart rate accelerated as I felt my body being pulled under the surface of the water. I saw Mic and her parents swimming toward me. I tilted my head back and struggled against the undertow like a child just learning to swim. Comfort flooded through me as Michel stretched out and grabbed my left hand. Her dad grabbed her around the waist, and we all swam toward the beach in a cocktail mix of pure adrenaline and peaceful relief.

That was the last time I ever swam in the ocean.

THAT MORNING, before that swim, I was in the condo, talking with Jilly (Mama Jill's new name post grandkids) and my sister-in-law Julie. During breakfast, I told her about the effort it took to do something as simple and easy as talking, and in that moment of honesty, the chaos of the disease overtook me.

"Everything is changing so fucking fast, it's mind-boggling," I said, burying my face in my hands as tears filled my eyes. "Time is closing in.

"Instead of waking up *from* a nightmare," I said, "every single morning, I wake up *to* a nightmare."

I stood up, and they came in to hug me. As always in my experience, these truthful and unembellished tears were healing. Baptism and redemption.

That night, Michel and I lit the fire in our master bedroom. Another day in our lives was in the past. What would the next day bring us? We lay in front of the fire as it warmed our feet. We fell asleep in each other's arms.

At dawn the next morning, I woke up early and sat on the balcony to watch the sun rise. Later, I sat out there eating breakfast. I stood up, leaned on the railing, and watched people migrate to the water. A glorious sight caught my eye: a father and son playing catch in the sand. It brought back fond and vivid memories of doing the same with my dad. Then, it hit me: *I will never play catch with our child.*

Baseball was my favorite sport. Football was a business, an

extreme workout. But baseball is a boys' game, fun and carefree. Center field, the only position I played after I was fourteen, is the most sacred ground in all of sports. Racing and sacrificing every ounce of myself to dive and catch an elusive, well-hit, low-trajectory fly ball was my most fulfilling experience in sports.

I couldn't remember the last time I'd tracked and laid out for a fly ball. But I knew I would never do it again. I also would never play catch with our child. Alone on the balcony, this realization obliterated me. *NEVER!* This was not simply about how *I* felt. What about our child? How would he or she know this sacred love? Standing alone, watching the father and son casually throw the ball around, I mourned and moved through another death of the boy I once was.

In retrospect, this process of mourning was like a healthy, brilliant game of catch with one of humanity's closest friends: Grief. But at that moment, all I could wonder was if I could continue to leave "that boy" I'd been behind. And how many losses could I sustain before I completely lost myself?

IN LATE SPRING of 2011, Michel and I embarked on one more epic adventure: a 15,000-mile road trip from New Orleans to Alaska in a customized, four-wheel-drive camper van we named "the Iron Horse." We dubbed the three-month adventure "the Shunpike Experiment," a nod to Stanley Shunpike, the Harry Potter wizard. A shunpike is defined as a side road used to avoid the speed and traffic of a superhighway, an apt metaphor to describe the trip in the context of our soon-to-be chaotic lives.

On the surface, this journey appeared similar to our past trips. The undetermined, meandering route. Our exploratory mindset. The camper van. It all fell in line with previous adventures. But physically we were changed.

In 2005, on our first trip to the ski area of my youth, Schweitzer Mountain, Michel marveled at my ability to change a flat tire so quickly on the side of a highway in the middle of a blizzard. Now, she had to hold my hand every time I climbed out of the Iron Horse. I was still walking, but unsteadily. Once out, I used a walking stick we bought at a park ranger station in Texas. We named the stick Louie after Michel's grandpa, Big Lew.

Michel had always been a hundred-pound dynamo, agile and competitive. In the past, she had regularly tried to keep up with me physically, but that occasionally backfired. During our 2008 trip to New Zealand, we came upon a huge tree with spikes in the trunk so people could climb to the top and gaze over the entire forest. There was no safety net of any kind. Only spikes circling the trunk for hundreds of feet. Mic desperately wanted to climb as high as I did. But after she made it to the first little rest space about a quarter of the way up, she realized she was afraid of heights and started hyperventilating. I had to help her down.

Her fierce competitive streak revealed itself early in our relationship. During a pickup football game in the yard of my teammate John Carney's house in San Diego, Michel challenged me to tackle her.

"Steve, *do not* take it easy on me," she said in complete seriousness. "Just do it."

I looked at her and asked if she was truly up for this. She nodded and quickly said, "1, 2, 3 . . . Hut!" I rushed forward, lowered my head, and tackled her—and knocked the wind out of her. John thought I was crazy. I was concerned at first, but when I saw that Michel genuinely enjoyed the experience, I thought, *This girl is even more amazing than I thought! She is exactly who I want in my life.*

On the shunpike, Michel was still pretty agile, even with a size 2 soccer ball in her belly.

This cross-continent adventure was our commitment to live in the face of death, our way of watching the sun rise along this new journey with ALS. The disease, though, was progressing relentlessly. The strength in my arms and hands was getting weaker by the day.

On the way to Los Angeles, we made a pit stop at a NAPA Auto Parts store in New Mexico to buy a jack for the van. The clerk walked us to the jack, and I tried to grab it but wasn't strong enough to lift it off the ground. We all stood there. Michel fidgeted. The guy looked me up and down, seeming perplexed, almost offended.

After an awkward pause, Michel blurted out, "He's having hand issues. Can you please carry that out for us?"

She was learning how to navigate the disease publicly, as was I.

WE DROVE THROUGH California to visit friends, then meandered our way north to the Gorge Amphitheatre in George, Washington, where we met up with a group of my buddies from Spokane and their families. Matt Shaw, who has been one of my best friends since seventh grade, was the head of sponsorship for this weekend's event, Sasquatch Music Festival. Matt got us backstage passes for the Foo Fighters concert. I'd been coming to shows at the picturesque amphitheater for twenty years and had some amazing memories of this unique venue with this group of friends. This was the first time I'd seen them since I'd been diagnosed, so the beauty and preciousness of this moment, in this place, was not lost or not taken for granted by any of us. The Foo Fighters had just released an album—*Wasting Light*. One song on the album stood out as powerful and poignant for me: "Walk." As I sat on the grassy amphitheater listening to Dave Grohl sing, a tear came to my eye.

> *I'm learning to walk again*
> *I believe I've waited long enough*
> *Where do I begin?*
> *I'm learning to talk again*
> *Can't you see I've waited long enough?*
> *Where do I begin?*

Could this happen in my life? Could I dance on my grave, and learn to walk and talk again if this disease took them away?

At this point in my body's progression, peeing was starting to be an issue, especially if I was far away from the bathroom. On the festival grounds, we'd solved the issue by forming a human wall so I could pee in the grass. When I could actually get to the bathroom, I could pee on my own, as long as someone unzipped my pants. On the first night of the festival, my good buddy Dave Stewart helped me walk to the bathroom and dutifully guided me into the stall. Dave unzipped, and I was ready to pee. As I was about to unleash, I was pretty shocked to feel Dave's hand holding my penis.

In the quiet of the men's bathroom, I looked down, let out a little chuckle of nervous laughter, looked into his eyes, smiled, and whispered, "Hey, I love you, Dave, but . . . you don't have to hold my dick."

He hastily backed away as we both erupted in laughter. As we walked back and told everyone else the story, I looked out over the ancient and rugged Gorge, and the strikingly beautiful Columbia River. I took comfort that I was so damn lucky to have a lot of friends like Matt and Dave in the trenches with me.

The next day, Mic and I sat on the grass hill overlooking the main stage and the vast Columbia River basin. A moment of profundity for our future family blossomed as a local Seattle band, The Head and the Heart, took the stage. To end the set, they played a song called "Rivers and Roads."

"Rivers" was one of our top names if we had a boy, and it was easily my personal favorite. The rivers of the Northwest had shaped my life.

When the band sang the chorus—"Rivers and roads, rivers and roads. Rivers, 'til I reach you"—I felt a rush of joy, contentment, and certainty flow through me. I looked at Michel, and we both smiled. The decision was settled: If we had a boy, his name would be Rivers.

After the concert, we started the second leg of our trip in the Iron Horse and headed to Alaska. My dad and stepmom, Jackie, visited us in Denali. My dad brought his spotting scope and was eager to see some wildlife. Growing up, some of my most pleasant memories with Pops were watching nature shows with him. All his self-absorption and critical lashing out would dissolve, and he would marvel with wonder and excitement at the animals, especially wolves and grizzly bears, which were everywhere in this national park.

Michel has always loved my dad, and I love that she loves him. She appreciates his forthcoming nature, his ability to admit his faults, and even his childlike, crude, sometimes offensive humor. On the April Fools' Day after we started dating, in 2005, we called my dad. Michel and I were in her Volkswagen about to watch a show at Tipitina's, a rustic live music venue around the corner from my Uptown house. Sitting in the passenger seat, I had him on speakerphone. I absorbed myself in my role in this scene. As he answered the phone, the excitement of pulling this off caused me to laugh, but I was able to transform this to sound like crying. "Dad," I said, "Michel is . . . pregnant." We heard him take a couple of deep breaths and I knew we had him on the hook. Finally, he said, quietly yet sternly, "Stephen, I told you you shouldn't be dippin' your wick. And if you were"—he paused and took another deep breath—"you shoulda been using a rubber!" Mic and I were laughing hysterically, but as quietly as possible. He then said, "Stephen, I've been praying that God would bring you to your knees, so—" I quickly interrupted, still laughing, "Dad, Dad . . . April Fools, man!" Michel chimed in: "We love you, Mike! April Fools."

While we still have our moments of tension, I've learned to see my dad as "that guy"—crude and coarse, but oddly endearing and lovable.

In a way, I've learned to see him through Michel's eyes.

In Denali, winds started picking up as we rode out to Wonder Lake. Dad looked for a spot he liked. He excitedly and awkwardly leaned over an elderly woman in her seat to see out the window and yelled, "Driver! There's a bear! We're getting off!" The people on the bus watched quizzically as I carefully climbed down the steps. Even with Louie, my walking stick, it was difficult to stand straight in the wind. We slowly hiked up the tundra until we found a ridge overlooking a river drainage and a valley. My dad set up his scope and about forty-five minutes after we settled in he whispered, "I got a grizzly!"

We locked in on it with the scope—but then we lost it. Behind us, Michel blurted out, "There is a bear, right on the road." As I looked back I saw that she was eating a chocolate chip cookie, and that the bear was walking directly toward us. If this was the same bear we saw in the spotting scope, it had disappeared from the ridge in front of us and in less than two minutes reached the road behind us. As it got closer to us, in an effort to stay calm and poised, I remembered that one of our guides told us that no one had ever been killed by a bear in Denali National Park, because people didn't feed the wildlife. The bear moved closer, and then, after a few moments, it disappeared again. That was the last we saw of the bear. We made it to the road, exhausted but unharmed, and waited to get picked up by another bus.

That evening, Michel and I were with my cousin Brendan in the Iron Horse. We pulled over to a meadow overlooking a valley to have some dinner. We were telling him about the grizzly encounter while he cooked. I was standing outside the passenger side, which had double doors opening to the rear end of the Iron Horse. Holding on to one of the doors with my right hand, I was looking in at Brendan, enthusiastically describing our "escape." Excitedly explaining how crazy it was, I lifted my left arm and started to fall back. All I had to do was step back and steady myself, but my legs didn't move. I fell straight back, similar to the way my classmate Tim Aguilar had fallen off the cliff at Five Mile Prairie. Unable to move. And like Tim, when I landed, my head bounced off a flat black lava rock. I was OK. After I got up, I realized if that rock hadn't been flat, I could have died. As I collected myself, I thought how strange it was that something as mundane as telling a story could be as dangerous as crossing paths with a grizzly bear, or even more so.

My dad and Jackie left, and my brother flew into Anchorage to meet us. We were booked for a salmon fishing trip on the Kenai River. Kyle and I went down to Quartz Creek near our lodge in Cooper Landing to practice our fly-fishing techniques. The creek was shallow and full of sockeye salmon. Nearing the end of their life cycle, the fish had turned a deep scarlet red and swum upstream to spawn. This scene was like a sublime alien encounter: the clear blue of the river as a canvas, the scarlet fish hovering with an ancient and peaceful resolve to ceaselessly move upstream to their final destination.

The irony hit me. Am I any different from these wonderfully

evolved creatures? Swimming upstream at the end of my short life, while bringing my offspring into this world. I'd fished since I was very young, and grown to honor the rivers, the environment, and their sacred creation, but in this moment I felt an even more powerful kinship with this place and these alien beings.

As we walked to the river, I knew this would be difficult, but to land a salmon in Alaska on the legendary Kenai River was a bucket-list experience for me. Kyle positioned himself on the bank and showed me how to make a roll cast, a technique that doesn't require much of a back cast, which I was no longer capable of doing. But my rod was designed for a right-handed angler, with the reel on the left side, and I didn't have the strength in my right arm to maneuver it. I focused and made a greater effort. I wasn't going to give up. Those traits had brought me a lot of success on the football field. It didn't help me here, though. While Kyle was effortlessly flipping his line into the rushing water, I struggled to lift the rod; my feeble casts were going nowhere. Frustration swelled within me. The harder I tried, the worse it got. After several failed attempts, my emotions erupted. I threw down the rod and punched Kyle in the shoulder.

"Fuck you, I can't do it!" I said.

I left Kyle on the bank and retreated to the Iron Horse. I broke down to Michel and Brendan.

When I played football, in addition to focus and effort, I was successful because I clearly recognized my role within the team. Many players, especially younger guys, wanted so badly to be in the starting lineup on offense or defense, they weren't able to accept reality and scoffed at playing on special teams. They interpreted it as a demotion or even a chore. When I was unable to cast the fishing rod, I interpreted it as a demotion. I suffered because I didn't understand my role in this process.

The next day as we drifted down the river with our guide, Jason, my spirit connected with the vast and heavenly landscape and the camaraderie of being with Michel, Kyle, and Brendan. The cold, wet conditions made it impossible for me to cast a fly rod with either hand. I chose to make the most of the situation and scouted the river for the rest of the group, pointing out the shadowy salmon in the water with my walking stick. Once again, I accepted my role on the team and played it with the most effort I was capable of giving.

The fishing was slow early on, but our luck improved as the day progressed. Kyle snagged a sockeye, and Brendan landed a beautiful sockeye female. When Michel had a big sockeye snatch the pole out of her hands, I figured I'd now give it a try. Practicing with Kyle the day before had been frustrating because I'd been attached to the expectation of catching a fish. That broke me open. The suffering made it easier to sacrifice any expectations, and simply enjoy this hallowed ground. I gave myself to this process.

Wading shin-deep into the rushing emerald stream, I propped myself against the skiff to maintain my balance. Jason helped me improvise a casting technique, where I tossed the line into the current and let the river take it downstream. My casting range was no more than eight feet, but the technique was easier for me, and it was effective. Five minutes in, I felt a massive thump and pull on my line. *Unreal!* I raised the rod as high as I could and set the hook. The line went taut, and I could feel the unmistakable wobble of a shocked and angry sockeye on the other end. *This is happening!* The tension of the fish and the strain in my body swirled and danced with the overwhelming joy and wonder in my mind.

Brendan scrambled down the shoreline to see if I needed help, but I was able to use my left arm to leverage the rod and work the powerful fish in to the shore. In utter disbelief, with an overwhelming sense of gratitude, I high-fived Brendan and bent over, overcome by the sheer awe of the experience. I actually wondered if this could all be real. When I heard Michel shriek and cheer from the bank as Jason netted the feisty 17-pounder, I knew it was.

Our cross-continent journey reminded me of a passage from my favorite novel, *The Brothers K*, by author David James Duncan. One of the book's characters, a young girl named Vera, has a harelip, which makes everything she says sound like it starts with the letter *n*. Baseball becomes "nasenall" and Jesus becomes "Nyeesus." Despite her condition, she is one of the most passionate members of the local church and regularly asks to lead the closing prayer on Sundays. This leads to all sorts of chaos in the congregation. Young boys snicker and mock her. Their horrified parents scramble to correct them. Meanwhile, Vera continues her prayer, unaware or unconcerned with the clamor around her. "No one counted to her," Duncan wrote, "except maybe, you know, God, or something."

The Shunpike Experiment was our version of living a harelip prayer.

WE RETURNED HOME to New Orleans in early September to our "real life," which was a chaotic contrast to the vast, quiet life we'd been living. Michel was a month away from giving birth, and we needed to start preparing for our new role as parents.

While my voice was still pretty strong, I started voice banking with a Scottish company called CereProc to create a synthetic voice. I recorded 1,500 English phrases on my computer and sent them to CereProc technicians, who used what was cutting-edge technology at the time to create a customized voice that sounded similar to mine. The vast majority of people with ALS receive generic computerized voices. This voice-banking technology was a new development that I was extremely lucky to find. It allowed me to explore a way to maintain some of my identity and still remain "that boy."

While I voice-banked each night, we also kept busy with other tasks during the day. We finalized our disability claims with the NFL. I finished the necessary tests to graduate from Tulane with my master's in business administration. We retrofitted our house by the bayou with a handicapped-accessible ramp. During the final days of the Shunpike Experiment, we had created a support group of close friends and family named "Team Gleason." We now met every couple of weeks to discuss our life and future plans. And we made plans to go public with the announcement of my disease. We just didn't know exactly how to do it.

While I thought my story might be a national topic of conversation because of my time in the NFL, I decided that the news was best disseminated from New Orleans, my home. This was where I blocked the punt and became a symbol of the city's own healing. I wanted to be with my family, my New Orleans family, when I shared something so very personal with the world.

The New Orleans media and the Saints had been very respectful and had kept my diagnosis quiet. But now that we were ready, they were fully on board with our plans. We decided to announce my diagnosis in a feature story written by a local journalist whom both Michel and I trusted and loved, Jeff Duncan. I had known him for years during his tenure at the *Times-Picayune* newspaper.

A couple weeks before the announcement, we met with the Team Gleason crew and hashed out more details. On the last leg of the Alaska trip, Mic flew home to prepare for the birth, while I spent a week or so at my friend's Black Rock cabin on Coeur d'Alene Lake. One morning, I was brainstorming the mission of our foundation and how we could effect change for people living with ALS. I wanted it to be innovative and unique. I had called one of my oldest best friends, Jim Salters, who was now a successful entrepreneur. Jim has always been a great and trusted idea guy. As we threw ideas against the wall, two images came to mind. One was of the people I was committed to help—the "freak show" Michel and I saw at Forbes Norris in San Francisco. The second depicted the way that I wanted to help people like them live—so they could experience the joy and wonder I had experienced catching the salmon on the Kenai River. There were a lot of organizations pushing for a cure to ALS, but hardly any working to help people *live* with ALS. I saw this as an opportunity to create disruption and positive change in the "marketplace." The mantra that had become so important to me at Gonzaga Prep helped me shape this vision: *To serve yourself, first seek to serve others.*

Back in New Orleans, I continued to shape these ideas with Michel, her dad, Paul, and our friends and family over the next few weeks until we finalized our strategic plan.

The mission of Team Gleason would be tackled on short-, medium-, and long-term fronts. The short-term goal was to help people currently living with ALS. We wanted to raise money to buy communication tablets with eye-tracking equipment and assistive technology for patients who couldn't afford them. We also wanted to provide trips—Team Gleason Adventures—for patients. We thought these experiences could give them something they didn't think possible after their diagnosis. These activities would serve as a source of inspiration, not only for the participants, but for others with ALS.

The medium-term work was to continue improving the technology for ALS patients. We wanted to create a mechanism to fast-track the development of innovative products so we could transform as many lives in as short a time frame as possible.

And finally, long term, we wanted to help find a cure for the disease by coordinating efforts from various agencies and directing more money to research.

So we created the Gleason Initiative Foundation, a 501(c)(3) non-profit, to

1. Provide support through innovation to help people LIVE with ALS
2. Help accelerate a cure or treatment for ALS

We were also advised to create a trust, for funds to go to our family. Legally, we cannot receive benefits from our foundation, but we can contribute to our foundation. We established the Gleason Family Trust to offset incremental costs that were incurred due to my diagnosis.

During a meeting at the Ice House in Mid-City, I emphasized the need to establish a positive attitude and determined mindset along the way. Someone mentioned an idea about handing out white rally towels at a Saints game.

"There will be no white flags on this journey," I said.

A buddy, Sig Greenebaum, said, "There's your motto."

"No White Flags" became our mission statement. We immediately trademarked the phrase for Team Gleason. It would become our rallying cry, not just for myself but for everyone in our orbit.

ON THE DAY before the public announcement, our team was in full force trying to prepare for the day. The truth is, Michel and I were in way over our heads. We had reached out to Vinnie to help us, as well as Michel's friend from high school, Suzanne Alford. Realizing the state we were in—and as I would later discover, what a mess of a website I had created—they dropped everything for a week straight and worked with us, adding content to the Team Gleason web page, plugging in donation links, and creating Twitter and Facebook pages.

Meanwhile, Michel was weeks away from giving birth, and I was experiencing continued weakness in my muscles. It was getting harder to do the most basic tasks. Michel had to help me get dressed, shower, and eat. But this pre-announcement adrenaline kept us excited and moving forward.

That night, we had no idea that we were starting a movement that would last over a decade (and is still going strong), but we did fully realize that we were unconditionally loved by our friends.

One of my best friends, former Saints teammate Scott Fujita, sent us this note on the eve of the big day:

S&M,

On Sunday, a new chapter in your journey begins.
And as it is with many of the adventures you've embarked
on together, this too is filled with uncertainty, ambiguity
and unfamiliarity. But again, as with all things, you will be
fine. You will be fantastic. You will continue to inspire and
triumph as you have with every other challenge that's come
your way.

I imagine you're both feeling some anxiety. I feel it with
you. But if at any time you feel overwhelmed, pressured or
uncomfortable, here are a few things I think you should
remember. You control the message. You control the pace.
You control the tone and sentiment of your story as you tell it.
You can step back and take a breath anytime you want. This is
YOUR journey.

And know this: Everyone loves you both. EVERYONE.

Everyone wants what's best for you. Everyone is rooting for you. Everyone has your best interests at heart. This is another chapter in your incredible life together, and everyone who's about to catch a glimpse of that life will feel blessed.

I love you both, and I'm with you.

Keep runnin' bro.

Fuji

THE STORY ANNOUNCING my diagnosis ran on the front page of the Sunday, September 25, edition of the New Orleans *Times-Picayune*; it was the five-year anniversary of the blocked punt. The piece took up three full pages in the A section of the paper and also was prominently displayed on the paper's website, NOLA.com. That morning, our inboxes and phones were inundated with texts and emails from family, friends, and families of those friends.

The Saints had learned about the timing of my announcement a few days beforehand and invited me to serve as the honorary captain for their home game at the Superdome that day against the Houston Texans. I rode to the stadium with Michel, my mom, Suzanne, and some members of our film crew. I'd attended many games since I retired, but this was the first time I'd worn my black No. 37 jersey and been invited back on the field. I was excited—and nervous.

When we arrived at the Dome, Michel held my hand and led me down the tunnel to the field. We found Drew Brees on the Saints sideline. While we lined up to walk to midfield for the pre-game coin toss, the public address announcer introduced me to the crowd as the honorary captain. I put my left hand on the back of Drew's shoulder pads to steady myself and slowly walked to midfield between him and fellow team captain Will Smith.

When we reached midfield, as I always did on game days, I looked toward the crowd to immerse myself in the moment. Not long ago, this had been my office. I had been fast, strong, and confident. Now, with 75,000 people watching from the stands, I was half the man I used to be. Rather than bare my chest, I wanted to unravel.

After the coin-toss ceremony, Drew, Will, and I walked toward the north end zone to start the traditional pregame "Who Dat" chant. The energy in the stadium escalated as the sellout crowd rose to its feet and began to scream and applaud. This was my chance, the opportunity to share my physical weakness with the people of New Orleans, the family that had embraced me eleven years earlier, the community that had motivated me to be resilient in the face of tragedy. This was my chance to return that motivation to this beautiful family.

When we reached the 25-yard line, I thought, *The time is now Steve-O. No choice, dude.* I looked up to the faces in the end zone stadium seats, and I wanted to run. In the middle of the field, with everyone watching, I dropped my head. *Let this cup pass.* I felt my lips quiver. From somewhere, from nowhere, from Drew and Will, from the people in the stands and from within, I found a pearl of strength. I lifted my head and told Drew, "I'm ready." I raised my left arm as high as I could above my head and emphatically, as an act of defiance, slammed it down toward the turf to initiate the chant. The roar of the crowd overwhelmed me as they broke into the chant: *Who Dat!, Who Dat! Who Dat say dey gonna beat dem Saints?!*

A photographer captured the shot of me with my left arm raised. The silhouette of this image would eventually become the logo for Team Gleason. Interestingly, the silhouette used was of the back of me, showing my right arm raised, but we never changed it.

Michel, Suzanne, and I watched from a table behind the Saints bench as the Saints beat the Texans 40–33. During the game, Michel and I marveled as the announcement story went viral and responses poured in from across the country to the new Team Gleason website. Our Twitter account had 11 followers before the story was published. By the time the game ended, our follower count had soared to more than 1,300. That might not seem like much today, but at the time, it was unbelievable.

Afterward, Coach Payton invited me into the postgame locker room and presented me with a game ball in front of the team.

The next morning, I wrote an email to Team Gleason members:

Five-Year Anniversary: My Thoughts

In its simplest form, football is just a game of boys. But in this game there are so many lessons that correlate to life outside the game. For me that correlation has never been stronger than it was yesterday at the Texans-Saints game.

There are times in life, despite your efforts, things don't go your way. Yesterday, we found ourselves nine points behind late in the game.

In the past, I would have seen the crowd become unruly and coaches come unraveled and players lose their poise, resulting in an inevitable loss.

But against the Texans, despite bad luck, poor play and dire circumstances, I saw a team that stayed together, leaned upon its support and faced its fear head-on with a calming sense of certainty. We may not win every game when down 9 with 13 minutes to play but it is a winning formula.

The challenges that I face are real. This is no game. Physically, things have not gone my way, I've made mistakes in life and the experts tell me the clock is ticking.

But in the end, I think the formula is the same. I am staying close to the ones that I love and I am relying on support from my team and I am looking my fear in the eye and laying bare my chest.

I am not here to predict the outcome of my life, but I have a calming sense of certainty.

Love,
SG

The Team Gleason website received more than eight hundred emails in the week after the story ran. The messages ran the gamut. Many offered healing solutions, everything from nutritional supplements to miracle drinking water to stem cell treatment to massage therapy. Others offered prayers or their service as a volunteer for upcoming Team Gleason events. An eight-year-old boy wrote to tell us he donated his entire year's allowance at a local ALS walk. Someone delivered a blueberry cobbler to our house.

That Monday night, the Saints threw a private surprise party at Mr. John's Steakhouse and awarded me a ring from Super Bowl XLIV. Saints head coach Sean Payton and general manager Mickey Loomis were there, and a bunch of my former teammates flew in from across the country to attend. It felt like a family reunion as Scott Fujita went around the room, embarrassing us all with anecdotes and memories.

"When I think about the journey we've been on, it's not so much about the trophies, it's not so much about the games themselves, it's about each individual contribution and memory on that journey," Scott said.

New Orleans mayor Mitch Landrieu presented me with an official key to the city and thanked me for marrying a New Orleans girl.

"You have continued to just teach us and show us with great grace and dignity and strength what it really means to live a full life," he said. "It's a great lesson and you keep giving it to us. So we love you."

At the end of the night, Michel held the microphone for me as I spoke to the gathering and thanked everyone for their love and support:

"The last few days have been pretty overwhelming, in a great way. We can talk about the blocked punt, and we can talk about rings. But what's more important to me is what we do when we walk out of this room—BECAUSE ALS HAS FUCKED WITH THE WRONG DUDE!"

ON THE MORNING of October 19, 2011, I awoke to Michel whispering on the phone to her brother Vinnie, not wanting to disturb me. She wasn't due for another eight days but was experiencing some cramping and asked him what she should do. He told her to go poop. After Jilly told her to call the doctor, we got ready to go to the hospital. A young filmmaker named Ty Minton-Small had flown from Seattle two days earlier to film the events surrounding the birth. Since I could no longer drive, and Ty could not operate a stick shift, Michel was forced to drive me and Ty to the hospital in the Jetta wagon. On the way, I tried to negotiate with her to let Ty be in the room to film the actual birth.

"Are you out of your mind?!" Michel screamed at a stoplight, mid-contraction. "He's twenty-three. We just met him! I don't want him filming my privates."

"He won't have to stand *right there!* He can just be in there and work the cameras," I lobbied.

We compromised. Ty would set up the cameras but leave when things got too intimate. That seemed to make them both a lot more comfortable.

While we were still in the car with nerves still kind of frayed, my sister-in-law Julie, whom I'd broken down with several months earlier, called. Considering the timing, the question surprised me. She asked was I ready for this? In the NFL, coaches asked me the same question right before game time; I smiled and joyously answered her like I answered them: "No choice!"

We walked through Ochsner Medical Center to the seventh floor, Michel's hand on my back as I walked unsteadily with my cane. Dr. George Morris IV (Jody) saw us and told us to go home.

"The baby's coming soon," he said. "But not today."

Disappointed, we stood up to leave. Then Michel stopped, and said, "Oh, boy, oh boy, oh boy." And then "Holy shit!"

Her water had broken.

"OK," Dr. Jody said. "You're not going anywhere!"

WE WERE SET UP in a spacious room with a beautiful view of the Mississippi River. Ty and I set up cameras around the room while Michel got situated.

Next door, we heard primal, harrowing screams from a woman in labor. It sounded like a horror movie. I glanced at Michel. She asked the nurse, "That girl didn't have an epidural, right?" The nurse replied, "Yes. Yes, she did," and walked out of the room.

"Steve," she'd said to me, "I don't know if I can do this." I squeezed her hand and said, "No choice!"

As her contractions started getting intense, Michel got her epidural and calmed down.

The doctor came in around 7:30 p.m. Everyone left except me and Jilly. I put on my scrubs.

At a dinner a few weeks earlier with Drew and Brittany Brees, Drew had told me that delivering his kids was one of the most amazing experiences of his life. A lot of men may find it too tough to take—too bloody, too visceral. I figured this was the truth of life, and the truth is always beautiful. So, I was all in. My hands and arms were not strong enough to do it alone, but I was ready to do everything I could.

At 8 p.m., Michel started pushing. I helped her stay focused and follow instructions. By 8:10, Dr. Jody told me to come to the foot of the bed, to get in there for the delivery. This process—giving life to a new human being—was truly miraculous for me to witness. All I felt was gratitude for being able to participate, for being there with my family. At 8:19, with Dr. Jody's help, I gently pulled our beautiful baby from Michel.

"We've got a baby boy!" Dr. Jody announced.

"It's Rivers!" Jilly exclaimed.

Feeling pure, infinite joy, I cried out, "That's my boy!" *Holy shit balls! I'm not going to BE a daddy, I AM a daddy!!* I thought, *I'm here for you right now, my son, and I will love you forever, Rivers.*

"That was so easy!" Michel said, shaking. "I'm ready for baby no. 2!"

After all was cleaned up and the baby put on Michel's chest, the room was flooded with family and friends.

Later, as the excitement of the birth transitioned to calm and quiet, it was just me, Rivers, and Michel. I pulled up a chair to sit and just be with them. They were both sleeping and I sat there in some form of worship during this holy moment. I reflected on my life and how the rivers of the Northwest and southern Louisiana had influenced me. I quickly wrote some notes in my phone, starting with a title: Why I Love Rivers.

I finished the notes. There would be more in the coming weeks.

Then I stood at the bedside, leaned over to Rivers, who was lying on Michel's chest, and whispered the words I'd just written in his ear: "I am from the mountains and wandering rivers, yet I am aware of this life's sacredness, no matter where I sit. With every breath that I am given, I am free. I am cleansed and baptized by rivers. I'm most at peace, at the river's edge.

"I rarely think about WHY I am filled with this peace. I have disappeared into Life. The sacred. Plants, animals and all creation abide near the rivers. At the river's edge our cup runneth over.

"Years ago I decided rivers are the source of fire. Fire's fuel is wood from the tree that drinks from the river. You, my son, are the rivers for my fire—my fire that burns so bright."

ON THE ONE-YEAR ANNIVERSARY of my diagnosis, I recorded a "300 Seconds" video for Rivers:

> We've had a lot of tough days and nights in the last 365 days; we've cried a whole bunch, but we've laughed much more than we've laughed in any other 365-day stretch. I've lost a lot of things. Lost a lot of muscle. I've lost some ability to do certain things like put on a T-shirt, take off a T-shirt, touch my pinky, lift my hands, clap, snap. But I've gained a lot of things, too. I've learned to accept others' support and help. I've learned to share myself with other people; it can be difficult at first when you can't do something. You look funny. Or you can't walk. Or you talk funny. Part of me wants to not go outside or not talk with anyone or not walk anywhere. But I've gained the ability to say, "Hey, I'm kind of embarrassed about this," or "I know I look funny, but I'm gonna do this anyway." And that is something that I maybe never would have learned or gained without this diagnosis. I think I've learned more than I've lost, and I've gained more than I've lost in the last 365 days. That's especially true, Rivers, since you've shown up.

Michel and I have had to make more crazy decisions in the

last 365 days than any young couple should ever have to make: What kind of bed to buy; How to get a wheelchair; Whether I should put a feeding tube in my stomach; Whether I should fly to India for stem cell research; Whether I should quit jobs, or stay in school, or quit school and stay with the job; Whether we should move to a different part of the country; What kind of treatments to decide; Where to go see a doctor; How to pay for certain things; How to help other people; How to let people know that this disease is brutal, and it's common, it's out there, tens of thousands of people across this country have it.

I also think that I'm gonna get better, and what better way to continue life than experiencing something as challenging and difficult and frustrating and stupid and lame as ALS? To beat it, to win, to come back and to share what I've learned during the process, and to live a very, very long time after that; it's gonna be an incredible gift for me. I consider myself lucky on Jan. 5, 2012; I consider myself a very, very lucky boy. I have an incredible, amazing wife who does everything for me, from washing my hair, to putting on my shirts, to putting a spoon in my mouth to feed me. And she brought me an incredible, beautiful, sweet, smart son—Rivers Varisco Gleason—and I have as much love surrounding me as anybody. My soul is pure. My soul is safe. I'm on fire. I love life. What more could I ask for?

A couple of days later, I celebrated my soul's pure fire and love of life by skydiving out of an airplane with a group of twenty friends and family to commemorate the one-year anniversary of my diagnosis.

14

Losing Control

There are moments in life when it is all turned inside
out—what is real becomes unreal, what is unreal becomes
tangible, and all your levelheaded efforts to keep a tight
ontological control are rendered silly and indulgent.

—ALEKSANDAR HEMON

Despite the drastic changes I'd endured over the past year,
I was still shocked and ambushed by the continued progression. You'd think I would have learned that this shit
wasn't stopping.

The disease, which started in the extremities on my right side,
had gradually progressed to other parts of my body. The muscles
of my upper legs, shoulders, neck, and jaw were growing weaker by
the day. Only weeks after our skydiving expedition, I was also having trouble talking, slurring my words as if I were drunk.

I wrote in my journal, "I've noticed that speaking, especially in
louder environments, is a struggle. I get tired trying to talk because
I have to project my voice. It's like I am losing my timing. Now I'm
like 'Delayed Conversation Man' from *Saturday Night Live*. When
I have something funny to add to the conversation, by the time I
get it out, it's just in time to fall awkwardly flat." I had to release
my anger.

On January 28, I walked into the living room of our house, lay
down on the couch, and just let it all out. Wailing and convulsing,

trying to shed my skin and tear myself away from the reality of what was going on.

In frustration, I started vigorously and angrily swinging Louie No. 3, my carbon-fiber walking stick, yelling, "Fuck this! Fucking fuck! Leave me alone! Let me be! Fuck you!" Then I swung him against my aluminum walker—over and over and over. "How. Is. This. Possible?"

Louie finally broke. He cracked in half, flew silently and gracefully across the room, and almost hit the TV screen. I fell on the couch and cried and yelled and screamed.

That experience of feeling deep, primal frustration, and working to shed the pain of this disease caused me to reflect upon a Pearl Jam song that was extremely meaningful for me, "Release." Eddie Vedder wrote the song about his biological father, whom he never knew about until after his father had died. He has said it's the most personal song he's ever written. The lyrics are powerful: "Oh, dear Dad, can you see me now? I am myself, like you somehow. I'll ride the wave, where it takes me. I'll hold the pain, release me."

When I first heard it in high school, I identified strongly with the song because of my relationship with my dad. Before he moved out, after the divorce, it felt like Kyle and I were stuck under a heavy cloud of crushing judgment and criticism from him.

That day, after I killed Louie, I recorded a couple of video journals.

My dad is like a fundamental, wacky, literal dogmatic Christian. He's a good man but I don't believe the same things he believes. So my whole life I've tried to convey and communicate that even though I don't believe some of the same things he believes, my soul is still free and safe. So in that way the song "Release" has been a soundtrack for our relationship. I feel God more in the experience of music, or at the top of a mountain, or in deep, honest conversation with family, friends, and even strangers, than inside a church, or in some concept of prayer. "Release" always helped me, inspired me to continue to communicate with my father in such a way.

Additionally, we now have a son, who if the experts are correct, I'll never have an actual face-to-face conversation where he'll speak to me, I'll hear him and speak back to him, he'll in turn hear me and speak back to me. So, I have this fear that he'll not know the essence of who I am. I'm working to share my heart, my mind, my essence to him.

So those two scenarios, my father, and, in turn, my son, are pretty heavy for me. That song spans three generations. Mostly, I'm working to share with Rivers, and let him know that he's free, his soul is safe. He is released.

"Release" took on new meaning after I was diagnosed with ALS. I would sing it in my head: "God, release me from this horrible, fucked-up situation. Please, please, release me from this burden. Or if you won't release me from this suffering, then show me how to be strong enough and ingenious enough to be happy or creative or purposeful or loving in this situation."

Not long after I killed Louie, I expressed my frustration for not feeling any release on Twitter late one night.

"Eloi, Eloi, lama sabachthani?"—Jesus of Nazareth. My God, my God, why have you forsaken me?

I figured if Jesus felt this right at the moment of his death, it was perfectly OK to acknowledge that I felt forsaken. I had always enjoyed and been able to relate to the humanity and suffering of Jesus, not as someone only to be worshipped, but also as inspiration, a model or even a brother. When I was playing with the Saints, I had a shirt that said "Jesus is my homeboy." I certainly felt a kinship with Jesus's dying words, according to the author of Mark.

As always, for me, this process of grieving and shedding tears allowed me to *release* the pain of the past and move forward. But it did strike me how ironic it was that I took out my frustration on my walking stick, Louie. Of all the things that had let me down in life, mostly, at that point, my motor neurons, and then consequently my muscles, Louie had been loyal, stable, and consistent. As my "left-hand man," he didn't ask for much and never complained. And there he was: fucking dead on the floor, cracked in half. That was sad. Louie didn't do anything, except serve his purpose exactly as he was supposed to, with no questions asked. He never tried to do too much, never abandoned me or was absent when needed. I felt bad that I annihilated Louie.

The good news was that Louie No. 3 had a twin brother, Louie No. 4. I retrieved Louie's brother and promised to never beat him against any floors or walkers, at least not anytime soon.

A TERMINAL DIAGNOSIS can cause people to deny the truth of death, or to attach themselves to some mental belief construct that provides distracting comfort from their fear of the ultimate unknown. Our ego wants to feel like we know what is ultimately unknowable.

My diagnosis intensified the conversations I had about religion and faith with my dad. He thought I should believe exactly what he believed in order to be saved.

This subject came up again when Pops visited our family in New Orleans a few days later. We talked for a while in the small bedroom of our yellow house on Grand Route St. John, and the conversation grew intense at points. Over the years of living with ALS, I've learned that this fear of death can be greatest for those who love and are closest to the person given the diagnosis. Michel was with us, so as the conversation turned emotional and Dad wrapped his arms around me, she started filming for our planned documentary film.

"Stephen, you're my son!" His voice cracked as he wept. "You don't know what it feels like inside that I might lose ya, man! You don't know what it feels like! It's killing me!!"

I'd always respected my dad's willingness to express vulnerability and to cry. My voice was weak, my speech garbled. The emotion and frustration of the moment exacerbated the situation. I took a deep breath, closed my eyes, and strained to push out the words.

"Dad, don't ever again say I need to get on my knees and give myself to God! Don't ever say that—EVER! . . . NEVER! . . . EVER!!" My voice was trembling and escalating in pitch.

"OK, Stephen," Dad said. "OK!"

I had been working to be released from his oppressive beliefs since adolescence. Now, facing the reality of a terminal diagnosis, I didn't know if this would be one of our last conversations, so it seemed important that I express myself.

The muscles in my neck were tired, so I rested my head against the wall I was using for support and took a few breaths. Words were rolling into and over each other. I had to open my mouth wide and make extreme movements with my lips to enunciate. Every word was difficult.

I leaned back and took another deep breath.

"When you tell me those things, it fuckin' CRUSHES me!" I said, as Dad turned his head and leaned in to try to understand my garbled words. "I called you a year ago. I said, 'Dad, I've been diagnosed with a terminal illness, and I know that when you get scared you want me to pray like you, and you need me to believe all the same things you believe.' You told me I needed to save my soul. But I told you then that my soul IS saved. I told you that then. And you promised me that you would not question my faith. You promised!"

"You're right," Dad said.

"Every time you question my faith it crushes me!" I said, trying futilely to scream.

"I'm sorry for anything I've ever done that's making you feel like I'm crushing you," Dad said, his voice quivering. "To hear I am 'crushing you,' those are pretty severe words. I don't ever want to do that."

"Because here is the thing about faith," I said. "You can't argue with someone's faith. You can't debate what someone else believes. Because there is no proof either way."

Dad replied, "Well, it says, 'According to your faith, be it unto you.' That's exactly what Jesus said."

"Exactly!" I said, and I finally felt that my release was possible. "So let me have my faith!" I cried. I couldn't make a fist and could barely raise my arms, but it didn't matter. I tried to punch Dad in the chest but my arm fell weakly to my side before reaching the target.

"Promise the next time you see me, you will not doubt, in your mind, my faith," I said. "That's your mind just trying to get in the middle of my heart. Stop trying to understand the relationship between my heart and God. Your mind . . . CANNOT . . . understand that. Do you understand me? My soul IS saved!"

"Don't be angry at me, Stephen," Dad said. "Please!"

My Dad had held rigidly to his interpretation of faith. But is holding tightly to human concepts, ideologies, and beliefs what faith is? It seems our ego wants to possess a certainty of faith. In the religious and spiritual texts I've read, and even in my own life, the faith experience is beyond mental concepts. Beyond belief. A stepping into the unknown. The unseen.

I think we both felt good about our heart-to-heart exchange.

Afterward, Pops and I went outside to pee. Dad commented on how handsome I was despite being a year into this disease. Behind us, Michel said, "Who can pee farther, boys?!" Dad grunted, and said, "I can!" Then quickly he said, "His dick's bigger, though!" My dad, a human highlight reel.

AT THIS POINT in my progression, I could still stand if supported, but now I used a walker, which we named "Walkie," to get around the house and a push wheelchair called "Wheelie" for longer distances. But we still were adventurous.

Michel, Rivers, and I flew to Schweitzer Mountain Resort in Idaho, the mountain I'd grown up on, for my final alpine adventure. My friends Dave Martin and Dave Stewart arranged for us to take an early ride down the mountain before opening. I was lifted and strapped into a snowcat, an enclosed machine built with tank-style rubber tracks that are spun by rows of hard rubber wheels, and rode up a slope called Ridge Run. At the top, I was lifted and strapped securely into a ski patrol toboggan. Dave Stewart, an ex–ski racer, got permission to strap Rivers to his chest, and they skied down Midway Run alongside me. We made the first tracks of the day, overlooking the magnificent view of Lake Pend Oreille.

I took it all in. I was immensely grateful for this opportunity with our son, but I was also flooded with sadness because I understood that this would be my last run. I thought of a happy college memory. A couple times every winter, my buddies and I would drive to the lodge with our GT Snowracer sleds. These are not typical sleds. They have two rear skis and one front ski that's connected to a small steering wheel. A small plastic seat sits about four inches off the ground. We used to hike up one of the runs and then race down the mountain, about 300 yards or so, reaching speeds of 40–50 mph. Whoever finished last would have to ride back to the condo on the roof of the car in his undies!

All those days were behind me now. This would be the first and the last time I would ski with Rivers. I would have to depend on friends like Dave to teach him to ski. It was a beginning and an ending for me.

Requests for media interviews and public appearances continued to grow.

Peter King, one of the most famous and respected sports journalists in the country, came to town to record an interview for *Sports Illustrated* and NBC Sports that was going to air during the Super Bowl XLVI pregame show.

He knocked on the door of our little thousand-square-foot yellow house one morning. Michel opened the door with a towel on her wet head, and Rivers on her hip. I was in the bathroom waiting for Michel to brush my teeth. It was not the typical way Peter and his crew of three met their subjects, but he came right in and made himself at home.

We spent the first day conducting an interview on the floor of the Superdome and then having family dinner at the Varisco house with Peter. On the second day, the crew somehow managed to set up its camera equipment in the small front room of our house to interview me and Michel on the couch.

I'd been doing media since high school so I was comfortable in front of a camera. Michel, on the other hand, was a nervous wreck. She was talking a mile a minute and complained about a ringing in her ears as she sat down for her solo interview. "Don't worry," I told her. "Only millions of people will be watching this."

On February 5, 2012, the Super Bowl game between the New York Giants and the New England Patriots drew a viewing audience of more than 111 million people, making it the most viewed show in TV history.

During the feature, Peter asked Michel, "What's the thing that causes you the most worry, or the most pain?"

"I don't even pray any more for Steve to have full healing," she said. "I pray for him to keep his voice. Because I love hearing his voice. And I want him to talk to me all the time. And be able to talk to Rivers.

"That's when I feel like," she continued, as tears welled in her eyes, "as positive as we always are, and as unfair as it is that he loses control of his body, I mean, to take his voice, too? It just doesn't seem fair."

The segment ended with Peter asking me if I ever thought about how long I have to live. "Yeah," I told him, "which is a really good thing to think about as a human, because we all have a timeline, Peter. Most of us don't live like we have a timeline."

Peter King and I were at the Super Bowl in Indianapolis when the story aired. Michel, too anxious to watch herself on TV for the first time, hid in the kitchen while Jilly screamed, "Mimi, it's OK! It's good!"

I'd flown there with my brother, Kyle, and a filmmaker to meet two ALS patients to help our foundation host its first Team Gleason Adventure. Scott Fujita secured the flights, tickets, and sideline passes. He also spearheaded media coverage for the event. Drew Brees arranged to get us a special tour of Indianapolis Motor Speedway, where we rode in a race car around the world-famous track.

"I want to be able to help ALS patients lead better lives. So many of them, when they get diagnosed, stop living the sort of full life that they still should be able to live," I told reporters at the event. "They don't have the resources to do it. I hope to be able to help some of them do the things they love to do. I refuse to give in to the disease. If I can help others do the same, I would be very happy."

The Super Bowl feature story elevated our profile to a national level. It blew up our social media platforms and launched Team Gleason into another orbit in terms of engagement and brand awareness. We had 28,750 visits to the page and more than 300 merch sales in an hour. Our newly upgraded website couldn't handle the load and crashed for 30 minutes. We gained 8,000 new Facebook followers and "Steve Gleason" was the trending subject on Twitter for an hour before being overtaken by Madonna. The eight-minute feature story gave us a platform that we could not have had otherwise. It also began a public conversation about ALS.

A MONTH LATER, Michel and I had our annual joint birthday party at Mosca's, the legendary Italian restaurant in Westwego. Six years earlier, I'd driven Michel to Mosca's for a Varisco family dinner in my Ram pickup truck. I jumped out of my truck, a muscled 210 pounds in a floral shirt I'd bought from a thrift shop. As we were waiting to be seated, a guy at the bar said, "You must have a lot of balls, wearing that shirt."

Now, six years later, my shirt and pants were fitted with Velcro buttons to facilitate the dressing and disrobing process. Michel drove our new MV-1, a black modified-wheelchair van resembling a London taxi, to the restaurant. I rode in the passenger seat in my new electric wheelchair for the first time. With us was Blair Casey, a friend, whom we brought on to relieve Michel of some of the physical burden of caring for me. I think I took for granted that Michel would always be there for me, despite my growing needs. I complained and vented to her when things got hard, as if she were a punching bag. She was now showering me, dressing me, brushing my teeth, wiping my butt, feeding me, and driving me. This, along with taking care of eight-month-old Rivers, was starting to wear her down.

I was still able to somewhat navigate the house with my walker, but the process of getting me in and out of the bed took Michel up to 30–45 minutes. She would drag me by the feet to get closer to the edge of the bed, lift me to a sitting position, then push her legs against the bed and grab my arms with the goal of putting both of my hands on the walker. Sounds easy, right? Sometimes it would take ten repetitions to complete, and lots of times she fell right on top of me, which, as irritating as it was, made us laugh.

I was also falling more. At times, as hard as Michel would try to push and pull and lift, she was unable to get me up from the position I lay stuck in. A couple times she had to go find a friend or neighbor to help stand me up.

Blair was a family friend of the Variscos. I met him when I was playing for the Saints and we held our training camp at Millsaps College in Jackson, Mississippi. Blair played safety for Millsaps and worked in the concession stand during our practices. I walked by the stand one day and he yelled at me, "Hey, Steve, I know your girlfriend, Michel. She used to babysit me as a kid and her dad was my confirmation sponsor." Blair and I hit it off. I hired him as an assistant during my playing days with the Saints and called him "Shortcut Sawyer" because he worked quickly and was able to pull off any task given to him, even if it was retrieving the engagement ring my brother left in a hotel room an hour before our wedding. Blair was strong enough to lift me in and out of my wheelchair when needed. He looked like Thor, with his muscular build and long blond locks, but we called him "Manny," after a flirtatious girl asked him if he was our male nanny.

As fun as it was getting together with all of our friends and family to celebrate our thirty-fifth birthday at Mosca's, going out to dinner had become real work. It was difficult for me to socialize because of the delayed timing of my speech and the strain it caused to project my voice. Michel would do her best to speak up for me, but after a while, the outcome was not worth the effort. It was also getting more difficult to swallow food, since the muscles in my throat had weakened so drastically. In restaurants, Michel had to focus on feeding me carefully. Going out to dinner was such a huge part of connecting to the Varisco world, but we started to opt out regularly, which was a hard loss for Michel. We'd had several years of glorious memories of communing with friends and family at restaurants like Mosca's, but now things were getting so twisted up. It was like we were on our own island.

I had stepped away from chasing a cure, but I was still open to unconventional options for healing.

We'd gotten multiple emails about the possibility of Lyme disease being misdiagnosed as ALS. A friend from high school who was battling Lyme set up an appointment for me with a specialist, and Michel, Rivers, and I took a road trip to a small town in North Louisiana to meet with him. After filling out a questionnaire and doing some blood work, he said my blood tests were consistent with Lyme and recommended treatment. We questioned him, because the paperwork was not indicative of Lyme, but he remained "confident" that a six-week daily treatment of pumping antibiotics through a port surgically installed on my chest might cure the Lyme and stop the ALS-like symptoms. A local infectious disease expert, Dr. Tom Moore, strongly advised us against this, saying it was a health risk because of the antibiotics I was already taking. However, at this point, with my voice and physical condition deteriorating every day, we clung to any hope we could get. I was only thirty-five years old. I did not want to leave Michel by herself. We decided to move forward with the treatment.

At the same time, with donations in our trust, we wired $23,000 to a pharmacy in Thailand to secure WF-10 sodium chlorite, an underground treatment that had produced promising results with some ALS patients. Both treatments failed miserably.

Our last-ditch effort was a stem-cell treatment in Alabama. A doctor there reached out to our team and offered me free therapy. Having gone through the failed experiences with the Lyme and WF-10 therapies, we were definitely apprehensive. But a friend of ours, Dudley Jourdan, had undergone stem-cell therapy and his progression completely stopped. To this day, Dudley's ALS has plateaued.

We decided to undergo the treatment. It did not go well. If anything, it felt like it accelerated my progression, although it was impossible to know that for sure. The aftermath of the treatment was brutal. I was in such pain the night after the procedure. I yelled out in agony, "I love you, Michel and Rivers!" not knowing if I would make it through the night. I was so constipated we had to recruit a professional nurse to literally pull poop from my rectum with her gloved hands.

As she dug in, I did my best to lighten the mood and relieve the awkwardness of the situation. I asked her, "Am I the hottest guy you've ever ass-fingered?"

When people asked me the most humbling thing about ALS, my go-to response had always been "Having someone else wash my balls."

After the visit from the nurse, I had to reassess my answer.

Stem cell. Lyme disease. WF-10. We knew these alternative treatments were long shots, but what other choice did we really have? If we hadn't gone through with these therapies, we would have stayed up at night, torturing ourselves with questions like "What if we'd done the stem-cell therapy and it worked?" We were doing the best we could to navigate our lives. Better to regret something you did than something you didn't do.

ALS was relentless. Nothing stopped its progression, but as I lost abilities, I was able to welcome change. Michel has told me that she always appreciated this. Instead of trying to walk longer than I should when I started falling, I was fine using the walking stick, then the walker, then the push wheelchair, then the power wheelchair. When feeding myself became too difficult, I let her do it, rather than try too hard myself. And when swallowing became too difficult and I began choking on my food, I opted to get a feeding tube surgically implanted in my stomach.

Life became a dance with change and loss. I would lose abilities, we would adapt; I would lose more abilities, we would adapt. Each loss forced us to develop new routines.

Brushing your teeth, for example. While this is important for everyone, it only takes an ordinary person two or three minutes to brush their teeth. As important as brushing your teeth might be, it's an afterthought for most people.

On the other hand, for someone with ALS, developing an efficient and effective way to brush your teeth is an arduous process. As I started to lose the ability to move and lift my arms, brushing my teeth would often take fifteen to twenty minutes. Logistical questions would arise, like how are we going to get toothpaste in my mouth? How the hell are we going to get toothpaste out of my mouth with my inability to spit? As frustration mounted, the next question would be, why the fuck are we even using toothpaste?!

Over the next several months, we got advice, and our own routine evolved. We figured out a concoction using Dr. Tichenor's mouthwash, created in New Orleans, switched to an electric toothbrush, and developed better brushing techniques, so that it only took three or five minutes to brush my teeth.

This process took several months, even years, to perfect, all just to develop an efficient routine for simply brushing my teeth. And that same deterioration was happening for every aspect of my life. Taking a shower. Taking a shit. Getting dressed. Getting in the car. Getting comfortable in bed. Every aspect of our lives was in chaos.

But we continued moving forward. I recruited Michel's brother Vinnie to push me in the Rock 'n' Roll marathon in a customized wheelchair for the 26.2 miles.

I did end up in the hospital after I turned pale white as we sat at a Saints game the following day, but it was only a short visit to get IV fluids. The media reports stated: "Former Saints safety Steve Gleason has been taken to a New Orleans hospital after becoming unresponsive at the Superdome while watching Monday night's game against the Philadelphia Eagles."

I also completed my voice banking with CereProc and made my synthetic voice. To this day, creating this voice has been one of the greatest decisions I've made.

With this new voice, I delivered a speech at the Social Innovation Summit at the United Nations in May 2012. We left Rivers for the first time and traveled to New York to make a presentation with Scott Fujita to some of the leading business and political leaders in the country. We pitched them on the importance of assistive technology to improve the lives of ALS patients. Part 1 of the pitch was made with my labored voice; part 2 with my synthetic voice.

At this point in my progression, I was losing the ability to move my thumbs. This was an especially tough and scary loss, as it was how I was able to control the joystick on my wheelchair; and more importantly, it was the last functioning part of my hand that I could use to operate my cell phone, which was a lifeline for communication.

At the end of my speech in New York, I told the group: "Save my voice, my lungs, and my thumbs, and I promise to change the world."

The message must have resonated. They could not save my thumbs, but we did receive a standing ovation and a $25,000 Chase Community Giving Award for Team Gleason. We also forged a partnership with Chase Bank that we still have today.

A week later, Michel and I took a loan from her parents and bought our first home, a three-bedroom ranch house in Lake Vista, a leafy neighborhood a couple of blocks from Lake Pontchartrain and City Park. We'd grown out of our little yellow house. We felt sad to leave the bayou and the bridge, but we could no longer fit there, especially with the addition of the power wheelchair. Michel would sometimes have to crawl over me to get to Rivers. It was time.

The one-story house was perfect for our growing family and was located less than a mile from Michel's parents, making it easy for family members to visit on short notice. The backyards of all the homes in Lake Vista were shared community spaces, with connecting walkways canopied by towering oak trees, perfect for taking walks with the family.

Despite the frustration of coping with the disease's progression, we were still living a fast and fun life. Michel, Rivers, and I traveled from event to event, with Blair faithfully by our side and videographers David Lee (Dewey) and Ty Minton-Small filming our every move. Michel and Blair loved to inappropriately perform for the camera, and Rivers was an easy and fun baby. We weren't exactly an inconspicuous crew, and because of our media appearances, people started to recognize us in public. A new type of celebrity was forming for me. Michel and Rivers were also being swept into the torrent.

During a visit to the Babies R Us store in Metairie, a starstruck lady behind Michel at the checkout counter stared at her and asked, "Are you Steve Gleason's wife?" When Michel answered, "Yes, ma'am," the woman replied, "You look just like her."

But as "celebrated" as we were, we did not live like celebrities. There were days where we went from high to low very quickly.

The afternoon of July 27, 2012, was a perfect example of the frustrating duality of our life. I was scheduled to attend a ceremony at the Superdome that afternoon to unveil the "Rebirth" statue, commemorating my blocked punt in 2006.

The Saints owners, Tom and Gayle Benson, commissioned sculptor Brian Hanlon to sculpt a nine-foot bronze statue of the blocked punt from the famous photograph of the play by *Times-Picayune* photographer Michael DeMocker. Michel thinks they didn't do my butt justice, but otherwise the statue was pretty incredible.

Coaches, staff members, and the entire 2012 Saints team, all clad in Team Gleason shirts, attended the event.

At a pre-event gathering in Champions Square, Drew Brees opened by saying, "Thanks, everyone, for being here. I have had the blessing of being able to play with many great players. But none more than the guy you're looking at right here, Steve Gleason. As a player, as a teammate, as a friend, Steve Gleason encapsulates everything that you would want, someone that you could look to for motivation or inspiration to lead you through some of the toughest times that you might face."

I spoke briefly to the crowd of friends, family, teammates, and VIPs:

"Well, this is pretty amazing," I said, straining to project my voice in the noisy room. "The last time I had a nine-foot statue of me unveiled was . . . well, uh . . . *never*. So this is a little bit overwhelming."

The crowd of reporters gathered at the scene inched closer so their microphones and cameras could pick up the audio of my labored speech.

"I think that statue is a symbol of the fact that other people see a situation that is wasted or worthless or tragic and the people of a community can take that tragedy and turn it into something heroic," I continued. "I think in some ways I'm in a similar moment here, where people say, 'Oh, Steve, this is such a tragedy what's happened' with my diagnosis. Then I'm driven to say, 'What can we do to turn that tragedy into heroics?' So I also want to recognize the four other ALS patients that are here. My message to you is that despite what other people say about our situation, we can take this and turn it into something inspiring and impactful to all the rest of the world. That's what that statue is."

A few minutes later, everyone moved outside for the official ceremony on the apron of the Superdome.

Drew Brees took the mic and read the inscription at the base of the statue to the crowd: "On Monday, September 25, 2006, Steve Gleason was responsible for one of the most dramatic moments in New Orleans Saints history. He blocked a punt in the first quarter of the team's return to the Superdome, following Hurricane Katrina. The blocked punt that season symbolized the rebirth of the city of New Orleans."

Right before my teammates pulled the large black drape off the statue for the official unveiling, I told the crowd: "As I like to say, 'It won't be easy, but it can be awesome.'"

It was an epic day. But on our way home from the ceremony, I was losing the ability to control my bowel movements. As soon as we rolled into the house, I pooped all over myself in my wheelchair.

This was life with ALS. One minute I have people celebrating my achievements and saying, 'You're my hero." The next I'm having to be helped onto a toilet by my wife and caregiver with my pants full of shit, a stark example of the polarities, dichotomies, and juxtapositions that are my life.

———

THE DISEASE'S RELENTLESS progression was causing me to feel frustrated, isolated, and irritable. The loss of my voice was particularly crushing.

Only a few people could actually understand me. I would find people nodding their heads or answering questions I didn't ask, so I began communicating more frequently through the tablet.

When I was diagnosed, the available assistive communication devices were heavy and very basic. They were originally glorified voice boxes, nothing more: basic word processing, no web connectivity, nor applications to allow someone to do any real work. At Team Gleason, we pushed to add speed and functionality to allow people who can't move or speak to remain as productive as possible.

Assistive technology devices work by shining an infrared beam of light into my eyes through the pupil. The light reflects off my cornea and projects back to the computer, allowing it to track my eye movement. By fixing my gaze for two-tenths of a second on a letter or function key on the onscreen keyboard, I can activate the keys and type words just as I used to do with a mouse and keyboard. When I complete a sentence or command, I "click" a command button to activate my synthetic voice to "speak" what I have typed. Using this technology, I can also open apps, scroll the Internet, write emails, and post on social media.

The technology is downright miraculous, critical to my daily existence. But it's not the same as normal communication. Not even close. An ordinary person speaks at around 180 words per minute. Even though I quickly mastered the eye-tracking process, I still could only type 15–20 words a minute, making my communication about eleven times slower than regular human conversation. Still to this day, by the time I answer a question or comment on a conversation, eight times out of ten my response falls into an empty room. People walk away before I press "talk."

This loss didn't affect just me. It also affected Michel. Communication was one of our strengths as a couple. That strength was being threatened.

Michel and I loved to talk about everything. I liked to talk about things like philosophy and sustainability. Michel, more about books, movies, and telling stories. More importantly, I was the person Michel wanted to talk to. Now this was being stripped away. Speaking by mouth was physically draining, and speaking by tablet was slow for conversing, at least compared to normal human interaction. Our connective communication was being replaced by short requests for the help I needed from her. And her storytelling slowly began to fall on people who could actually respond.

I could still move my head, but I started using a neck brace to prevent my head from falling forward. I could still drive my chair with my left hand but would tire easily and need help with that as well.

It became more dangerous to swallow, so I began eating less and losing weight, which wasn't good. The reality was setting in: I would have to move permanently to the feeding tube for daily nutrition.

Nutritionists strongly recommended commercial liquid nutrition formula to fatten me up, but we chose the whole foods route. We blended the foods into smoothies. Michel obsessively made spreadsheets to calculate what healthy foods could add up to the 3,000 calories in the smoothies necessary to gain weight.

In October, Drew and Brittany Brees invited us to dinner at Rock-n-Sake in the Warehouse District. We'd spent many fun nights during my playing days with Saints teammates at this popular sushi restaurant. The chefs there supported me when I was battling ulcerative colitis and had to follow a very strict gluten- and sugar-free diet in order to heal my gut. I discovered that most sushi rice contains sugar, so they accommodated me by serving my fish on regular rice.

At this point in the disease's progression, I hadn't swallowed a bite of "regular" food in weeks and was eating solely via feed tube. Michel fed me a smoothie at home before we left for the restaurant, so my plan was to just enjoy the night and not worry about eating.

But as the plates of delicious salmon sushi arrived at the table, the spirit of the night inspired me. My adrenaline flowed and Michel excitedly encouraged me to take a bite, so I went for it—and succeeded without coughing to death! It wouldn't be an exaggeration to say it was the tastiest fish my 6,500 taste buds had ever encountered.

If this, indeed, was my "last supper," then I could do worse than enjoying fresh salmon sushi at one of our favorite restaurants with great friends.

We toasted the occasion with a round of sake bombs. Michel poured mine down my tube.

WHILE I ACCEPTED the losses that resulted from ALS, I was committed to continuing to embrace new adventures.

Pushing limits had been a lifelong obsession. And while it was becoming more difficult than ever to test these boundaries, I refused to give in or let the disease define my life.

Our first Team Gleason Adventure took us on a canoeing expedition on the Little Missouri River in Montana with fellow PALS (People Living with ALS) Jay Rink and his sons. The trip replicated the sixty-mile canoe journey by Lewis and Clark two hundred years ago. At times it was challenging for me and Jay. The guides ingeniously strapped us into retrofitted lawn chairs in the canoes so we could sit comfortably upright for long stretches on the water. We stopped at the same places along the river that Lewis and Clark had hung out. Our guides entertained us with stories as we traveled and educated us on the habitat and history of the area. During the weeklong trip, we saw fewer than ten other people, so it was easy to imagine Lewis and Clark's journey two centuries ago. It was a glorious week of water play, spectacular scenery, spiritual sunrises and sunsets, bald eagles, star gazing, soul searching, and peace, lots of peace.

The nightly ritual was to gather around the campfire and share our favorite moments of the day. One night, I asked everyone to share their "top three favorite travel destinations." Our public relations rep, Clare Durrett, the only woman among eleven men on the trip, mentioned Machu Picchu, the famous Inca citadel in southern Peru. It piqued my interest.

Our successful canoe trip inspired me to keep exploring. Could an ascent of Machu Picchu be possible? I wasn't sure. But I wanted to find out.

It would be an incredible challenge, an audacious idea for someone in a near-paralyzed state a year into an ALS diagnosis, and with a toddler in tow. But, as I like to say, "awesome ain't easy."

IN DECEMBER, I flew to Cleveland with Blair and my first friend in New Orleans, Benny D., to undergo surgery to implant a device called a diaphragm pacing system (DPS) into my chest to regulate my breathing. The DPS acts the way a pacemaker does for the heart. Michel stayed in New Orleans to look after Rivers. Scott Fujita was playing for the Cleveland Browns at the time, and he met us at the hospital. My friend Jim Salters flew in from Cincinnati to visit, as well.

While I was there, I also switched out the long feeding tube attached to my stomach and replaced it with a small Mic-Key button, a low-profile tube that goes directly into the stomach through the wall of the belly and is used for nutrition, fluids, and medicine. I also added a suprapubic catheter to my body, which is basically a plastic tube that is passed through the power part of the abdomen into the bladder to drain urine to an outside bag permanently attached to my leg. My days of peeing on walls were over. My body was looking like a medical experiment.

After the procedure, Scott emailed Michel updates. He sent a photo of my insides and said, "And here's his appendix wrapped up in mesh from his hernia surgery years ago, so . . . Steve had his appendix taken out today, too! They're just finishing up his penis enlargement now. I'll let you know how it looks once I see it."

Scott also snuck beers into the recovery room. Benny D. inappropriately flirted with the nurses, broke out his guitar, and turned the entire wing of the hospital into a party. Nurses wandered in from other parts of the hospital and joined the festivities. *If I was going to die soon, I was committed to laugh and smile while I cried and died.*

Reveling in the beauty of this night, I thought about the conversation on the canoe trip.

"Hey, Fuji," I said to Scott. "The morning after I was diagnosed, you said you would follow me to the ends of the Earth. I want to hike Machu Picchu. Will you go with me?"

He looked at me, perplexed.

"Machu Picchu?" he said. "Like Machu Picchu in Peru?"

"Yeah," I said. "I want to climb it for a Team Gleason Adventure. Let's do it!"

"I'm in!" Scott said.

Upon my return to New Orleans, I sent an email to a thread of doctors:

> The following will not be a typical ALS inquiry. As you may know, part of the mission of our foundation is to raise awareness on a global scale by producing and documenting epic life adventures for PALS. Assuming the world does not end at the finish of the Mayan Calendar, we are planning a trip to Machu Picchu for April 2013. I want to check if this altitude will affect my breathing over a period of 7–10 days. Lastly, we would like to have a medical representative on the journey and I can't think of better representation than one of you.
>
> That's it.

To prepare, I flew to Durham, North Carolina, and underwent tests of my lung capacity at Duke University. The Duke Hyperbaric Chamber is the only civilian hyperbaric facility in the United States and specializes in the physiology of human exposure to extreme environments. The doctors subjected me to the simulated altitude conditions in Machu Picchu and Cusco and cleared me to make the trip.

When I called Kevin Swan, the ALS patient we were inviting on the trip, he thought he was being punked.

In April 2013, Michel, Rivers, and I and a team of twenty-two friends and colleagues set out for Peru. Rather than bringing a single backpack like we were accustomed to, we flew to Lima with a power wheelchair, two custom push wheelchairs, a tank of oxygen, several breathing devices, a feeding tube, a week's worth of feed tube formula, a catheter bag, a neck brace, baby gear, pill crushers, an ass pad, and a film crew from NFL Films.

I had not traveled extensively at this point in my progression, and was not conditioned for it. After a long flight to Lima, followed by a flight to Cusco (where I was given a broken wheelchair upon arrival), from a bus to a train to a bus to a hotel—every time being lifted from my chair to a seat, adjusted, and then lifted back into my chair—I was absolutely toasted. As we were preparing to meet our group for dinner, I shit my pants. I was done. Blair and Michel sat with me as I desperately wept.

We were scheduled to take the train into the mountains the next day and start the trek to Machu Picchu, and we were starting to seriously question the wisdom of our plan.

After cleaning me up, Michel and Blair, my cheerleading support team, talked me into going to dinner. Begrudgingly, I obeyed.

The cobblestone streets of Cusco made the three-block journey miserably bumpy in my wheelchair. When we got to the restaurant, there was no accessible access up the curb, so a couple of our guys had to lift me from my chair into a dining room seat, and then lift my 200-pound power wheelchair into the door. My chair was running on two bars of power, so before my tablet died, I typed a message to Michel:

"I'm questioning God. He's either forsaken me or he's absent."

Weary from traveling with Rivers and spending the day waiting for my Liquid Hope feed tube formula at a local customs office, Michel and I were both about to lose it.

But shortly after we sat down, half a world away, in the corner of a restaurant in the middle of Cusco, Peru, a young woman approached our table and started enthusiastically showing us pictures on her phone. I could see Michel smile and take a deep breath of relief.

Her name was Jenny Gonzalez. The picture on her phone was a shot of her and her fiancé, Tommy Dudek, at the summit of Machu Picchu from the previous day. Gonzalez was wearing a gray Team Gleason T-shirt with our motto, No White Flags.

"Oh, my God, I can't believe I'm meeting you!" Jenny said as she approached me. "You're so amazing—AMAZING!"

Jenny was a Tulane University graduate. She had learned about my story from Tommy, a New Orleans native and ardent Saints fan.

"I am so terrified of heights," she explained, "and I knew, coming here, that that's the shirt I wanted to wear, because somebody like Steve, who can do so much and not be scared of life, I want to be like that. I want to be like him."

It was humbling. Jenny, to my knowledge, does not have ALS in her family, but my story and the work we do at Team Gleason had had a great impact on her.

At the end of the dinner, the boys effortlessly lifted my chair out of the restaurant and carried me to my seat, and we drove home. The cobblestones seemed much smoother. Maybe God wasn't absent, after all.

JENNY SINGLE-HANDEDLY had changed the mindset of our group. We were now full of excitement and positive energy as we rode on the comfortable train that would drop us off at the start line of the seven-mile hike up Machu Picchu.

The train dropped us off in the middle of the Peruvian jungle. We had three minutes and a four-foot drop to disembark the crew and the two wheelchairs onto two yards of space between the tracks and a cliff, leading down to the Urubamba River. Kevin and I were lifted off the train and strapped onto our chairs as the train car swiftly sped off, the smiling attendants waving goodbye. Blair assessed the situation and said, "Is this some kind of joke?"

After positioning us in our custom wheelchairs, we all huddled for some quick words of inspiration. Our goal, Fuji said, was to be out of the jungle, and at our destination, Machu Picchu's Sanctuary Lodge, by dark. And so we began our journey.

The first thing we encountered was a set of forty steep steps leading down to the bridge that crossed the water.

Four small men from Amazing Peru, the company we hired to

lead us, approached my chair. My first thought was *Are these poles that we fabricated really going to hold up?* My second thought was *Are these guys really about to lift me on their shoulders and take me down this staircase?*

By the time I processed what was going on, they were lifting my chair on their shoulders.

The hike is essentially a goat trail. The path is eighteen inches wide, and the drop off the trail is hundreds of feet almost straight down. It is considered one of the more dangerous treks in the world. As I looked over the edge, I thought, *I can resist this. Or I can accept it. But either way, it's happening.*

If Michel or her mom had done more photo research of the route, I don't think that they would have said yes to me and two-year-old Rivers doing this. Our pace was a glacially slow one mile per hour because we had to constantly stop to stretch my legs, move my pads, and inflate my neck brace.

Halfway through the trek, the welding fell off of the back of my chair, so one of the poles was no longer usable. Fortunately, this did not cause us to fall off the cliff. Using Peruvian knowledge and our guys' muscles, they jerry-rigged the chairs using zip ties, rope, and bamboo. Not long after, that ingenuity came in handy when one of the poles broke away from Kevin's chair.

Fujita reminded us again that we needed to be out of the jungle by dark, but at 5:30 as the sun was going down, we asked Hector, our guide, for the thirtieth time how much longer before we were out. He, for the tenth time, said, "Three more hours."

In the dark, lit with a few dying headlamps and the two phones that still had battery life, the guys faced their biggest challenge, carrying me and Kevin up "the stairs of death." Everyone on the trek gathered to help in any way they could to achieve the final push.

The spectacular view of Machu Picchu that people look forward to seeing from the famous Sun Gate was not that spectacular at 11 p.m. More importantly, though, we could see lights from our hotel, the Sanctuary Lodge. The people at the lodge were told to expect us around 6 p.m., so by 9 p.m. they sent people with torch lights to look for us as we were ascending to the lodge. For most people, the hike takes six to seven hours to complete. It took us eleven. The light from the hotel workers was tremendously helpful during our final descent.

Rivers was a champion. My friend from Tulane Business School, Kyle Brechtel, carried him in a backpack, with only a short lunch break on the way. When they finally reached the hotel, Rivers was nearly unconscious and dehydrated.

Our team had achieved a remarkable feat: carrying two grown men along the Inca trail for eleven hours into the night. As we all convened that night at a celebratory dinner, I thanked my team and said, "I think the word is 'relief'—no one was hurt, we made it. I believe that challenge is our opportunity. And we have faced and overcome some enormous challenges here. Turning tragedy to triumph, but that's the last time I put my life in the hands of people who make $3 an hour." (In retrospect, they probably saved mine and Kevin's lives more than once.)

After we said our goodnights, we headed to our hotel rooms, which were located on the second floor. Michel asked the porter, "¿Dónde está la elevadora?" He said, "No elevator, only stair," and pointed to a steep set of stairs. Turns out our adventure was not done yet.

WE ARRIVED HOME in late April and settled back into our lives. The disease's progression was merciless. My care was ultra-high-maintenance at this point. During the day, even though I was trying to be productive, I was mostly entangled in logistical BS, like figuring out how to clear mucus out of my lungs, since I'd lost the strength to cough. Just a few months earlier, after getting me settled in bed, Mic and I would watch TV or listen to music and talk and laugh with each other. Sometime in February, we decided to smoke marijuana. We were talking, and I couldn't speak clearly, but Mic knew everything I said. We laughed so hard I started lightly choking. Michel wrapped her arms around me until I said I was OK, then she affectionately laid her head on my chest. We both started laughing again, and that harmonic laughter was pure heaven.

But now, I was almost 100 percent dependent on my tablet. The only time I would make any noise, usually a moan, was to get Michel's attention in the middle of the night. She understandably struggled getting up multiple times each night, and I hated waking her. I would wake up, feel whatever pain was there, and move toward it. Only sometimes could I fall back to sleep; I would just lie there, trying desperately not to wake her, feeling horrible if I finally had to do so. Our face-to-face conversations were less frequent. We communicated mostly by email and text, and the topics were almost always about logistics or my care. We were the strongest, most unified couple I'd ever encountered, but this disease was devouring us.

I suppose many people were shocked to hear that I was a virgin until I met Michel. For me, it was less about following rules. The decision was based on my earliest relationship with Jen Austin, so I chose to wait until I was connected with someone as a friend, a connection of heart and mind rather than just physical attraction. That helped me see that sex and even romantic love were not roads to lasting happiness. But this ALS progression tore me up so much, the perspectives and insights I'd acquired in my previous life were turned upside down and inside out. Although our sex life had been wonderful, that wasn't the loss that was ripping us apart. Losing the beautiful back-and-forth conversations with Michel on any and every topic from food to movies to deeper topics like love and God and heaven caused our friendship to vanish. This didn't tear me up. It obliterated me. It imploded me to dust.

Michel was also obliterated. The years of wiping my butt, showering and feeding me, clearing mucus out of my mouth, had taken a heavy toll. We were more like nurse and patient than husband and wife. The physical changes to my body. The ultramuscular boy who hugged her tight and lifted her, touched her, and whose smell she loved was gone. That boy had died right before her eyes, despite her endless care and hope that it wouldn't be.

One night in early May, I was desperate for some kind of connection to Michel, some replenishment of our happiness together. We were home with Rivers, who was sleeping. Seeking escape from my pain, I asked Mic to have sex. She acquiesced, too ashamed to disappoint me.

ALS does not affect your sexual organs, desires, or functionality. It does, however, force you to be creative because of its effect on your mobility, mood, strength, and breathing. Michel and I were in our bedroom, in my chair, rather than on our bed, where we would have been just a year ago. It was ugly. I couldn't move. Michel had to awkwardly navigate the headrest, my pants, the catheter tube coming out of my bladder in my lower abdomen, the feeding tube coming out of my stomach. This ugliness was pitiful. There was no connection, pleasure, or happiness. As I finished, I looked up at Mic, and saw a silver tear fall from her eye.

Before she walked out, steely faced, she said, "I'm sorry, Steve-O, but I can't do this anymore."

I used the joystick on my chair to hastily roll into the bathroom and look at myself in our huge mirror. On the way, I ran into the wall of the bathroom, crushing my right big toe between the footrest of the chair and the wall. The pain in my toe hurt so fucking bad. But as terrible as it was, it felt logical and orderly. It made perfect sense to me. I'd encountered pain like this thousands upon thousands of times, so I knew it was temporary.

But my emotional pain felt elusive and incoherent. I sat there by myself, alone with my reflection in the mirror. I was lost. Bewildered, I didn't cry. I looked down at my crooked sack of a body. I was now the freak.

How much more of this pain could I endure? I didn't even know what to focus on. Anger? Sorrow? And where? Michel? Myself? ALS? *I missed her so much. I can't fucking take this. I can't take this! FUUUUCK!!*

This was the last time I had sex.

———

A FEW DAYS LATER, I wrote this in my journal:

> *We are choosing to be here right now*
> *Hold on, stay inside*
> *This holy reality*
> *This holy experience*
> . . .
> *Choosing to be here in—This body, this body holding me*
> *Be my reminder here that I am not alone in*
> *This body, this body holding me*
> *Feeling eternal, all this pain is an illusion*
> . . .
> *Recognize this as a holy gift and*
> *Celebrate this chance to be alive and breathing*
> —MAYNARD JAMES KEENAN

May 9th, 2013. "300 Seconds."

Rivers, you probably won't appreciate this until you're much older, but I think you will, at some point, find this comforting or useful, or both. If not, maybe you can laugh at me, and my crazy ideas. That's fine by me. A good fucking laugh is as valuable as anything.

It is inevitable that at times you will get caught up in something that hurts you emotionally. Maybe it is a broken heart, rejection or some epic failure. Poor financial choices. Feelings of envy. Athletics. Academics. Social media. Public or family judgment. Deep grief. Regret. Anxiety. Embarrassment. All of which I have experienced.

I have an exercise that helps me when I am struggling with this type of pain. Currently I have feelings of confusion and despair.

When I feel sad or afraid I imagine that I am from some other time and place, or even a timeless, formless dimension, and I am a different being. As such, I imagine that this being I am exists as sacred Love or always in intimate, transparent communion.

Basically, this being has never experienced isolation, loneliness, separation from the sacred, separation from Love.

So, this being chooses to do an experiment to understand what it is like to experience individuality. So, I become human. And experience all the beauty and horror, the joy and the agony, of being human. I am here to take notes, like a scientist observing an experiment, and take these notes to my previous existence. In this way, I can fully commit to being human. I am here precisely to feel the brutal suffering, or boundless elation of human circumstance. I'm passionate about this "experiment." The twist is that in committing to being human, I have the perspective that each and every moment is precious and holy. I am able to shine the sacred, loving presence that I know from my real existence.

Essentially, I rise from Love, become human, learn to live and embody Love, then return to Love.

Rivers, the perspective in this story seems to give me (Dad) some perspective, strength, and trust that I can continue.

In truth, if we're honest, courageous, and humble, no one knows what occurs before Life, or after death on a personal level, if anything. So, we are free to create our own version of those potential existences. Especially when you wonder why this is happening, they can help lead you from weakness to strength, from victim to hero. I think, if they are useful for you, Rivers, to grow to be more loving and wise, that's what is important.

> But there was no need to be ashamed of tears, for tears bore witness that a man had the greatest of courage, the courage to suffer.
> —VICTOR FRANKL

By the winter, my world, which had once been a cosmos of strength, friendship, community, love, and curiosity, was rapidly shrinking to a bubble of weakness, frailty, isolation, and complete loneliness.

With all of the changes and the high-maintenance, 24/7 care I required, our house was feeling more like a hospital than a home.

Instead of sleeping in our king-sized bed, next to Michel, I slept alone, in a tiny hospital bed, which had bars on all sides. This was the recommendation from doctors, and I didn't know any better. My prison, to sleep in.

I vividly remember the first night in that bed. I was staring at the ceiling, with no ability to move or communicate. All I could do was moan, like a zombie.

Staring into the darkness, I felt lonely and powerless. I had lost the ability to move or talk, and breathing was labored. I had learned to enjoy pushing the edges and boundaries of my mind and body to grow, but this was so exponentially beyond anything I had encountered, it was devastating. The fear was suffocating. Fear of being bound up inside this sack of flesh: imprisoned. Afraid of losing everything—being muted and silent. Losing connection with everyone, especially the people I loved most—Michel and Rivers. My chest was so heavy. The anxiety caused my breaths to feel as difficult as ever. It was like I was at the bottom of the pile on an NFL kickoff. Everything that seemed to be me was slipping away—my identity, my humanity, my life—the ultimate, existential fear. The effort it took to breathe made me feel like I was burning up. My head was on fire. As sweat beaded off my forehead, I felt the cold rubber of the inflatable mattress below my fingers and legs. The extremes of heat and cold added to the fear. I was living a nightmare. My mind raced. *What am I now? This pathetic body?*

Is this what dying is like? I hope I can escape? There is no escape. Holy shit, there is no escape. No no no.

There was so much fear. Separation, loneliness. I felt utterly insignificant.

I started openly, silently, remorselessly weeping.

My arms and hands, unable to move, lay useless by my sides. All I could do was feel gravity pull the warm tears down the sides of my face.

In that moment, lying awake in that cold and sterile bed, the darkness, the silence, all alone, surrounded on all sides by the bars of this tiny hospital bed, every ounce of grief poured out of me. I was so tired and weary of all of this, I just gave up. A surrendering to the moment.

There is no escape. If this is what dying is like, maybe escape is not the way.

From somewhere within, from nowhere, I was able to allow the fear in. As I did, something extraordinary occurred—a miraculous shift. As I looked into the darkness, the idea of hoping, trying to resist or control anything, suddenly seemed futile.

The surrender led to a transformation. I disappeared.

Breath by breath, it was as if I was poured into the night, or it was poured into me. I can't say why, but strangely, it felt as if I were underwater. There was muted silence, but the silence was a symphony. There was stillness of my body, but the stillness was everywhere, unbound. Through this communion, nothing remained but the night, open and free. Reality anew. Unfathomable awe and wonder. Suddenly the insignificance of me was entirely liberating.

The irony was that the purpose of the bars of the bed was so patients didn't roll over and fall out of the bed, yet here I was staring at the ceiling without any ability to move. What a tragedy, a hilarious fucking tragedy! I had no choice but to smile and laugh at this. The tragedy. The humor. All of it was perfectly freeing.

In some way, I had felt similar, much less dramatic versions of this experience in other aspects of my life—snowboarding on the peak of a mountain, riding a wave, cliff jumping, sitting in saunas then plunging in freezing water, even playing football—where I could lose myself in the flow, but I'd always sought these out as *external* extreme experiences, where I dove into the challenge. This came unbidden, from within.

There was a strange, temporary shift in perception. My relationship with life, and with the world, shifted. Whatever I was, it was clear that I was not imprisoned in this body. Fear and resistance fell away. There was only the night. Empty of me. Breaths came easier.

As powerful and profound as it was, I had no idea what to do with it, or how to integrate this into my life. So the separateness and suffering continued.

This experience did ignite a spark of curiosity within me that long winter night. A subtle call to explore and discover insight into the mystery of what happened.

The intimacy of that experience is indescribable, but the word that seems most appropriate is "peace." An unknown peace. Magically, this peace was within me and within the darkness. Indivisible.

Through tears of grief I was reborn.

15

Darkness

No tree can grow to heaven unless its roots reach down to hell.

—CARL JUNG

January 5, 2014, was the three-year anniversary of my diagnosis. It was an unseasonably warm day, even by New Orleans standards. With a cold front approaching in the week ahead, I asked Blair to take me outside so I could enjoy the springlike weather.

Our house is in a unique neighborhood. Lake Vista was built in 1939, and its design follows that of the "garden city movement." The entire four-hundred-acre neighborhood is literally one single "super block" with no through streets, intersections, or arterials. Pedestrian-only walking lanes (or if you're living with ALS, rolling lanes) run along five massive parks that converge in the center of the neighborhood, where there are two schools, two churches, and a kid-friendly coffeehouse. There are no fences, and the fronts of the houses are technically on the opposite side from the roadways, which encourages neighbors to hang out. Kids can roam free and explore, or walk to school without ever crossing a street.

One of the best aspects of this spectacular neighborhood is the oak trees. Many of the oaks were planted during the planning process nearly a hundred years ago. Mighty live oaks canopy the yards and line the lanes and the parks in the neighborhood. I'm lucky and grateful to be able to commune with nature, through the oaks, on a daily basis.

I love oaks. They are such a mysterious and majestic part of creation. Francis of Assisi called trees his brothers and sisters. I agree. Especially the oaks of the Gulf Coast. My spiritual brothers and sisters are deeply rooted and connected to the earth while reaching to the light of the cosmos. Some oaks in New Orleans are nearly a thousand years old! Their massive limbs stretch so far toward the horizon that they touch the ground and bend back toward the sky. In the most beautiful way, I saw my allegiance to the oak as an acknowledgment of my new life in New Orleans, the transformation of my West Coast roots. The oak tree connects me to this area, it connects me to this new version of nature, it connects me to life. At one time, Michel and I even talked about naming our second child Oaks.

Two years earlier, I planted an oak in our front yard as a gift to Michel on our fifth wedding anniversary. It was an expression of my appreciation and love for her. The traditional five-year anniversary gift is wood. Instead of some dormant slab of maple or cherry, I wanted to have a living, growing, breathing symbol of our marriage.

After I planted the tree, I visited it almost daily to observe, worship, and admire it. A communion. I would hear the lyrics to one of my favorite Pearl Jam songs: "Do you see the way that tree bends? / Does it inspire? / Reaching out to catch the Sun's rays / A lesson to be applied." I inspected it for new growth and to make sure it was healthy. For eight months, there had been nothing.

THREE YEARS INTO my diagnosis, the disease had stolen nearly all of my physical abilities and affected every aspect of my life. I used a wheelchair to get around. I ate strictly by feeding tube and I rarely spoke with my own voice. Breathing was difficult. The increased salivation in my mouth made me drool and cough incessantly.

I worked to be positive. We all did. But there was only so much chin-upping we could do. The reality: ALS was a motherfucker.

Michel and Blair were my primary caregivers, and we had developed something of a routine to get through each day. Blair worked daily during the week from 7 a.m. to 3 p.m., and from there, Michel would take over and care for me until nighttime.

We depended on Rick Crozier to help get me into bed every night and out of bed on the weekends. Rick played safety at Tulane University in the late 1980s and competed in triathlons. He was strong enough to lift me in and out of the wheelchair.

On Sundays, for as long as I was physically able, Blair, Rick, and our close family friend Tommy Capella would take me to the Saints facility. They helped me do the morning routine I had done when I played football. They put me in the sauna, cold tub, hot tub, and shower. It was beautiful, to push my mind and body like I had done in my playing days.

Rick lived across the street from us so it was convenient for him to come over and help when needed. Every night, Michel brushed my teeth, gave me meds, changed my clothes, and prepared the bed. Rick would then lift me into bed, and together, they stretched and positioned my body so I was comfortable enough to sleep. The process was complicated by the fact that I could barely talk.

During the night, I would moan to wake Michel to help me, whether it was to administer 2 a.m. meds, reposition me, clear my lungs, or kill a bug that had crawled on my cheek. Ty and David, our documentary film videographers, assisted when they were around, but Michel needed more help. Although family and friends urged her to seek professional caregiver assistance, she repeatedly shunned the idea. As my wife, she felt she could and should handle it.

One night after a brutal session of trying to clear my lungs of mucus with a cough machine, I slowly typed these words on my tablet to Michel and Blair, "Guys, I'm struggling. I don't want to die, but this is so hard. I fear the night, the days are unbearable. I don't know what to do. I'm so tired of asking for help. I can barely breathe. I'm so tired, mentally. Everything frustrates me, even watching Rivers. I am wearing you down to bones."

I sobbed. Michel hugged me, tears streaming down her face. Blair held on to my shoulders.

ALS is a training ground for wanting only what you have. As you have less, you must learn to want less. You must find new creative ways to explore and expand.

To cope with this unbearable existence and to compensate for my physical losses, I sought new avenues to fill the void. Other than journals, poems, and video blogs, I struggled to find new creative outlets to replace the physical things I used to do—football, cycling, swimming, photography, and drawing. And while my work with Team Gleason was purposeful and impactful, it didn't satisfy my creative desires.

To try to fulfill this need, I became more active on the Internet. The social media platforms we created for Team Gleason were an outlet for me to interact with my online followers. Finding new ways to inspire them filled a gap in my life and gave me a sense of purpose, something I desperately needed. I enjoyed it. Most importantly, it was easier than interacting with people in "real life" because people talked and moved too quickly for me. Now, texting with friends and using social media were my speed.

However, as I gravitated to the online community, the lack of communication was affecting my relationship with Michel.

I would assert that free, open conversation is the ultimate power that sets humanity apart from other animals. It also sets free, open communities (families, friendships, companies, countries, and societies) apart from oppressive, unfree communities. And it was at the heart of the relationship between me and Michel.

Now, darkness was creeping into our lives. Michel confessed her feelings in a private journal entry:

> The lack of communication is so sad. And lonely. It separates us. The eye technology is good, critical, and I am grateful for it, but it's not fast enough. I find that we only talk when he has to tell me what he needs. Not much actual conversation. It depresses me. I miss my old Steve. I miss his touch, his voice, the comfort of his strong body taking care of me, making me laugh. I miss his handwritten letters. I miss his handwriting. I miss the ease of rid-

ing bikes to get breakfast or last-minute movies. I miss long conversations. I miss his smell. I miss dancing with him and kissing
him. I miss his hugs. I miss our laughter. I miss sharing responsibility. I feel so heavy trying to be so strong. I want to weep when
Steve struggles, but I can't. I have to be strong for Steve. I have
to be strong for Rivers. I will do this. I miss our future. I long
for him to hold Rivers and play guitar and play sports with him.
If I dwelled on what I miss all the time, I'd be in a very bad place,
as would Steve. So I don't. I can't, and I won't. We have to live
in the present. We have no choice. Rivers—I pray that the older
you get, the more you understand how much your dad loves you.
That you are the reason he chooses life despite how hard it is,
every minute. But I also don't want this to be a burden on you.
This is so heavy. We are both so lucky to have you, Rivers. You
make life worth living.

While Michel didn't communicate these issues to me, I sensed
her sadness and exhaustion. She was a fierce fighter, but the burden
of caring for both Rivers and me was taking a huge toll on her. She
poured every ounce of herself into being a mother, wife, and caregiver. By the time she finished dealing with me and Rivers, there
was no time left to invest in herself. One night, as we hectically got
ready to go to a Team Gleason event, our crew arrived to pick us
up and Michel fainted from exhaustion. From my chair, I watched
her, looking gaunt, stand back up, fix herself, finish getting me
ready, and announce to the group, "OK, let's go. We're going to
be late."

While privately our lives were being turned upside down, publicly we maintained a brave face, keeping busy with Team Gleason
duties and our documentary film project.

In February, we made another appearance during the Super
Bowl broadcast, this time in a commercial for Microsoft. This was a
major production. Our entire street was overtaken with box trucks,
SUVs, and catering services. We hosted an entire production team
for a couple days at the house, as videographers took close shots of

my eyes and of Rivers sitting on my lap. This was Microsoft's first-ever Super Bowl commercial, and they wanted to highlight how technology helps those with disabilities, injuries, or illness.

The project launched our partnership with Microsoft and opened doors for us to push technology further to help those with ALS, a tiring yet exciting mental boost for all of us.

We needed the encouragement. The disease had made its way to my respiratory muscles. It was becoming more and more difficult to breathe. I spent hours each day using a suction machine to clear the clogged mucus from my throat. At night, my routine had become much more involved and time-consuming. Rick and Michel had to spend forty-five minutes to an hour meticulously situating me in bed with pillows both for comfort and to prevent pressure sores. Michel had to carefully position me to make sure I could breathe and place hand-sewn stuffed animals around my neck to keep my head from moving.

I needed to wear a retainer that positioned my jaw in an under-bite so I could breathe while sleeping at night. Michel used a bar-baric scissor tool to attach the rubber bands to the retainer in my mouth that kept my jaw in the proper position to maintain an open air passage. She then put on a chin strap to secure the face mask connected to the BiPap breathing machine.

The complicated apparatus only increased the amount of help I needed from her. My incessant needs at night robbed her of sleep, making her increasingly almost too exhausted to care for three-year-old Rivers in the morning.

On the night of Michel's birthday, I expressed my struggles in a private family blog entry:

> I am having serious problems getting situated in bed. It's my head mostly. My lips blow open from my mask. Saliva drips down my chin and seeps down my throat, causing me to swallow every 5 minutes. My right ear keeps getting crushed by my pillow, due to my head being rotated to the right.
>
> Torturous. It feels like too much for me to handle. It's starting to affect my sleep. I'm afraid to yawn because I'm nervous that

it will fuck up the position I am in, in bed. I feel terrible asking Michel for help. I have to vent, but I can't or shouldn't vent to Michel because it grinds on her. I am so fucked! It's so draining to spend an hour directing people to adjust me in bed.

What a waste of a life. I understand why some people choose to fade away. I pray all day, yet God hasn't intervened on my behalf, which I would be fine with if society hadn't created the story that God does intervene. God works in mysterious ways is religion's way of confessing that God is absent. Neutral, holy.

Michel was the one who bore the brunt of this frustration. She spent endless days and nights caring for me. She would help me and then finally sit down to take a break; by the time she sat, I would need her again and she would stand up, help me, and sit back down.

The synthetic voice I used to communicate only made things worse. It sounded flat and lacked inflection. Even if I wanted to try to compassionately ask for help, it would take too long to type "can you . . ." so my requests always sounded curt, like demands.

As the days and nights piled up, the compassion in our relationship started to wane. Michel and I entered a dark tunnel of resentment and contempt.

In mid-March, I expressed my concerns in my journal:

I need to do something to help my relationship with Michel. I fear we are growing so distant we may break from each other's orbit. Somehow I need to engage her on how to restore the strength in our relationship. I feel like I have tried this before, but nothing changes. I will try again, with better technique. Maybe a letter for Easter. To Michel: Sorry, I brought you a terrible nightmare life. I can't take it any longer. It will be better for you when I am dead. We can be together then. Enjoy your freedom. No guilt for your freedom.

This led me and Michel to have a conversation about having a second child. I'd brought it up a couple times and she was against it. "Steve," she said adamantly, "look at me. I'm barely a hundred pounds. I am nowhere near mentally or physically strong enough to carry or care for another baby."

She feared that adding a second child to the mix might break her. Her points were valid and logical, but it saddened me. I desperately wanted Rivers to have a sibling. I did not want him to take this journey alone. I knew if I were healthy, this would not even be a question, which only added to my guilt.

On our sixth anniversary, Michel wrote me an email, confessing that she was "struggling deeply" with our relationship.

> There is still this reality of missing you. I mourn for the loss of you. But you're still here. Does that even make sense? It's so hard. And I'm not proving strong enough to get past it.
>
> I miss having a husband who can do these things with me. You know all these things. If I do go places without you I mourn you not being there. It's too heavy and wears me down. I have this huge layer of guilt and shame because I feel depressed.
>
> I worry about our future. I wonder how long you'll be here, how old I'll be when you're gone and if I'll be too old to find someone else? Will I be alone when Rivers leaves me? Will I find someone to love us? A weird part of me copes by thinking and planning for our future without you. Then I feel like I'm an evil person and feel even more ashamed.
>
> This is an awful anniversary letter. I'm sorry if I'm failing you. Please know I love you. And always will.

I replied via email and told her it was a "great" but "sucky letter":

> I think I understand. It sucks royally, but I think I understand. You will explode if you stay, but you will implode if you go. I feel guilty for putting you in a situation that I have no answer for.
>
> I think it must be a mind-fuck to feel trapped but are not, when you are stuck with me at the house. Whereas, I really am trapped, so I don't entertain many thoughts like, "Man, I want to hop in a car and drive to Austin."

I will say that I rarely if ever am depressed when you are out doing stuff. My hardest times are when y'all are right in front of me, and I can't keep up. Maybe that helps with giving you freedom to be happy during those times.

I have no idea what to do about our/your future. No idea. I want you to be happy, and if I die before you, I hope you find someone to grow old with. Or maybe find someone now, is that crazy?

I think it's important that you keep projects outside of Rivers, but I think he will stay close to you. I worry that you will find someone Rivers doesn't like.

I don't know how to unshroud your depression and guilt. I wish I did. I am sorry if my response is too upbeat or evangelical. This really does suck, but I feel like I understand you and your feelings better. Thank you.

Michel replied:

I don't know what to do. Really. There is nothing to do besides change my attitude and feelings toward my life. It's just hard. I'm turning into someone I don't like. I go hours a day feeling hopeless, like, I don't have anything to look forward to. I am like a zombie when playing with Rivers. I've never felt depressed before, I don't know what to do. People liked when I was a machine and a perfect wife. People don't like when I'm sad and struggling. They want me to go to therapy and fix it. It's not that easy. I do know that I want us to love each other 'til you (or I guess, one of us) dies. I'm really scared.

At this point, my physical regression had reached a breaking point. I was still getting mucus plugs in my throat and lungs, and my blood oxygen had decreased from 99 percent to 95 percent. Consequently, I wasn't sleeping well and was constantly fatigued and irritable. Michel was equally irritable.

One day she impatiently walked away to do housework before I was finished talking with her.

I wrote to her, "Hey! I type faster than anyone else using this tablet!"

She responded: "Yes, I know! But you speak slower than everyone not using that tablet!"

In late May 2014, as Rivers played on the ground with his trucks, we could not clear a mucus plug. The machines were not working. One of our new caregivers, Lauren Bowman; Anna Campo, our respiratory therapist; and Michel took turns leaning me forward and punching on my back, then leaning me backward and punching me on my chest. I feared the hospital. I didn't want to get sick at the hospital or be told I'd have to get an emergency tracheotomy. But at this point, we had no choice. Luckily, the hospital visit was quick and effective.

I was constantly anxious, afraid that something simple, like having my head in the wrong position, would lead to suffocation. I was tired of living with that fear.

Ultimately, I was dying. It was time to seriously consider getting a tracheotomy. Without the procedure, which implants a breathing tube directly into my windpipe so I could breathe through a ventilator, I would not be able to breathe on my own for much longer.

I had to decide: Choose life, or death.

This is a decision that many people with ALS are forced to make at some point. Ventilation was an option to continue my life, but it would come with a cost. Once ventilated, I would be attached to the ventilator 24/7 and need full-time assistance. I could never be left alone. Few nursing homes or residential care facilities are equipped to care for people on ventilators, and in-home health care would be required, which would cost hundreds of thousands of dollars a year. Plus, the procedure couldn't be reversed. There was no turning back.

For these reasons, the vast majority of people with ALS—95 percent—decide to forgo the procedure and allow the disease to take its course. If the patient makes it that far, getting trached is essentially a live-or-die decision.

Life as I knew it was painfully difficult. Not just for me, but for everyone around me. My physical condition had become increasingly unbearable, and my relationship with Michel was rattled. Our house, once a place full of family and friends and life, was shrouded in grim sadness.

Something had to change.

For me, there was no easy answer. I wasn't ready to die. We had the resources and support to continue. I had more I wanted to see, do, and accomplish, but I was worn out, Michel was worn out, and I saw no light in the darkness. No playbook and no guide.

I also wanted to continue to make a difference in peoples' lives through our work at Team Gleason. For better or worse, people looked to me for inspiration. I was a role model for many of them. Most important, I wanted to be there for Rivers, in whatever capacity I could as a father.

Michel and I met with our respiratory therapist, Anna Campo, and our pulmonologist, Dr. Stephen Kantrow, who told us, "I know when we first met and you could communicate very clearly, you were very clear that as things moved forward you were going to utilize any technology to stay in the game. I know that has been your goal but I wanted to revisit that with you."

I told him, "I have had the opportunity to contemplate my own death quite thoroughly these past few years. I'd say it's an opportunity because I think understanding one's own mortality can help open a person to lead a more meaningful life. I fight to stay alive for my son, for my wife, my friends and family. I am not giving up."

On May 19, 2014, I checked into East Jefferson Hospital to undergo a tracheotomy procedure. Dr. Knight Worley performed the procedure the next day.

I announced my decision to the public in a tweet to my 80,000 followers: "We've lived this ALS journey publicly, no reason to stop now. I am heading in for a semi-planned tracheotomy tonight. . . . I believe in the power of intention, prayer, meditation, etc. I appreciate your unified focus on healing."

I trusted our doctor, but there was a lot of fear as I was rolled back for surgery. Michel hugged me, sobbing and drenching my shoulder with tears. Though she had been getting more distant, she now dropped her guard.

The surgery provided immediate relief. I no longer had to wear anything on my face, my breathing opened up, and I didn't have to worry about head placement, choking, etc. As alien as this procedure was, in many ways, I was energized mentally.

Michel, on the other hand, was not. For her, the decision meant more years of this arduous existence.

We had brought on a team of caregivers to help her and Blair: Jay Holland, Lauren Bowman, and my occupational therapist, Jenni Doiron. I also recruited Jared Gros, the able-bodied cheerful nurse from my hospital stay. But their aid wouldn't free her from the binds created by the disease. And it added strangers to our family, so Michel resented the lack of privacy.

While the trache and ventilator improved my physical and mental health, it required a massive adjustment to our daily lives. Having a hose connected to my throat and a ventilator box on the floor limited my mobility. It also made the coordination of my morning "workout" decidedly more complex. Getting from my bed to the shower, then to my wheelchair, now required a handful of people and took nearly two hours to complete. Through trial and error, we learned new tricks and made adjustments to improve the process, but the daily task required an inordinate amount of time, patience, and money, all of which were increasingly scarce. We were fortunate to collect disability from the NFL and for the money raised in our trust, but with funds dwindling, I started accepting paid speeches as a source of added income.

The accelerating demands only made things more difficult for Michel. We were together—but separate. Our daily interactions had become almost procedural. She was often distant and vacant. She showed little passion or compassion toward me. Everything was brief and "professional." A pat on the head. A peck on the cheek. A tap on my hand. She could barely look me in the eyes. We were roommates—not husband and wife.

As Michel and I drifted further apart, I tried to fill the void with other ventures: social media posts, "300 Seconds," journaling, growing Team Gleason, and working on the documentary film with David and Ty. My schedule kept me busy and provided an escape from the reality of my struggling marriage.

As the Ice Bucket Challenge, a global ALS fundraising phenomenon, took off, Bill Gates, who had taken the challenge and learned about my story from our work with Microsoft, asked to meet with me. One of his business partners, Larry Cohen, was also a friend of Pearl Jam guitarist Mike McCready. Mike and I had met in 2003 through a mutual friend, Erica Perkins, at a Pearl Jam show in Atlanta. Michel and Mike's wife, Ashley, met soon after and they loved each other. Our families have become close. They, as well as the other guys in Pearl Jam, have been big supporters of ours and Team Gleason.

Larry called Clare Durrett, our PR director at Team Gleason, to see if I was interested in meeting with Gates in Seattle. Getting there was going to be tough, so through a network of people a private jet was arranged.

The jet was first-class in every way. We were excited and grateful for the use of it, as I had not yet traveled with the trache, and we were apprehensive about flying commercially. Blair and a group of firefighters loaded my wheelchair into the cargo hold at the back of the plane. Mike McCready welcomed us on the tarmac holding a portable speaker above his head, like John Cusack in *Say Anything.*

The night before our meeting with Gates, I typed to Michel to stop talking over me, and said it loud enough in the hotel lobby for our whole group to hear. I received an email from her mom, Jilly, that night.

> TT [My Varisco family nickname]. It's been bothering me
> all night, and I must let you know, it was very hurtful and
> embarrassing when you told Michel she was "rude" for talking
> over you. What was "rude" was the way you called her down in
> front of us and your caretakers.
>
> Love—Jilly

The note was unusual for Jilly. Her natural instincts were to nurture and pacify. It was out of her comfort zone to call me out, so I knew my actions had hurt. I felt regret and immediately penned a reply with my eye-tracking software.

> I am sorry Jilly. We are really struggling. I feel lost in our relationship. I know lots of it is my fault, and some of it is just ALS's fault. I feel like she will not take time, stop her daily life, and talk to me, listen to me, or put her hand on me. I feel like I am watching her drift away and am powerless to stop it. Then I do stupid stuff like say she was rude, and that pushes her farther away. It's terrible. I know this trip stresses her out.
>
> I am sorry. I don't want you to be mad at me. I was rude, you were right. I know she misses the old me. And I feel like she thinks the current me is hideous. I just get so frustrated with her impatience and how she doesn't want to be around me, but it's no excuse for saying that out loud. I wish I could wake up and this would all be a dream, and me and Michel were like beans and rice again. . . . I can handle the physical destruction, but what ALS has done to my relationship with Michel is nearly unbearable.

We met with Gates for close to an hour in his private Gates Ventures office in suburban Seattle. One of my goals was to secure a commitment for funding Answer ALS, a program that originated at the Team Gleason ALS Summit in 2013. We'd brought together leading researchers, patients, caregivers, and advocates to create a business plan that would lay the foundation for all future research, to accelerate treatments or a cure. Answer ALS is the single largest ALS research consortium in history, but it desperately needed funding.

I had nothing to lose, so I pitched him pretty hard to contribute. He was more interested in geeking out about the technology I use to live my life. I showed him how I type, communicate, and browse the Internet with eye-tracking software.

"I can do anything," I told him. "What's your favorite song?"

"My Favorite Things," he said, referencing the song sung by Julie Andrews in *The Sound of Music*.

I found the John Coltrane version of the song on Spotify and played it for him. "I really want to improve this technology," he said.

At the end of the meeting, I asked him for a $125 million contribution to Answer ALS to ensure the program's scale and longevity.

"ALS is so complex, it has to be approached like the original moon shot," I said. "President Kennedy did not ask for more studies on how to get to the moon. He empowered a large-scale, collaborative, and goal-oriented initiative to land on the moon."

He didn't commit to Answer ALS at the time, but now supports the program.

WE RETURNED TO New Orleans and dove full-tilt into the planning and production of the documentary.

At the same time, we started to reach out to friends who had ALS for counsel on how to improve the relationship between me and Michel. Other couples had been through this situation and somehow managed to make it work so I struggled to come to grips with what had caused things to go sideways.

One of the people I advised Michel to contact was Eric Valor, a Team Gleason board member and former IT manager for Mercedes-Benz, who was diagnosed with ALS in 2005 (Eric died in 2019 from complications from the disease). Michel emailed Eric, who lived in California, and told him she was struggling in our relationship. Eric responded the next day.

Michel:
First and foremost, you are absolutely entitled to feel how you feel.

Yes, we say the "for better or worse" bit while getting married, but nobody anticipates this living death situation. It's the most difficult thing a couple can go through. And it's not uncommon to be the death of relationships. The daily chore of caring for a severely disabled partner is extremely wearing. And the daily loss of physical ability is emotionally destructive for the patient.

But you have to know that Steve isn't gone. The essence of ourselves is our minds, not our bodies. Our bodies are only a life-support system and physical manifestation mechanism for our minds. That's why Team Gleason is so important. And it's very important for Steve to have a mission to keep him engaged with and in life. Rivers is also incredibly important to him as you already well know. That's all I will say about this for now.

The key to my relationships is communication. It always has been. So that is the key. The Steve you fell in love with is still there but the body he once had isn't. He can still touch you in the ways which are important. Daily intimate communication is key.

This is a horrible situation to live with daily. Not everybody can handle it. Do not deny your feelings or they will perforate your soul. At the end of the day, you have to take care of yourself or you won't be able to care for Rivers.

Eric

Nevertheless, the undercurrent of our spiraling relationship was starting to affect how I viewed the film project.

In August, I sent a tough email to our production team:

I am troubled about this documentary. As if we need any more obstacles. I think the following needs careful consideration:

Initially, this doc revolved around a love story. Love between a father and son. Love between a husband and wife. Love between a young man and his family and friends. The story will inspire as it shows these relationships strengthen despite obstacles and adversity. The audience will walk out refreshed and compelled to rethink their purpose and their relationships.

Problem.

If we are honest, ALS has disintegrated most of my close relationships.

Consider:

My cousin (Brendan), who went on the Alaska trip, I no longer speak with. We aren't angry with each other. More, a dissolution of a friendship.

My brother, Kyle. Probably my best friend over our lifetime, I now see 5–10 days a year, max. We talk online, but our relationship was based on our activities together, our exploration of the physical world, as an avenue to explore the spiritual/philosophical world. Smoldering.

Michel. I don't think it's a secret. We are struggling. One could argue that our relationship is in complete shambles.

Now, that relationship is a distant memory.

I can't believe I am saying that.

It's fucking heartbreaking. A good old-fashioned tragedy.

How did it happen? And so quickly? Even less than a year ago, we were strong. Facing adversity, but together. In fact, last year, I was concerned that our footage was too glorified and didn't reflect the struggle ALS patients face.

That concern is long gone. It tears me to pieces. Again, how did this happen??

My thoughts . . .

Among other theories, I think we absolutely failed at bringing on adequate help soon enough.

I am concerned that my relationship with Rivers is next. It's a very real concern. For me to do anything, there must be planning and logistical foresight. Parenting is hard. With ALS, it's nearly impossible. With disunited parents, it might actually be impossible. Impossible is not a word I use. Ever.

Since Mic and I are not cohesive, we are much less of a team as parents, and I feel I am losing my grip on fatherhood. As I lose that grip, my heart is beginning to crack. If it happens, I will seriously consider waving the white flag.

The competitive side of me just can't understand how this can't be fixed. It says, "Just push harder!" I am deeply confused.

Am I optimistic that the story can end well? Although my optimism has faded recently, my answer remains yes. It took time to get here, it will take time to move forward.

So, I am disturbed about the movie. It's either a depressing tragedy about how ALS can take down even the strongest marriage. Or, it's a flat-out lie. Either way, not the sort of something I am proud to share.

So, I am at a loss. If we don't make the film, I will feel terrible for the people that have worked so hard to get us here, especially Ty and David, who have given their lives to this film and have no money.

Inspiring the world, while I lose my family.

WHILE THE TRACHE improved my quality of life, it did not eliminate all of the challenges of living with ALS. Every day was a learning experience—and often a struggle.

One day, I would be constipated and spend hours with a nurse having poop dug out of my butt. The next, I would shit the bed after taking a laxative to combat the brutal "impaction."

"This is so hard to watch," Michel said. "I can barely take this, seeing you in this pain."

I was feeling so weary, inadequate, and needy. I would ride Michel, doing things like insisting that she change her last name to Gleason, which just separated us further. When we got married, I loved that she wanted to keep Varisco. As if changing her last name was what would heal me; us.

In mid-October, we went to see Pearl Jam at the Austin City Limits Music Festival in Austin, Texas.

A few weeks before the show, Michel had told me how much she loved the Pearl Jam song "You Are," and played it for me in our living room. I had never really connected with the song, so it was powerful for us to listen to it together.

This broken wheel is coming undone,
And the road's exploding
But you're keeping me strong,
Rolling along with you
Love is a tower,
And you're the key
Leading me higher,
Will you let me in?

That was *us!*

The song inspired me to believe our love was strong. We could heal.

The day of the show I texted Mike McCready: *"If I may be so bold, I have a request. Can y'all play 'You Are' for Michel? Totally understand if it doesn't happen. Luv u."*

Mike responded and told me that drummer Matt Cameron wrote the song and that the group was working on the set list for the show. He made no promises.

"Sweet, man," I replied. *"I think it would be pretty special. This ALS journey is a fucking grind. So, to have you share that song with her will mean a lot to her, I think, and me."*

Not only did they play "You Are," but Eddie Vedder talked about me and Michel before the song. He dedicated "this powerful love song to our good friends, Steve and Michel."

I was hoping it would help Michel understand how good our life actually was. And while she definitely expressed excitement and kissed me on the face several times, I wanted there to be more.

A few weeks later, after Michel had gotten home from going out to a show with her brothers, we started a Google Chat, which had become the main form of communication for us.

Michel: "I feel guilty about not being happy when I'm home. I feel bad because I feel like you're making an effort to try harder, and I'm not reciprocating."

Steve: "Thanks for acknowledging that, Mic."

Michel: "Thanks for trying."

Steve: "Of course."

Michel: "Steve, tonight at the show one of Pauly's friends leaned over, put his hand on my back, and asked me if he could get me a beer. I said yes, and then I felt my eyes burn. It felt somewhat thrilling to be touched. And cared for. He literally just asked me if I wanted a beer, and I felt like it was the nicest thing anyone has ever done for me. I think I am starving for something. I know we are both good people, Steve-O, who love each other. But you have to acknowledge that we've been through more than most people could handle. And, yes, we were good. But things are different now, Steve. And the pain and loss and fear and anxiety and frustration and suffering are real. I need you to acknowledge that. And the difficulty of communication and loss of intimacy have proven, for me, to be very, very difficult, if not impossible. I imagine it has to be the same for you."

Steve: "Yes. You're right that what we've been through breaks most relationships. It is very different. And very real pain. Damaging pain. And we can't go back."

Michel: "I want to be good parents together with Rivers, but I also want us to be happy."

Steve: "And you think it's either/or?"

Michel: "I don't know."

Michel: "I do know that we both have needs that aren't being met, and that I want to be better around you, but when I feel like I'm trapped I get distant and resentful. But I don't know a solution. Not trapped necessarily because of you, but because of the world watching us."

Steve: "What world is watching us? Caregivers?"

Michel: "Ha. Caretakers. Team Gleason. Team Gleason followers. New Orleans. Washington. 80,000 social media fans. We created a world that isn't ours. So I feel like any decisions we make are not ours."

Steve: "Do you feel that our world isn't ours? This is new to me. Thanks for sharing."

Michel: "Yes, I do. We didn't really have a choice, because taking care of you takes a village. But any decision that we used to make alone soon evolved into my dad, Clare, Su, Lauren, Blair, Liz, and our Team Gleason therapist, etc., etc. Which is fine. I think it just damaged our family unit. But again, not anyone's fault. This is too big to do alone."

Steve: "Do you think we can consciously make an effort to make some S&M decisions?"

Michel: "I guess. I mean, we do now with Rivers stuff, I'm more concerned with the world being involved in our private life, which is just a normal result of 'celebrity.' "

Steve: "Can you give an example of the world involved in our private life?"

Michel: "Facebook. People recognizing Rivers. People commenting on what a super wife I am. Both make me feel uncomfortable, as I know I'm not a super wife anymore. At the same time, I know I have been an incredible wife for a very long time. I feel like I've given my everything. And when I stepped back and started thinking about myself—I went through the depression of losing my old Steve, then to the realization of how much I gave to you, how my life revolved around you and my whole self became living to make sure you were the best you could be at all times. And it was great. I don't regret any of that. But also draining. And realized I didn't get enough in return. And now it's like I've distanced myself and have nothing more to give. I think it's part of the reason I feel trapped. Like, I don't think I'm depressed anymore. But let's say things just got unbearable between you and me. Yes, the public opinion of what decisions we would make can make me feel trapped."

Steve: "I feel pretty terrible about this. You never really shared this with me. I'm so sorry. I can't go back and fix it. But I'm sorry. You were amazing, and I wish I would've acknowledged it more. I just miss you so much."

Michel: "Thanks, Steve-O. It's my fault too. I've not been good at expressing what I need. I keep it bottled up 'til it destroys my insides."

Steve: "I just yearn for my best friend."

Michel: "Me, too, Steve. But it's hard giving that to you. I'm trying to figure out why."

Steve: "Why do you feel like you have to conceal your feelings?"

Michel: "I should have been talking more openly. Because I'm afraid of how it would affect you. If you didn't have ALS, it would be different. Since we are talking openly now, I might as well get other stuff off my chest. You up for it?"

Steve: "Of course . . ."

Michel: "OK, give me a second, I have to go check on Rivers."

As I lay waiting in my hospital bed, I could hear Michel lulling Rivers back to sleep. I reread the conversation several times. As difficult as it was to hear what she had to say, it was encouraging to have Michel speak so openly. Deep down, I knew these thoughts existed already, and it was helpful that we were able to connect through our pain, even if there was no solution. She was convinced that I couldn't satisfy her physically, and obviously I couldn't force her to change.

Michel: "OK, I'm back. So I think this is something that has messed me up. In the beginning we've always talked about you getting trached. And we were in. But when the time came for it to actually happen, we were distant. Not a team. Watching you for the month before was fucking traumatizing. I could not imagine you living like that. I could not imagine having to live with you living like that. I think I brought it up once, like 'Are you still 100 percent in on this?,' and you said, 'Yes.' But you never asked me for my feelings. And it's something I really don't have the right to say yes or no on. Ultimately it's your life. But it involves me and Rivers, too. So I felt like we should have been a team with this. And, honestly, I didn't feel it or really know what I wanted at the time. It's really terrible to admit this, but you were in a bad state, and I didn't know what post-trache life would be like. If it would keep you in the same state but alive for the next twenty years. The day you came home from the trache surgery I felt the weight of the world on my shoulders. If I was completely open I might have said something like 'I'm scared of continuing on this way. I want you to do what you want to do, and I will always be there for you, but I may have to move on with someone who can take care of me in the way I need.' More importantly, I wanted to hear that from you. This is heavy shit, Steve. But most importantly I want to become friends again, and I know we have to be honest, if there's any shot of it."

Steve: "OK. Although that's shocking, I'm not shocked."

Michel: "Yes, I can imagine it's shocking, too. That's why I haven't had the guts to say it. . . . I also feel like we've gotten nowhere in conversations sometimes because you ask me to say things that are too hard to say, so I stop talking. I'm obviously not meeting all your needs, either."

Steve: "I need blowjobs."

Michel: "Haha."

Steve: "Kidding."

Michel: "It's hard because 'needs' could, in all fairness, be food, shelter, clothing, love. So I'm asking you the same question while I type mine."

Steve: "I need compassion, someone who says, man, I know you're struggling, but I recognize it, and am here if you need to yell. I need someone who will cry on my neck. I need someone to share their fears and weaknesses with me. I need patience, while I type my feelings. I need to be touched, like when you used to put your hand on me in bed. I need to be laid next to. I need my hands taken and pressed against your cheek. And then my fingers wrapped around your arms, then on your sides. I need to be kissed on the lips, like we practiced one night in bed, when we were high. I need someone willing to try unorthodox ideas, to enhance a friendship, even simple things like Google Chat."

Michel: "Good list, Steve-O. I want you to have all those things. I'm not in a place to give you most of those right now. I have too much resentment. I am very sorry about this, Steve, and will work on giving you what I can. I need all the physical stuff, too. I need to be held, hugged, fucked, taken care of, taken out to dinner, danced with, kissed, bike rides, out to bars, playing outside. I need compassion and empathy. I need to feel a connection with someone. I need to get it, and not just to give it to you, because then I feel like it's not fair and start feeling the f-ing resentment.

"I know this is obviously a desperate and difficult situation. I know you'd give most of this to me, but you can't. And it's not natural to have a husband who cannot do most of these things. God, I'm so sorry to even be saying these things, but I don't know what else to say or do. I know in a way I should just shut up and be happy because you love me and provide for me and you love Rivers and do your absolute best to be a great dad. But these are my feelings and they are real. I'm sorry, Steve-O."

At this point in our lives together, I was still trying to make it work, and hoping Michel would see my perspective.

Steve: "I can do most of those things—in unorthodox ways, I think. But only if/when you try."

Michel: "OK. Shit!"

Steve: "I'm sorry that you feel like you only gave and never received. I want to know how to fix that."

Michel: "I just don't feel that way about you physically, Steve-O. I'm sorry. I'm sorry!! And it's not because you're not hot. I think your face is still one of the most handsome I've seen. And your body is looking great, too. It's just not there. We've been through too much."

Steve: "I'm trying to understand. You think I look cute, but we've been through too much. Are you saying, so, if I got better, you still think we've been through too much?"

Michel: "I think it's stemmed from being a caretaker. Then, I thought maybe it would come back, taking away caretaking. But it didn't. . . . I know it would be easier to work on if you got better. Clearly. I imagine some of your attraction to me has gone away since I've grown cold and distant?"

Steve: "Not really. I think you're smoking hot, and every time you walk by me, I want you to hug me so tight."

Michel: "Ugh."

Steve: "Well, you can't force it. You . . . of all people."

Michel: "WHAT ARE WE GOING TO DO??!!!"

16

Compassion

Redemption is found in truthful speech.
—JORDAN PETERSON

On January 5, 2015, the four-year anniversary of my diagnosis, Scott Fujita sent me an email. Scott, as always, was thoughtful, insightful, and funny. He also offered his support, which had been steadfast throughout our friendship.

After reflecting on this, and our friendship, I emailed him back.

Fuji,

I was diagnosed four years ago with ALS. I think I can say, it has become the worst news ever received.

I am not even sure how to feel about the "anniversary." My first thought is, it feels like 40 years. It doesn't feel like a celebration. More like a 23rd or 38th or 47th birthday. Just another notch on the ladder.

I clearly remember you telling me, "I will walk to the ends of the earth with you." While I feel we have more exploring to do, you have certainly remained true to your word. Thank you, Scott.

It's been a long 4 years, but because of you and a handful of others, it's been very fruitful. From Machu Picchu to Microsoft to our fucking awesome son, we have made the most of a brutal circumstance.

I often wonder why this happened to me. There is no right answer, but the answer I/we choose: This happened to me so that I can inspire people to be great fathers and husbands despite adversity and shortcomings. This happened to me so that it won't happen to millions of others.

You were right and will always be right: "There is nothing more powerful than the human soul on fire."

Thanks for keeping my fire burning. I love you. Forever.

SG

Later that night, I watched *Finding Nemo* with Rivers. On this anniversary, there would be no skydiving, no Machu Picchu. Just me, my son, and an important life lesson, "Just keep swimming, dude."

A FEW WEEKS LATER, I traveled to Washington, D.C., on behalf of Team Gleason business to meet with Sylvia Burwell, the U.S. secretary of health and human services, the most powerful health official in the country.

Traveling can be rewarding, but also incredibly stressful for me and my care team. Travail. Flying with a power wheelchair and ventilator is complicated. My care staff has compiled a 7-page, 2,400-word checklist of protocols and procedures for the experience.

Upon reaching the hotel room, our crew had to set up my rented hospital bed and my tablet, then get my chair adjusted. If anything couldn't be adjusted correctly or I couldn't get positioned comfortably in the hospital bed, it was a sleepless nightmare. Fortunately, we avoided any major issues, and after a planning session for the meeting the next day, I made it through the night just fine.

Senator David Vitter had arranged the meeting with Secretary Burwell to give me and Team Gleason staff members a chance to visit with her, Senator Lisa Murkowski, and Kathy Holt, associate director of the Center for Medicare Advocacy. Our goal was to update them on a recent Medicare rule that cut off funding for people with disabilities who use tablets to communicate and how that rule was negatively impacting their lives.

The meeting went extremely well. I even got a belly laugh out of Burwell when I told her that she needed to find a solution or I would tell our mutual friend James Carville about it. Burwell said her office would look into it, but the fastest way was a legislative solution. From this conversation, Team Gleason began work on what would eventually become the Steve Gleason Act.

That afternoon I told our crew, "Let's go check out some of the monuments nearby."

I thoroughly enjoy history and love to dig into the mystery and stories of the past. It fascinates me.

The Lincoln Memorial had an impact on me because of what an incredible thinker Abraham Lincoln was. I am guessing there were more progressive presidents or global leaders, but I found his clarity of thought on slavery and the union remarkable, all the while dealing with depression.

As we made our way around, I came across a Lincoln quote on the interior of the memorial that struck me:

"I am loath to close. We are not enemies, but friends. We must not be enemies. Though passion may have strained it must not break our bonds of affection. The mystic chords of memory, stretching from every battlefield and patriot grave to every living heart and hearthstone all over this broad land, will yet swell the chorus of the Union, when again touched, as surely as they will be, by the better angels of our nature."

The quote was about keeping the Union together, but it was the perfect analogy for my marriage and relationship with Michel. ALS had torn our marriage apart. It was a smoldering battlefield. Wounds were raw. Yet, I still held on to the idea that both of our hearts "will yet swell the chorus of union, when again touched, as surely they will be, by the better angels of our nature."

It was important that we unite, not just for our sanity and happiness, but most importantly for Rivers's development. He was our top priority. I wanted him to know and understand love.

Reuniting would not be easy. Michel had become traumatized by ALS and the deterioration of my physical body. It wasn't her fault. It's like watching someone you love get disfigured in war. The difference was when soldiers leave traumatic situations they can often begin to digest and process the trauma. Michel was still a prisoner of war.

ALS had done this. It destroyed "us." My worst fear is that it would somehow destroy Rivers, too. The passion between us certainly had been "strained," but we couldn't allow it to "break our bonds of affection." Too much was at stake.

ON VALENTINE'S DAY, I took a slightly different approach to connect with Michel and spark a reconciliation.

Dear Michel,

More than any other Valentine's, I hate this one the most. What's hard is where we are emotionally, on a day like today. Do you know how much I love you? I know you are tired of trying to be happy. I don't blame you. This is not the life you imagined when you married me 7 years ago. I feel guilty every day for turning life into a nightmare.

I am proud of you, Michel. You often say you are weak, but I see your strength. I see you trying to be happy. I see you not giving up. Do you know how much I love you?! I love you as you struggle.

It's our 10th Valentine's Day together. Maybe we'll have 10 more, or 30. Or maybe this is our last. But 10 doesn't feel like much, considering people live for 80 years.

Michel, we can't do this alone. I know you can't fake your feelings, and I don't want you to. Shit, that's part of why I loved you so much when we first met! At the risk of sounding religious and self-righteous, and not that you asked, but I know you feel bad/guilty for how you are at times. I forgive you. Will you forgive me, for being overly critical, and "looking at you, like I wanna kill you"? Please forgive me, Michel. Do you know how much I love you?

This is what I believe. I believe that, while my ALS may not end, we will break through this . . . this . . . emotional prison we are in. Keep your heart strong. I am here, loving you, as your friend, as your mover. Always and all ways. Forever. That's how much I love you.

Happy Valentine's Day, Michel.

A FEW DAYS LATER, I started to feel sick. I was hyper-cognizant of my body in my playing days, and now even more so. My care team is equally vigilant. So as soon as I started to feel "off," we contacted my doctors and they advised me to head to the hospital.

I was admitted to the emergency room at East Jefferson Hospital with a low fever of 99.7 degrees. As we waited to see a doctor, my temperature kept rising and eventually climbed to 102.5. Finally, after a couple of hours of testing, the doctor diagnosed me with a touch of pneumonia and started pumping me with antibiotics.

We then settled into the room and started the movie *Whiplash* on my tablet. About an hour into the movie, though, I started to get lightheaded. I started typing as quickly as possible on my tablet, "I-m . . . n-o-t . . . f-e-e-l-i-n-g . . ." is what I managed to get out and pressed speak. My vision narrowed and I started to lose consciousness. I heard Liz reply, "You're not feeling the movie?" Liz Chapoton was a friend who came on board the day after I was diagnosed. She knew nothing about ALS at the time but is now one of the most knowledgeable patient advocates in the state. At that point, my vision was gone and I heard Michel frantically call out for the doctors. Everything went blank.

I awoke to a bunch of doctors and nurses, Michel, Liz, and Dewey looking at me. Everyone looked very shaken. And understandably so. They all thought I had died.

We learned that I had fainted because of a sepsis attack, a serious infection that caused my blood pressure to plummet. I had pneumonia, which led to sepsis, both of which can be lethal. Scary shit. The doctors surmised that I wore down my body during Mardi Gras the previous week, and my immune system was weakened. I could easily have died.

I was released from the hospital after sixty-eight hours.

The incident further traumatized Michel. Over these years with ALS, she had watched "that boy" wither away in a figurative death; now she watched him literally die right in front of her. She had run out of the room and wailed to David, "He's dead!"

In a strange way, living with ALS was easier for me than it was for Michel. After all, I didn't have much choice.

One night I went to see *The Theory of Everything*, the Academy Award–winning movie about the life of Stephen Hawking and his first wife, Jane.

The movie, which was based on Jane Hawking's memoir *Traveling to Infinity: My Life with Stephen Hawking*, profoundly affected me. It changed my outlook. I felt like I was watching our own life play out on the big screen as I sat in the Elmwood Palace Theater that night.

When I got home and settled, I immediately texted Michel on Google Chat.

Steve: "I think you need to leave this house."

Michel: "What do you mean?"

Steve: "You're miserable around me. You need to be happy. I try to deny it, but you're not in love with me. And I want you to be happy. You need someone else."

Michel: "Oh, man, Steve-O. I'm so sorry. I love you. I just want to feel like me again. Thank you for wanting me to be happy. I want you to be happy, too. Did the movie make you think this?"

Steve: "Yes. Except I'm no Hawking."

Michel: "What do you mean?"

Steve: "He has a purpose. The movie was our life, except they had people to go to. As they divorced, they both had a girlfriend and boyfriend to be with. She lost her life to him. She chose to marry another man, and she's happy now. So go be happy."

Michel: "I don't think I could live with myself for leaving you."

Steve: "Pretty obvious, you're already gone. Other than physically leaving."

Michel: "But I do love you. I think I fell out of love with the way of life."

Steve: "My mom loves me."

Michel: "Steve, I wish I could verbalize all of the things I need to say. It's so hard. For a second, I let myself feel the feelings of seeing you and missing you and it was brutal. I don't want to be divorced. But I don't feel alive a lot of the time here."

Steve: "You want to leave but not get divorced?"

Michel: "Wait. . . . What? I don't know if I want to leave, Steve. I don't want you or Rivers to hate me for feelings or decisions I make. God, we should not have to be dealing with this. I contemplated leaving for a while to feel less trapped. But I think it's a bad decision. I worry about my future. My and Rivers's future."

Steve: "I understand."

Michel: "How hard is it for you without physical intimacy?"

Steve: "Hard. Worse than that, no emotional intimacy."

Michel: "Yes. Both. I think they are a very necessary part of feeling alive and happy."

Steve: "Well, I'm right here."

Michel: "I know. I'm not a bad person for losing those feelings. I'm so sorry. It feels unnatural. I cannot help that. The last time we had sex (in a chair) kinda messed me up."

Steve: "I'm fucking sorry. This sucks."

Michel: "I wanted to be a great, loving wife for you until you died. And I'm failing."

Steve: "It's just hard trying to be the optimistic one, like, fuck, we keep having the same convo over and over. You're miserable. You need intimacy. In the movie, they went through the same thing, and were happier after they split. So, if the options are 1.) You're a miserable black hole; or 2.) You leave and be happy, I choose no. 2."

Michel: "I can't imagine us not being a unit, I think with some modifications we can still exist."

Steve: "Currently, we're not a unit."

Michel: "Well, we are one right now."

Michel looked for an apartment close by, so she could have her own space, away from both me and the caregivers. She'd grown weary of the lack of privacy—no more walking around in underwear, parenting without the feeling of people watching or judging, having private phone conversations, going to the bathroom with the door open, or even sleeping without people walking in and out of our room. Ultimately she only stayed there a handful of nights. Michel started seeing a therapist and I sought counsel from other PALS (People with ALS), who had been through similar experiences. I talked to them about how they managed to survive as couples.

But as much as we tried, nothing worked. We continued to drift apart. And as we did, the inevitable happened. Lonely and yearning for connection and emotional intimacy, we both sought others to provide what we couldn't give each other at the time. Our lives were playing out like *The Theory of Everything*.

In early July 2015 on a Friday night, we went to see the movie *The Overnight*, a brash, dark comedy about two couples experimenting with swinging. One of the lead male characters, Kurt, played by Jason Schwartzman, is well-endowed. The other, Alex, played by Adam Scott, is not. It's a running theme throughout the movie.

Afterward, Michel came into my room and sat cross-legged on the corner of my hospital bed.

Michel: "I thought we had a good time (tonight)."

Steve: "We did. But that doesn't change the fact that you'd rather be with someone else."

Michel: "What can I say to that? I'd rather be with you to do the things we used to do. I'd rather be at Coeur d'Alene jumping off boats and going to eat. But we can't. I'd rather be going on adventures than just hanging out at this house. I'd rather be with you—when you were *you*. I cannot help it. I can't help it! What am I supposed to do?"

Steve: "I am trying hard to be accepting and forgiving, but I don't think I can. Nothing will change the feelings of insignificance I feel around you."

Michel: "Well, great. Here's to a long, fun Fourth of July week-end. And a lifetime of neither of us being happy."

Steve: "Don't try to guilt-trip me."

Michel: "Whatever, Steve. I've lived with a guilt trip since you've been diagnosed. Any time I've felt anything besides the times I'm doing everything in my power to make you happy. This is a fucking endless nightmare. This is a lot more than me 'dumping you,' and you fucking know it."

Steve: "Yep. You're right. Thanks."

Michel: "Good response! We've got all the punching gloves out right now. Do you think this is healthy at all?"

Steve: "I feel like the small-penis guy in the movie. That's not funny. I can't take this. Fuck!"

Michel: "What do you want from me? What do you expect from me? I am not sick, but I might as well be."

Steve: "I expect you not to want to have sex with other people. Sorry to be so demanding."

Michel: "I want to be with someone who can move. This disease has taken that away from us. Steve, you cannot move. And I am not OK with not having sex again in my lifetime. I am thity-eight years old! You should not expect that of me. We would not be having this conversation if you were healthy. But you are not."

Steve: "But you expect a different reaction from me? I have a perfectly working dick."

Michel: "Damn it, I feel like a monster having to be so graphic with the things I am saying. Yes, I do expect a different reac-tion. We are both trapped. And that's the truth. ALS is killing us both."

Steve: "It's just too hard for me to let go. I am sorry. I was hoping to be more gracious. I *do* want you to be happy. It just hurts that I am not making you happy. I do want to be better, stronger, and kinder. Ugh. I feel like I just went 10 rounds with Mike Tyson. I'm sorry. I think maybe it's good to get that stuff out. I just hope we didn't say something we can't take back. I love you, Mic. Let's keep climbing this trail."

———

A FEW DAYS LATER, something remarkable happened. The oak tree that I planted for our fifth anniversary sprouted for the first time. The bright green shoots were sprouting everywhere—beautiful, young, strong, new growth.

Why would our oak be blossoming just as our marriage was crumbling to dust? As strong and youthful as our oak stood, our marriage was the exact opposite: weak and withering.

Not long after I was diagnosed, I told friends and family I didn't intend to bankrupt my family, financially or emotionally. Yet, holding on so tightly was ruining our marriage. Feelings of failure often suffocated me. My parents got divorced when I was fifteen. I vowed that I would never have a marriage like that.

Obviously, our situation was vastly different. Black and white. Light-years apart. My parents never had a true connection and got married because "God" told them to. Michel and I got married because we were best friends. I knew that if Michel didn't get free of this, that friendship and once-invincible connection would be decimated. Vaporized.

I had been obstinate. I never imagined our breakup was a possibility, so I did not include Michel enough in the "Steve: ALS Poster Boy" life. Fuck, man, I never wanted to be anyone's poster boy. I didn't even want to be an advocate for the disease. I also realized I hadn't asked Michel what her thoughts were on the trajectory of our life. Basically, I was pressuring her to connect and love me, as if it were her duty.

I felt defeated. I didn't *want* to let go. But holding on so tight was annihilating us. We needed to heal.

What would happen? I didn't know, but whatever happened, the most important thing was for us to restore our friendship and be a strong parenting team that nourished and guided Rivers from a boy into a man.

Friendship. That's what catalyzed our love. We were instantly friends from the first words she said to me: "You're cuter than you look." Friendship. This is what propelled us to our ultimate union. Friendship is what will endure throughout this life—and beyond.

Because it was a symbol for our marriage, which was smoldering, I had thought that we needed to cut down our oak tree. Maybe turn it into firewood. As Michel and I started to truly understand each other's pain compassionately, my thinking changed. I realized we should look at our oak, not as a symbol of our marriage, but rather as a symbol of our connection and love for each other and our ever-present love for our family. As with everything that is affected and undone by ALS, we had to reinvent "us."

17

Being the Light

Let me run into the rain
To be a human light again
—MIKE MCCREADY, "Inside Job"

One night in February 2018, Michel and Rivers snuggled next to me in bed with the popular Dr. Seuss book *Did I Ever Tell You How Lucky You Are?*

As Rivers lay on his stomach between us, Michel read aloud, "You're lucky, indeed, you don't ride on a camel. To ride on a camel, you sit on a wamel. . . ."

"Rivers," I said, interrupting. "Mommy and I have something to tell you."

Michel put the book down and turned to Rivers, whose head peeked out from under the covers. "Wanna know something pretty cool?" she asked. "Guess what I have in my belly?"

Our six-year-old son just looked at her quizzically.

She tried again. "What do mommies grow in their bellies?"

Rivers asked, "Babies?"

We smiled.

As he started to understand, he said, "For real?! You have a baby?!" Rivers had expressed his desire to have a sibling fairly often over the last couple of years, and I could sense he was about to explode with joy! I was right there with him on the brink of detonation.

He jumped up and down on the bed in his Flash Underoos. "My

first baby ever!" he exclaimed in perfect childlike wisdom. "Can I see?" He reached over to touch Michel's exposed stomach.

"It's very, very early," she said. "So it's just slowly but surely going to get bigger and bigger."

"When he gets to be, like, three years old, I'm going to be his big brother at school!" he said.

"So, Rivs," Michel said, breaking the other news, "it's gonna be a little girl."

Rivers jumped up and down again, "Oh, man. This is gonna be so ginormous! I can't believe it."

He then stopped, looked at both of us, and asked inquisitively, "But why is it going to be a girl?"

THE DECISION to have a second child was a significant step for me and Michel. We both wanted Rivers to have a sibling with whom he could navigate life. I had expressed this to him in a journal entry a few years earlier when he was four:

Rivers, I want you to have a sibling.

I fear ALS may scar you, as it has scarred Momma, and scarred or potentially killed me. That may be a difficult burden to bear. You should have a sibling to walk that path alongside.

Shit, man, maybe you're fine. Maybe you have come through this mostly unscathed. Or, even flourished despite this tragedy that struck. I hope so. But hope is no strategy of mine. Hope takes no action. Hope relies on others, or Life, or something "out there" for our happiness. I know this, Rivers; growth and flourishing are possible after trauma, if we can explore being responsible and accountable for our minds.

New Orleans is a city of family. I see not giving you a sibling a tragedy on top of a tragedy. There will be times you need support more than your mom can give. More than your crippled or potentially dead father can give. More than the lifeless pages of a journal can give. More than two-dimensional videos can give.

In 2011, we had one embryo left over from the in vitro fertilization (IVF) treatment we did for Rivers, so we froze it as a blastocyst. Five years after that, after much prodding from me, Michel started an IVF process. On the day Michel was scheduled to get her progesterone levels checked to make sure she could move along with the pregnancy cycle, she sat alone in her car outside of the fertility clinic, listening to the song "Madness," by Muse, with the trigger needle in her hand. She'd skipped her last injection that morning, but still had time to inject before walking into her appointment. However, on the way in, she dropped the needle, filled with fluid, in the trash can. Without telling anyone, she purposely canceled the cycle, a secret she kept from me for years.

Michel wasn't ready. She didn't feel strong enough to carry and raise another child. She was still filled with too much sorrow and resentment. She still lived in limbo, hoping for a different life.

But in January 2018, Michel was healthier, feeling stable, and our relationship was growing stronger.

The brutal nature of this life had separated and traumatized us. When Michel and I weren't communicating transparently, she could barely look me in the eyes. Yet, after we had those tough, truthful conversations, the tense barrier that existed between us started to dissolve. We were able to enjoy being around each other again.

As we began to heal, our dark humor returned. We started belly-laughing again. There was a day I was in the front yard tilted back in my chair, catching some vitamin D, as I saw Michel pull up in our driveway. She always seemed to be in a hurry, so I saw her run out of the car, leaving the driver's door open, and sprint past me into the house with only a quick hello. Once she was inside, I noticed her car moving, ever so slightly. I was confused. My mind tried to make some sense of this. *Why is the car rolling down the driveway? Shit, the emergency brake!* I felt myself try to get up and run. Of course, nothing. *Hey, Michel! Your car is moving!* Oh, yeah, I can't talk either. I turned my eyes to the house with a look of distress. No one. As the car slowly gained speed, I pictured Rivers playing in the driveway behind the car, but thankfully, no one was in the vicinity.

I felt a wave of relief rush through me, but all I could do was just sit there silently, waiting for the inevitable. It gained speed, went down the driveway, and onto the street. From the corner of my eye I saw a frantic Michel race out the front door of the house, jump into the car, pull the emergency brake, and stop the car, inches away from the vehicle parked on the other side of the street. She walked up to me, eyes wide, mouth agape, like "Holy shit, did you just watch that?" I was beet red, smiling ear to ear. Laughing on the inside. I hadn't Lol'd since 2014. She started howling. The ease of our laughter continued until it became the norm again.

Our documentary film was also a catalyst in Michel's healing. As with most of my crazy ideas, she was open-minded when I thought it would be a good idea to have our life filmed nonstop. The process was not easy. The documentary consumed almost five years of our lives.

For almost four of those years, Ty Minton-Small and David Lee, the directors of cinematography for the project, essentially lived with us. Ty, who had answered an ad on Craigslist in Seattle for a videographer, was immediately dropped into the fire, given the responsibility to film Rivers's birth three days after meeting us. David, a local New Orleanian, came on board a few months later.

They became embedded in our lives. Michel was happy to have the extra sets of hands to help with me and Rivers, in exchange for being filmed every day. I appreciated their patience and willingness to work with me creatively. The project was originally designed as something permanent to leave to Rivers, and he loved Ty and "Dewey" like big brothers. They experienced the extreme highs and lows of our life. These dudes were in the trenches with us, and we trusted them completely. As a result, they were able to capture footage that otherwise would have been impossible to get.

We wound up with plenty of content for the project: 1,500 hours of footage, plus 27 hours of the "300 Seconds" video journals, as well as 220 written journals I had made to share with Rivers. We were creating something real, raw, and personal, but we didn't know where it would lead.

Michel loved these boys and was on board to be filmed at all times—until she wasn't. One day, as she and I were arguing about something, David picked up his camera to shoot. She walked over to him, put her hand on the lens, and said, "Enough." He put the camera down and didn't film another moment.

Things went to another level when we decided to hire a production team from L.A. to make a full-length documentary to be shown in film festivals and theaters all over the world.

Michel and I agreed that if we were going to do this, we needed to do it the truthful way. We wanted to portray the reality of life with ALS, the struggle to live despite a terminal diagnosis, and not sugarcoat it into a "heroic" tale or some feel-good Hallmark after-school type special. We wanted to share with the world our mission to live and flourish in the midst of hardship and tragedy. Not only did we believe the film *Gleason* could bring awareness to ALS, we thought our situation could benefit anyone who has experienced life's adversities. Through the years, I'd come to believe that our greatest strength as humans is our ability to share our weakness and vulnerability with one another. This helps us know we're not alone in our experience of adversity, loss, or tragedy.

But the footage was so raw, so personal, it was terrifying for both of us to share with the world. (Similiar to the way we feel about this book right now.)

The documentary was scheduled to debut at the prestigious Sundance Film Festival on January 23, 2016. On the night before we were scheduled to fly to Utah for the premiere, I was engulfed by anxiety and fear. I tried to cancel the trip. I told Michel, "I don't know if I can do this. It's too much. I have a bad feeling about this. The same feeling I've had before I'm about to make a terrible mistake."

Michel looked at me with a wry grin and bluntly told me what I'd told her countless times: "Steve. No choice!" It was time to show up.

We traveled to Sundance that weekend with an entourage of friends and family members. At the premiere, we watched our life story play out on the big screen. Michel and I had experienced our share of media over the years, but this was different. Seeing myself on film while sitting in a room full of strangers was scary and awkward. I watched myself lose the ability to talk, scream in agonizing frustration, weep, and have poop pulled out of my ass. Michel saw herself give birth. It was a terrifying, exhilarating adventure for the both of us.

Gleason received strong reviews at Sundance, and Amazon bought the rights. We went to opening nights in New Orleans, Los Angeles, New York City, San Francisco, Seattle, and Spokane. Suddenly, we were living a very public "celebrity life." Mega celebs like Matthew McConaughey, Jeff Bezos, Vince Vaughn, and Courteney Cox showed up to our premieres. We met with Brett Ratner at his office at Warner Bros. studios, which was the original office of the Rat Pack. Brett poured a beer down my feed tube as we toasted the film.

Our lives were inundated with media requests and publicity appearances. Michel took on many of the commitments, as it was easier logistically for her to do so. She traveled the country for interviews and film festivals and to conduct Q&A sessions. People in caregiver roles thanked her for being so honest and for shedding light on how brutal caregiving can be for people.

People felt really connected to her after watching the film. Being able to talk about her story, to reveal her own vulnerability, gave fresh meaning to the deep trauma she'd been through. It felt rewarding for her to offer some wisdom that came from her experience of pain.

Michel also unexpectedly became an artist. What started as a coping mechanism to pass the time during my many hospital stays became an important and necessary step toward healing and wholeness for her. She had no art training but had always doodled. During times when she felt overwhelmed, she would use a set of colored pencils to draw, which quieted her mind. Eventually, she began filling pages with intricate symbols, resembling Egyptian hieroglyphics. Her work looks chaotic, but also perfectly symmetrical. She thought her art resembled what she craved in life—order within the chaos.

Art provided a sense of self-worth, a creation of her own that had nothing to do with me. I *love* her art. I named my favorite piece

"Logistics," a defiant play on our conversations during our darkest times.

With the help of friends, and some enthusiastic cheerleading from me, she curated her first art show during the Sundance premiere after-party. She was in disbelief at how much people loved the beauty she created from her pain. I beamed with admiration as I watched her float around the room.

Through art and the *Gleason* experience, Michel regained her strength. Additionally, once she felt a sense of freedom, she no longer felt trapped. She was able to love our life once again, no matter how ugly it could get. She described it well in a speech on accountability commissioned by Northwest Farm Credit Services.

"I started holding myself accountable," she said in the speech. "I knew I had to get better, especially for Rivers. Even though I was with him all the time—I was not myself. I was not present. I was not being the mom he deserved. I was not the person I once was.

"I'd been doing what all the wise people told me to do: Spend time with your friends, go to therapy, eat a good diet, journal, exercise! That all helped to a certain degree.

"More importantly, I began to find acceptance—accepting our life for what it was. In my depression, it was hard to find and feel gratitude. I distinctly remember my mom telling me over and over: Think of all the things you DO have! And I knew it. I knew that, but I couldn't accept that gratitude, which made me feel even more ashamed.

"Slowly, with a different mindset, though, I was able to feel it. And it felt great. Accepting our life for what it was and not wishing for a life I didn't have helped me to actually start enjoying our life and to become a stronger and better person."

Holy shit balls! As I watched Mic deliver this message, there was pure admiration and love for her. *This* was my mover! She was shining her light of healing to help other people move through tragedy.

I also experienced healing during this period. Not physical healing, but maybe more importantly, healing of mind and heart.

Even during times of the deepest and most tormenting pain, I think I was always seeking ways to refill the reservoir of strength within. As I was losing all of my abilities, especially talking and breathing, I found a deep hunger to be at peace. One of the silver linings of living with ALS is it didn't affect my mind. I could read. And I was "retired," so I could pursue any avenue of learning or growth that interested me.

Viktor Frankl stood out as my guide in the darkness. I read his book *Man's Search for Meaning* nearly every day. I would read it in the middle of the night, if I wasn't able to sleep. As a Jewish concentration camp survivor, he endured incomprehensible personal suffering, but he transformed into the apotheosis of strength, through his acceptance, surrender, compassion, and forgiveness.

I was motivated by his example. He was stripped of his identity and utterly dehumanized, yet he still managed to find great meaning within the suffering of his life, primarily through helping others. He emphasized that it was up to us to be accountable and find meaning within our own experiences.

The greatest thing I learned from Frankl was his remarkable ability to transform by accepting his circumstances for what they were. His quote, "When we are no longer able to change a situation, we are challenged to change ourselves," epitomized this ability to transform for me.

In the bleakest moments of darkness, these ideas helped me continue. I was inspired seeing how his transformation led to happiness. He also said that art would lead to meaning in life, so I thought it was fascinating that Michel had found that path on her own.

IN AUGUST 2016, a couple of months before the Cubs broke the curse and won the World Series, we traveled to Chicago to see Pearl Jam's concert at Wrigley Field. Before the show, we were hanging out with Mike McCready. Mike said, "Steve, we're playing 'Inside Job' tonight, and we'd like you to introduce the song."

I'd loved the song since I first heard it on their self-titled 2006 album. It found new power and importance in my life after my ALS diagnosis.

Both Viktor Frankl's wisdom and the lyrics of "Inside Job" suggested we have the freedom to train our minds to keep showing up in any circumstance.

> *Pursuing the greater way for all human light,*
> *How I choose to feel*
> *Is how I am*
> *How I choose to feel*
> *Is how I am*
> *I will not lose my faith*
> *It's an inside job today*
> *Holding on*
> *The light of night*
> *On my knees to rise*
> *And fix my broken soul*
> *Again*

This song was a literal light in the darkness. When I expressed to Mike my experience of suffering and how those words helped, I learned that he wrote the lyrics! Those are the only lyrics he's written for Pearl Jam, and they were about his emergence from addiction.

Eddie Vedder introduced me to the sellout crowd and said some kind words about Michel and Rivers, too. I rolled out to the middle of the stage and cued up my prepared speech.

"Hi, there, Wrigley Field . . .

"If you want my opinion, this stadium and this field are most sacred ground.

"Like all of you, I am inspired and strengthened by the music of these guys.

"Mike and I have been friends for almost fifteen years, and I'm grateful for the relationship that my family has with the Pearl Jam family.

"This next song is one of my all-time favorite songs—ever. Everyone who has a heartbeat will face adversity, but when you experience those moments, like the message in this song, please remember this: How we choose to feel is how we are. And personally, I feel fucking awesome."

The roar of the crowd and Pearl Jam's epic performance of "Inside Job" was an adrenaline rush I'll never forget.

Experiences like this have become pretty common for me on this journey. I had a cult following during my NFL days, but my profile grew immensely when I chose to go public with my story. Our documentary film *Gleason* resonated with people across the globe, and my social media accounts skyrocketed with followers, almost half a million and still growing today. I've learned to accept this quasi-celebrity status because it provides a powerful platform for me to reach and inspire people, to motivate them to reimagine what is possible in their lives. It's also allowed me to do some really cool stuff, like going onstage with Pearl Jam at Wrigley Field.

There was a time when I was conflicted about these events. During a 2011 interview, I told the *Times-Picayune,* "People ask all of the time, 'How does it feel?' I think about Pearl Jam. I know Mike [McCready]. We kind of go back a little bit, but if I wasn't diagnosed with this disease he probably wouldn't say, 'Hey come onstage (during their twenty-year reunion in 2011).' Part of me was like, 'This is sweet.' And then another part of me felt like, 'Well, that kind of sucked.'"

Now I realize this: Life gets ugly at times, so when we have the chance to do something amazing in the midst of ugly, go for it.

A FEW MONTHS AFTER the premiere of our documentary, the Archdiocese of New Orleans asked me to deliver a speech to their parishioners on the topic of faith. Yikes! I assumed they had seen the documentary scene where I tell my dad, "My soul is safe." I was tentative, reluctant even, but I hesitantly agreed to do it. I'd grown to understand the value of doing things I was afraid to do. I've experienced some of the greatest moments of growth by taking a step of faith when life seemed chaotic, uncertain, or out of control.

I found that I enjoyed the challenge of contemplating and organizing my outlook on the topic of faith. The faith in my blood rarely comes from buildings, church sermons, or homilies. The spirituality that fuels me has come from experiences, where the beauty of life overwhelmed me, as if I were part of something so much more vast and grand.

The speech was scheduled at a local high school gym. In the summer of 2016, five and a half years after being diagnosed with ALS, I rolled toward the bleachers and looked around at the people I was speaking to that morning, including Archbishop Gregory Aymond. After a quick hello and thank you to everyone, I dove right in.

"So, Archbishop, if I may, I would like to start today with a confession. Is that OK with you?" He nodded in agreement.

"This morning when I had to wake up at 5 a.m., I was cursing like a sailor," I said, which drew a good laugh from everyone, including the archbishop.

"Some of those curses were directed at you, sir." Even more rolling laughter, though I couldn't see if the archbishop joined in. I was grateful to be able to lighten the mood while speaking with a synthesized voice, using my eyes to pause and play for the audience.

I told everyone about my reluctance to speak publicly about my personal faith, beliefs, and prayer. I said that if a person speaks publicly about his or her personal experiences, it's no longer personal.

"I did wrestle with this request, and here's what I decided," I said. "This was, I believe, an honest and sincere request from the archdiocese and the archbishop. As such, if I choose to answer this call, the only honorable way to answer is honestly and sincerely, wherever and whatever that may end up being. . . . So, let's begin this journey together, if you're willing."

I then moved into the major theme of my speech, one that has guided the spiritual journey of my life.

"For me, there's a companion word that tags along with 'faith,'" I said. "The word is 'explore.' They simply must go everywhere together."

I've noticed that I've always felt this call to explore faith, even though it feels that most religions present faith as a rule or law not to be questioned. But they wanted my thoughts, so that's what I gave them.

"Exploration," I continued, "requires two simultaneous elements: a curiosity to gain knowledge and the admission of ignorance, which, to my ears, sounds like when Jesus said, 'I tell you, unless you change and become like little children, you will never enter the kingdom of heaven.'

"By definition," I said, "faith is believing in something you cannot believe in, which is pretty much craziness, like, you know, cuckoo. So, if this word 'faith' cannot be rationalized, there is an endless amount of exploring to do, because the truly faithful will never find their faith.

"So, if you walked in here, questioning your faith, join the club. I think you are on the right track."

At this point in my spiritual journey, I'd left behind the idea of some gnarly bearded male God. I lean toward the great Jesuit priest Karl Rahner's description, as the "Absolute Mystery." If one is certain of their version of faith, there is no Mystery. I was also sure that tactics of fear and guilt would never lead to anything resembling faith. My intention was to lead with love and inclusion, which is how I feel Jesus presented his teachings. After sharing stories about the extraordinary love and growth I experienced in the Catholic communities at Gonzaga Prep and in New Orleans, I took more risk, sharing some things "I think I think about faith." Among them:

"I think that unless you've completely lost your faith, wrapped yourself in new faith, at least once, preferably more than once, then your faith is no faith at all," I said.

"I think Jesus purposely did not say, 'Convert thy neighbor to yourself and your personal beliefs.' He said, 'Love thy neighbor,' which is a much more complicated and difficult command. Humans have the conquer-and-convert thing down to a science, whereas I think we've got a long way to go on loving our neighbors.

"I think any human understanding or interpretation of the great creator falls embarrassingly short of who or what God is. So, in that sense, we have no choice other than to present ourselves, not only to the creator, but also to our neighbors and our enemies, as little children."

I paraphrased David James Duncan, saying, "I think my heart is, by nature, inclusive, so I absolutely love Jesus and his teachings. I also adore Gandhi, the Buddha, the Dalai Lama, and their teachings and examples."

I finished by explaining how ALS had affected my faith.

"In the beginning stages, I certainly prayed to be healed," I said. "I also sought healing on nearly every level. My seeking healing was by faith, which is to say there was some craziness, like, you know, cuckoo. I rarely pray to be healed these days. Maybe I have lost some faith. Who knows. While I would love to walk and talk again, the creator can choose to heal me, or not. Most importantly, I enjoy my life. I pray for my daily breath, my strength, my ingenuity to continue living the life I love, my life with purpose."

I ended the speech on a less risky note.

"In my five years with ALS, with my wife, Michel, we have faced extraordinary adversity. I choose, possibly by faith, to see adversity as our opportunity. People often say, 'He's suffering from ALS.' I see it differently. Maybe I am just obstinate, but I never say I am suffering from ALS. I think ALS has given me and my family an opportunity to share our strength, our example, our love, with whomever may need to hear it."

HAVING MICHEL BACK returned life to our home. When we first hired caregivers, in 2014, it was emotionally harrowing for me to be alone with relative strangers; I was dependent on Michel and afraid to be without her. This caused her to feel guilty if she went out, and imprisoned if she was home, because of my reliance on her. Becoming more independent and comfortable with my crew gave Michel space and freedom to do what she wanted. I was happy that she chose to stay home more and more.

Our house, which for a few years had felt like a prison or a hospital, was growing more full of light and life. We made a baseball field in the park, which is about a hundred yards from our back door. We hosted Rivers's baseball and soccer team parties, Fourth of July wiffle ball tournaments, and kids' birthday bashes, which have included an 18-wheeler ride, *Star Wars* Stormtroopers, mechanical bulls, real unicorns, and real mermaids. Our day-to-day was still incredibly difficult, but our life started to return to the vast cosmos of curiosity and love, friendship, family, neighbors, and kids.

On a cold New Orleans night in early January 2018, Michel and I sat by the fireplace in our living room and she told me that she was ready to implant the embryo. She was going to turn forty that March, and she wanted to have a second child. There were more risks because of her age, and we weren't sure it would end up working, but we went for it.

The doctors implanted the embryo on February 2.

Although we'd made the decision, there was still fear on both our parts. Michel and I loved each other, but our life together had changed dramatically in the decade since we were married. We were now communicating more openly with each other, but ALS still made it remarkably difficult to do so. I had accepted not being able to move, and to be happy within my physical confinement, but not being able to talk spontaneously and quickly, or joke around with Mic, was painful for both of us. We had grown to understand each other's pain and wanted to help each other deal with that pain (my definition of compassion). That openness helped keep us together. It also allowed us to form a strong parenting partnership and to revitalize our friendship. But I wasn't much help with Rivers, and even with our amazing caregivers help with the kids, would Mic be able to parent two kids as something of a single mom?

I also felt pangs of concern because I had prepared all these videos and journals for Rivers, but I had nothing really for our second child. What would she think of that? Would she resent him? Feel less important?

Then there was the whole terrifying idea of having a girl, I was fearful that I'd be unable to provide what she needed. I knew how to be a boy's dad. I had a younger brother and knew what it was like to grow up in a boy's world. I had zero experience raising a daughter.

That said, I believed that a girl could grow up to be absolutely successful in any arena she chose. I knew that a father's presence, love, and understanding, along with providing a path that encouraged intelligence, boldness, independence, and strength could help instill those traits in a daughter. The more I thought about it, the more the thought of being a girl's dad invigorated and excited me.

On the seventh anniversary of my diagnosis, I wrote an email saying that I was doing better in the last six months than I had been in a few years. That the darkest days were behind me. This was largely because, as Michel and I began to emerge from the darkness, I was able to really focus on training and strengthening my mind, to have a greater sense of well-being.

I discovered one of my all-time favorite books, *Resilience*, by Navy SEAL Eric Greitens. If Viktor Frankl was my guide in the darkness, Greitens and this book guided me as dawn emerged. Greitens makes it clear that resilience is *not* becoming who we were before we encountered hardship. "What happens to us becomes part of us," he writes. "Resilient people do not bounce back from hard experiences; they find healthy ways to integrate them into their lives. In time, people find that great calamity met with great spirit can create great strength." This philosophy perfectly matched and defined my outlook.

The "Mastering Pain" chapter particularly resonated with me. During my early years of playing football, I found that I was able to move toward physical pain to inhabit it. "At the outer edges of excellence, the trained soldier is aware of the bead of sweat, just as the athlete is aware of pain, because they are the pain. This sounds abstract and almost spiritual, because, well, it is. In true mastery there is a transcendence at work: you actually are your pain."

Greitens takes it further by saying we could do this with emotional pain as well. As proficient as I had been with physical pain, I knew I could greatly improve how I dealt with painful emotions. I wondered what was possible for me. I also read *21 Lessons for the 21st Century*, by Yuval Noah Harari, which may be the most important book I've read. Harari mentions multiple times that the realest thing in the world is suffering. Strangely, this was not something that had occurred to me, but was blatantly clear given what Michel and I had been through living with ALS. "The big question facing humans isn't 'What is the meaning of life?' but rather 'How do we stop suffering?,'" he says. "When you give up all the fictional stories, you can observe reality with far greater clarity than before, and if you really know the truth about yourself and about the world, nothing can make you miserable. But that is of course much easier said than done." This was such a radically bold assertion—nothing can make you miserable—that I had to reread these sentences several times.

Harari goes on to say that suffering is a product of patterns in our own minds, and that suffering does not exist outside of our minds. Like Frankl and Greitens, Harari was proposing there was a path to train our minds to end suffering. It was becoming clear to me that the great wisdom to be free will always be—Peace of mind is an *inside job*.

He then offers a tool that has helped him alleviate suffering and be more resilient—meditation, specifically Vipassana, translated as "introspection." I learned that meditation can allow people to better understand reality and the mechanics of our suffering. In the past decade there has been a lot of scientific research on the benefits of meditation. It's been shown to reduce pain, anxiety, and depression; improve cognitive function; and even produce changes in gray matter density in regions of the brain related to learning and memory, emotional regulation, and self-awareness. I started looking for meditation practice resources, and I read a book by Professor Harari's teacher, S. N. Goenka. I found a guided Vipassana meditation album on Spotify that seemed to fit what Harari described, and I dove in.

I started practicing about 20–30 minutes a day, following Goenka's guidance: "Just observe the reality of the present moment, whatever it may be." I felt the rewards of this almost immediately.

Paying attention to the sensations of the breath brought a remarkable ease of mind. With all the sports I played, I was very in tune with my body, but this practice took my awareness to a new level. I felt an aliveness and vitality throughout my entire body.

During these meditations, while observing the breath and the body, there were times I'd entirely lose the shape of my body. Thoughts would soften, the ego would quiet, and I could just ride the wave of experience. I had moments, like the night in the hospital bed, where I would disappear. I trained daily in this way for the next two years. I'm not sure how much it was improving my "real life," but for a guy who was living with ALS, to have an hour a day of peace and even bliss, it was a welcome change.

I'd spent most of my life seeking the sacred and extraordinary, but this practice was showing me that the sacred is within us. Heaven. As much as I loved exploring the outer world, the inner world is easily as vast, mysterious, and miraculous. Perhaps even more so. I became committed to explore what was possible within my physical limitations to find heaven in our midst.

For up to sixty minutes each day I sat and focused on my breaths and body sensations as well as my mental state. When I felt resistance or judgment in my mind, the instruction was to do nothing, to just observe those reactions. This was so foreign; it seemed simple, but it was not easy. I gradually increased the time I practiced. I didn't realize it then, but as I started this practice of meditation, I was embracing the light, embarking on a practice of a lifetime.

Additionally, life, though still extremely difficult and sometimes impossible, was growing more manageable. Physically, the disease had fully progressed and robbed me of almost all of my voluntary muscle function. Only my involuntary muscles worked: my heart and circulatory system, sensory system, penis, and digestive tract, along with voluntary muscles in my eyes and eyelids and certain facial muscles, which allowed me to still blink, wink, and smile. For me, and perhaps paradoxically, the agony of losing my abilities, and the exhaustion of adjusting to the chaotic, ceaselessly changing losses, was over, at least for the time being. For the past five or six years, the brutally relentless progression had stabilized.

Assistive technology had also improved. As the technology developed, communication got somewhat easier. Better word prediction software led to faster, more efficient typing. Consequently, with my eye strength still intact, my communication improved.

We brought on Stephanie Capella, a close friend of Michel's, to our team to help with scheduling, which brought on happiness and some order in the chaos. With Kyle's structured systems, and Jenni's nutritional, medical, and therapeutic expertise, my daily routines have become enjoyable for me.

I WAS ABLE to orchestrate a move back to our king-sized bed. I worked with our care crew and the Home Depot staff to fashion a way for me to sleep on the right side of the bed, so I could see (in my periphery) through the massive glass slider to our backyard and the two ancient oak trees there. My nightly isolation from humans was gone. Sleeping in the big bed allowed me, Michel, and Rivers to snuggle and watch movies, Premier League soccer, and baseball together.

As Rivers grew, we began to have actual conversations. It was not always easy to keep his attention. He is an active boy and my speech is so slow, but at bedtime and dinner, and in the carpool, when he was contained to one place, I was able to engage with him. Michel and our caregivers helped me work with him on the superpower life skill—patience. Every day before we picked him up from school, I spent about an hour preparing questions to ask him. Some days the technology would not work, or he would not be in the mood to talk, so the effort was for naught. But some days, when both went smoothly, we would have great conversations. When he was five, our two favorite topics were the Chicago Cubs and Halloween.

All this said, when the time came for the newest member of our family to enter our lives, we were in a strong place to welcome her.

On the morning of October 16, 2018, I awoke at 4:45 a.m. for my caregivers Kyle and Colleen to prepare me for the day.

I was a complete wreck as we headed to Baptist Hospital at 7:30 a.m. I cried the entire way. I tried to tell Kyle to stop the van, but tears blurred my vision and I couldn't type the thought. For the past week I'd been suffering from C. diff, a hellishly wretched bacteria that causes a person to have diarrhea at any point and many points throughout the day. It's debilitating. If I didn't get cleared by the doctor before the delivery, I wouldn't be able to hold or touch my sweet baby. Instead, I'd just watch from afar, like a portrait.

I felt uplifted as I entered the room and saw Michel in a hospital bed with her back propped up. She was connected to a bunch of monitors. One of them monitored the baby's heartbeat! It was visible on the screen but also audible. Michel looked so happy she glowed.

As Kyle was setting me up, Dr. Eric Ehrensing, my infectious disease doctor, walked into the room, eyes twinkling and face smiling. "Your C. diff is under control, Steve!" Loud applause erupted in the room.

Michel's water broke at 12:08 p.m. We called her dad, Pops, to tell him to bring Rivers to the hospital. They arrived a couple of hours later, and energy started to build in the room. An hour later, a nurse told us that dilatation was complete at 8–10 inches. It was go time!

Michel was suddenly so insanely nervous, she was talking loud, and nonstop.

"Y'all, why am I talking so much? I can't stop talking," Michel said as everyone in the room laughed.

"Oh no. I feel like I'm going to faint?!" she said, turning white.

The nurse pulled out an oxygen mask.

I had previously typed up a request to Jody, our doctor, about wanting to be the umpire this time, since I couldn't be the catcher like I was with Rivers. He and the medical crew were totally in.

With some careful maneuvering of my wheelchair, I found a spot inside the stirrup on the lower-left corner of Michel's bed, just over Jody's right shoulder, a good view of the strike zone.

After four quick sets of three pushes, we started to see Gray's head.

"Good work, Michel," I typed. "You're doing great." A few pushes later, Jody pulled Gray to life. This birth lasted less than ten minutes. Incredible!

"That's my girl!" I excitedly proclaimed to the room, mimicking the line I used at Rivers's birth.

Gray wasn't crying so I asked the doctors if she was OK.

"Absolutely nothing is wrong," Jody said. "She's healthy and beautiful."

Gray was more than that. She was perfect, stunning.

The terror I anticipated the night before and earlier that morning faded, like a marker in the sand, washed away by waves of joy that had felt so distant just ten hours earlier.

I positioned myself next to Michel and held a bundled Gray in my lap as Rivers, his seven cousins, and a handful of close friends crowded around, gleefully watching over me.

It's hard to believe that as fragile as my life is, I not only get to have a son, but also get to experience having a baby girl. Bringing life into this world, when given a terminal diagnosis eight years prior, was a beautiful miracle.

This journey had been painfully agonizing and it had taken a long fucking time. But here we were.

As Michel and I grew closer, we confided our darkest secrets to each other. Michel acknowledged there were times when she seriously thought about driving her car into Bayou St. John, the sacred body of water that served as the backdrop for our wedding ceremony.

"There were nights right after I was trached I thought you might just turn the vent off," I replied. "And there were nights that I was so tired and exhausted, I would have been OK with it."

Ultimately, our decision to move through those times of brutal suffering was due to our commitment to keep showing up for Rivers. He was a light that guided us on our path. Now we had another luminous being in our lives, another reason to keep going.

18

Gratitude and Service

Gratitude is the understanding that many millions of things come together and live together and mesh together and breathe together in order for us to take even one more breath of air. —DAVID WHYTE

oly shit balls! What the hell am I even doing here?! Is this really happening?

H I had experienced thousands of moments of disbelief in the past decade. While most of them were painful, this one was full of wonder and glory. I sat in a waiting room at the U.S. Capitol on January 15, 2020. I was there to receive the Congressional Gold Medal, the most prestigious civilian honor bestowed by Congress. The list of previous gold medal recipients included some of the most powerful, enlightened giants in human history. I was the very first football player and only the seventh athlete to receive the gold medal. I like to think I brought some humanity and imperfection to the distinguished list. I was confident none of the previous recipients had worn a $7 long-sleeved black tuxedo shirt and brown Uggs to the ceremony when they were honored.

Like most people, I was aware that there are medals presented to citizens. I was mostly aware of military medals and some of their significance. After I first met with Senator Cassidy in 2018 to encourage him to help us with a Medicare issue, he showed me his proposed legislation recommending me for a Congressional

Gold Medal. Our volunteer policy advisors then educated me on the meaning and history of that. I've said I was humbled, but that's still an understatement. Not only that, I was told that to approve a Congressional Gold Medal, two-thirds of Congress must agree.

At that time, there had been fewer than two hundred recipients since George Washington received it in 1776. And until 1867, all honorees were connected to the military in some way. After that, philanthropists, inventors, pioneers in every field, and those who exhibited extraordinary humanity toward others were honored.

Upon arrival at the Capitol, a small group of us were escorted by Capitol Police through security to the Speaker of the House's office, which serves as a green room for Congressional Gold Medal ceremonies. Wide-eyed, surrounded by ornate gold mirrors and oak bookcases stuffed with leather-bound books, we all stood (sat) still, afraid to touch anything. There was a nervous energy in the room. Our friend Peter King from NBC Sports dropped by for a visit and a quick interview. While I spoke to him, Rivers played cards with our friends Tony Hazel and Liz. Gray had unfortunately been diagnosed with the flu the night before we left, so she stayed back in New Orleans. Michel mentioned numerous times how ravenous she was and was presented with a mound of vending machine snacks, which she ate while sitting at the Speaker's hardwood desk. We requested water to no avail and could not find a water fountain anywhere in the vicinity, so we left the office dehydrated, everyone but me with cottonmouth.

After taking group photographs with some political leaders in the Speaker's lobby, we headed to the ceremony. My crew took their seats. I was to roll into National Statuary Hall on my own.

As I drove my wheelchair with my eyes down the very long hallway and entered Statuary Hall, I was filled with anticipation and anxiety, exactly like I had felt before a football game. Excitement. Fear. Acceptance. *"Get some!"*

Statuary Hall is a majestic place, a cavernous, two-story semicircular room with floor-to-ceiling marble columns, towering twelve-foot statues of historical leaders like Samuel Adams, Amelia Earhart, and Huey P. Long from each of the fifty states and a second-story gallery along the curved perimeter. It was packed with hundreds of people, among them some of my closest friends and family that we were able to include in this "invitation only" event. As I made my way down the center aisle, the crowd delivered a standing ovation. The back of the chamber was lined with videographers and TV cameras from C-SPAN and every national network and local station in New Orleans. I had prepped my speech, and recited it multiple times for my team and close friends. The nice thing about this eye-tracking technology is that while it ain't easy to write speeches, I was fairly certain I wouldn't anxiously stu-stu-stu-stutter.

In two rows of chairs to the right of the dais sat some of the most esteemed political leaders in our country: U.S. House of Representatives Speaker Nancy Pelosi, Senate Majority Leader Mitch McConnell, Senate Minority Leader Chuck Schumer, and House Minority Leader Kevin McCarthy, U.S. senator Patty Murray and Louisiana natives U.S. senator Bill Cassidy, U.S. representatives Cedric Richmond and Steve Scalise.

The ceremony took place eleven days before the controversial impeachment trial of President Donald Trump was scheduled to begin down the hall in the Senate Chamber. Considering the heightened political climate at the time, it was unusual to see so many powerful Democrats and Republicans gathered side by side for a common cause. Statuary Hall is located between the House and Senate chambers in the Capitol building, where heated debates between the two political factions had been occurring for weeks. For at least one hour on this Tuesday morning, the Congressional Gold Medal Ceremony served as a peaceful respite from the current political environment. An hour after the ceremony, impeachment papers for President Trump were walked through the hall where we had been seated.

In the crowd to my right was NFL commissioner Roger Goodell; his predecessor, Paul Tagliabue; New Orleans Saints owner and Gray Gleason's godmother, Gayle Benson, and her entire executive staff. To my left was Drew Brees, a future Hall of Famer, who, along with his wife, Brittany, and their son Baylen, flew to D.C.

on his and Baylen's birthdays to speak on my behalf. Also there were leaders from Microsoft, Google, and Comcast, along with fellow ALS brothers O.J. Brigance, a former NFL player for the Baltimore Ravens, and Pat Quinn, a co-founder of the Ice Bucket Challenge.

After leaders from both the Democratic and Republican parties delivered beautifully crafted and humbling speeches, our friend Ben Schneider, from the band Lord Huron, sang an acoustic version of one of our family's favorite songs, "Ends of the Earth."

While I was aware of the statistics, it was still absolutely mystifying when Senator Schumer said that "only 163 people have ever received this honor: George Washington, Nelson Mandela, Mother Teresa, and now, Steve Gleason."

As Speaker Pelosi presented me with the medal and Michel, Rivers, and I posed for photos, I felt gratitude for the honor, what it meant to the ALS community and for all who were there and have been with us on this journey.

I drove to the front of the room to deliver my speech.

Hi there, everyone,

Thank you, Speaker Pelosi, Leaders McConnell, Schumer, and McCarthy, Senators Cassidy and Murray, Representatives Richmond and Scalise, and all members of Congress.

Also, thank you for coming to D.C. and speaking today, Drew. Just so everyone knows, today is Drew's birthday. So, Drew, let me wish you a very Capitol happy birthday, brother.

This award, from the elected officials who represent the people of the United States of America, is a sublime honor for me. But, more importantly, I feel that this honor represents some joy, encouragement, and even triumph for the tens of thousands of extraordinary families currently enduring life with ALS, the millions of extraordinary people in this country living with disabilities or other illness, and more broadly, all of you ordinary humans, who experience adversity, tragedy, or anguish.

No one is immune from anguish, tragedy, or adversity. Not even elected officials, NFL players, or even the most holy Saints.

I suppose I don't see my story as a football story, or even an ALS story, but rather, a human story.

The truth is that we all experience pain in our lives. But I believe that the problems we face are our opportunity and define our purpose.

I believe that adversity is our opportunity, because we will all face pain and tragedy. But it's clear to me that beyond the human capacity of imagination, our greatest strength as a species has been our ability to bravely share our weaknesses and vulnerabilities with each other.

Doing that, we're able to understand the issue and collaborate with each other to solve problems and overcome any obstacle.

While sharing one's weaknesses may not be common practice for people, especially for politicians in an election year, wink wink, sharing my weaknesses was entirely critical for me to play eight years in the NFL, and it has been unquestionably critical to my survival and purpose for the past nine years, living with a disease as dreadful as ALS. I am grateful to the literally thousands of people who have directly uplifted me, both emotionally and physically, in my forty-two years. Most importantly, I'm grateful to my parents, for instilling in me many of the values I've used to be successful. And, of course, my wife, Michel. This is not the life we imagined, and it hasn't been easy, but through communication and compassion, we're living an awesome life.

In addition to understanding that I had to share my weaknesses to survive and succeed, I'm fortunate to have a motivation and a reason to live. Our son, Rivers, and our daughter, Gray. They give me purpose, the purpose of a lifetime.

Some of you may disagree, but I believe there has been no greater time in history to be a human. At the same time, I don't think anyone here, or anyone watching, will disagree that we as a country, and more appropriately, we as a global species, face enormous challenges in the coming decades of the twenty-first century, challenges like exploring and colonizing other planets, or thoughtfully solving climate change, or positively harnessing the seemingly miraculous power of artificial intelligence, so people's disabilities are turned into super abilities.

These challenges provide us with an exponential opportunity, as Americans, and as humans.

Because if we can share our weaknesses with each other, and compassionately collaborate to solve problems, our human potential is boundless. If we can work to understand and solve each other's problems, and each other's pain, compassionately, then, truly, all things are possible.

Thank you again to the people of the United States of America, a nation I'm so proud to live in, for this unbelievable honor.

We held the post-ceremony reception at the Ronald Reagan Building and International Trade Center. People continued to stand up and give the most amazing, heartfelt, and hilarious speeches about our moments of triumph and ecstasy, our (mostly my) dipshit moments, and our moments of suffering. Smiles, all-out laughter and tears. Beauty. Love. Perfection. We even joked that it almost felt like it was my "still living" funeral!

I was able to help design the medal. The front side features what is essentially our Team Gleason logo—an image of me in my No. 37 Saints jersey, holding my left fist in the air. The back side shows an image of the Northwest, with a river running through evergreen trees, a mountain peak, and the full moon in the distance with my life motto "Keep exploring" inscribed across the bottom. Our friend, former Chicago Cubs and Boston Red Sox general manager Theo Epstein, somehow missed his handoff and dropped the medal on the floor. It was ultimately handed to someone other than Michel, as she has a knack for throwing away things that should not be thrown away.

That night after Kyle got me into my hotel bed, I asked myself *why and how this amazing ceremony ever happened.* I'm not sure there is a single answer, but it was clear that the work of Team Gleason and Answer ALS were the primary reasons.

I founded Team Gleason because I felt lucky to have overwhelming support from the communities of New Orleans and Spokane. Obviously the Saints were all in. I had dozens of NFL teammates and even opponents reach out to say they would help in any way they could. When I have time to reflect, I recognize how incredibly fortunate I am. This leads to generosity. After I was diagnosed in 2011, I realized my life might be over in a few years, but I was grateful for the massive love surrounding me, and I was committed to laugh and smile while I cried and died. This gratitude naturally led to a calling and a question within me. How could I help the "freak show" people like me I saw at Forbes Norris the day our family was diagnosed with ALS? It was clear that we were all in this together.

My introduction to the idea that we're all in this together was the teachings of Jesus. While I had mostly left the supernatural, fundamentalist dogmas (unquestionable claims of certainty without any clear supporting evidence) behind, Jesus's teachings and actions inspired me—to love, serve, and care for others as ourselves. The story portrayed by the author of Matthew of the sheep and the goats captures this well for me: Love and care for the least of our brothers and sisters to get to the kingdom of heaven. That experience in the U.S. Capitol, with our most powerful politicians in harmony rather than in contention, was pretty heavenly.

Founding Team Gleason was not entirely altruistic. I wanted to live a good, fulfilling life, so I wanted to help others do the same. Nor was it a chore. I was passionate about exploring ways to help people in the ALS community live. It poured out of me during our early meetings. The majority of ALS organizations and nearly all the funds raised were dedicated to finding a cure. There was a clear need for an organization that could help people with real solutions to live a better, more purposeful life, right then, there, and now. Team Gleason is now the leading ALS service organization in the country, with a staff of more than twenty, including a speech language pathologist, an occupational therapist, and an assistive technology specialist. Requests for services continue to grow exponentially and have come from all fifty states, a few territories, and several countries. None of us could have envisioned the global impact we'd make during those early days, meeting at Paul and Jilly's house over coffee and donut hole breakfasts. We were merely following the desperate need, like a river follows the landscape.

At this point, compassionately helping and serving others may be the most important thing for me, and perhaps all of us, even if one doesn't worship Jesus. His teachings on loving and serving others are radical and revolutionary to follow. Jesus didn't tell us to worship him, but rather to follow his teachings and example. This seems to be a far more difficult undertaking: to love all people, including the outcast, the rejected, our so-called "enemies," and ourselves, at the highest level of possibility.

I'm not sure about Jesus, but I'm not abdicating common sense. And it seems clear that there are people and even entire cultures that are following, and acting on, very bad ideas and beliefs. But, how would our world change if we all aspire to communicate compassionately, collaborate creatively, and find ways and innovative systems to help one another move from discontent and suffering to freedom and peace, from heaven to hell? A capital "L": Love. An ultimate, incomprehensible, and unconditional love. What might be possible if we committed to help one another live on this path? All things?

Our work at Team Gleason hasn't invented a lightbulb or perfected electricity, but with the help of others working together, we innovated far better technologies for all those with disabilities, passed laws to ensure assistive communication, and provided access to critical tools and life experiences for the ALS community. We have so far provided over $30 million in assistance to tens of thousands of people with ALS and an untold number of other people with disabilities around the world. Although no one has received the Congressional Gold Medal by developing a cure for any disease, we did help create the most comprehensive ALS research project in history in an effort to help make that an eventual reality.

For the ten-year anniversary of my diagnosis, I expressed this sentiment of gratitude to friends, family, and supporters in a letter on January 5, 2021:

Ten years ago I was diagnosed with ALS. Right at this moment, I feel a profound sense of gratitude, meaning, and responsibility in my life. I trust that I am exactly where I am meant to be, and I intend to live wholeheartedly for every breath that remains.

ALS has made me more vulnerable than I could have ever imagined. It has humiliated my body into a pathetic and alien heap of skin and bones. It has annihilated my mind, causing anger, frustration, and suffering that I had never known prior to January 5, 2011.

ALS is a remorseless disease. Yet, my heart remains. My spirit remains. From vulnerability, my spirit offers strength. From humiliation, my heart brings resilience. From annihilation, my spirit knows purpose. From suffering, my heart knows compassion and is driven to serve others who suffer.

My family—Gray, Rivers, and Michel—is my most important yet my most difficult work, under the circumstances. It's also difficult for them. Within me, there is an everlasting sense of commitment and responsibility to those three. A couple more decades, at least, if they'll have me. One day at a time. One moment at a time, knowing intimately how fragile and precious human life is.

I work to love my family unconditionally and eternally. At the end of each day, lying in bed, before I close my eyes for the last time, I have a deep sense of contentment and peace. Overwhelming joy.

I trust that my future is greater than my past. My past has been pretty fucking epic, so I have extraordinary expectations for my future, our future.

—SG

A couple weeks before I sent this email, I became a subscribing member of the Waking Up app, founded by author, neuroscientist, and philosopher Sam Harris. It's categorized as a meditation/mindfulness app, but for me, it's so much more. Mindfulness is simply training our minds to pay clear, nonjudgmental attention to every moment of experience, whether pleasant or painful. To be fully present and give myself to the moment is the practice.

In addition to teaching the Vipassana meditation, in which I had been training for a couple years, Waking Up also explores what is typically called "non-duality," which in the simplest terms refers to the experience of not being separate from the rest of life and the world. The essence of this teaching is that the "self," or ego identity, is an illusion, a construction of our minds. As my most influential spiritual teacher, Adyashanti, says, "There is no 'one' who is conscious. Consciousness just is." The "me"—that agonizes over the past, has anxiety about the future, and is afraid of death or nonexistence—this "me" can be investigated, recognized as an illusion, and deconstructed, even for a few seconds. Experientially, when this "me" is cut through, I disappear into the now. Indivisible. Unknown peace. This temporary disappearance has helped create a more enduring shift in perception and reduction of unnecessary suffering, for me as well as the people I interact with each day. It allows me to be more understanding, compassionate, and loving with others and myself. While people can say anything, I'm interested in the fruits and actions of people. With Waking Up, Sam Harris and dozens of other teachers are helping multitudes of people, including me, move from pain to peace, from suffering to strength, and from fear to freedom. I'm grateful.

Non-duality is an empirical truth shared by most religious and spiritual traditions, including Christianity. My favorite Christian reference to non-duality is on St. Paul's Monastery on Mount Athos in Greece, one of the most important sites of Orthodox spirituality. *"If you die before you die, you won't die when you die."* Additionally, Richard Rohr, a Franciscan priest and my most beloved contemporary Christian teacher says, "Nondual consciousness is a more holistic knowing, where your mind, heart, soul, and senses are open and receptive to the moment just as it is." I appreciated that the type of nondual training Waking Up offered had no New Age superstition, and I didn't have to believe in anything based on insufficient evidence. All I needed to do was curiously inquire and explore.

While gratitude and service have flowed fairly naturally for me,

Waking Up has helped me see why these two life skills will be anchors in my life for every breath that remains, rather than getting lost in thoughts of how people or life *should* be treating me.

I learn about trust and gratitude from everything and everyone.

One night in January 2022, Rivers and I were in my bed watching *The Mandalorian*. An overnight caregiver was on, but we hadn't been able to get any chemistry or easy communication up to that point. I started thinking about the difficulties of the next eight or ten hours, ended up pretty hysterical, and started to cry. Eventually, I collected myself and told Rivers, "I'm sorry I'm so weak." He got on his hands and knees, got right in my face, and replied, "You are not weak, Dad, you just need to improve your mindset." Wow, our son was dropping the great wisdom on me. Rather than paying attention to what mattered, being with Rivers watching one of our favorite shows, I was dominated by made-up thoughts of the future. I was instantly grateful to be present with our son.

In his book titled *Mindful Cognitive Behavioral Therapy*, Seth Gillihan writes, "*Add up all the good things we have in our life and then subtract the things we assume we're entitled to. What's left will correspond very closely to our level of gratefulness.*" I'd like to be a cognitive behavioral therapist when I grow up! This path to gratitude is something I now use every day. I'm entitled to . . . nothing. Not to move or breathe. I'm not entitled to be free of enormous or impossible challenges. I'm not even entitled to be alive! I live by grace alone, breath by breath by breath.

I shared this idea of entitlement with Rivers after I read this. He sat for a moment, then said, "I'm entitled to love." Wow. I think Rivers is right. Not so different than what Jesus tells us. To love people, including ourselves, and even to love life, seems to be the ultimate purpose, at least for me.

The best way I've learned to practice loving people is a style of meditation called Metta, translated as Loving-Kindness. The practice is to pick a person in your life who is easy to love and to wish them well. I use our kids and Mic all the time. I also use my mom, who was diagnosed with Alzheimer's in 2020. Metta practice is to repeat phrases like "May you be happy," "May you be free of fear," and "May you be free from suffering."

We're invited to create our own phrases, so some I came up with over the years include "May your mind be free of tension and pain," "May you know peace, the ultimate happiness," "May you know you are loved," "May you accept each moment of reality, as it is," and "May you know you are the source of love." This type of practice was powerful and transformative for me.

As the sessions go further, Metta expands Loving-Kindness to neutral people, the cashier or the delivery person, strangers you meet, and to all people. I liked this. To see people and truly want them to be happy and free from fear is a process that brings radiance, vitality, expansiveness, and joy to my mind and body.

I used to find that joy in giving people huge proper Gleason hugs. I'm not able to do anything physical like that these days, but I can invite others to join me in the act of Loving-Kindness. I call it Fo to Fo. This Fo to Fo started with Rivers and Gray, but it's grown to include nearly everyone. There's a wonderful picture of me and Drew Brees on the front page of the New Orleans paper. Fo to Fo is simple. You put your forehead on my forehead and we look each other in the eye. Fo to Fo is beautifully profound. Forehead to forehead. Eye to eye. Moving beyond body, language, or concept of anything. Just being. Embracing. Like Aristotle said: two bodies, one soul.

You'll often hear me say "Fo to Fo, Mo Fo!" You can interpret the last two words as you may.

The real kicker for me with this style of meditation is the invitation to practice this Loving-Kindness for ourselves, as well as for difficult people in our lives. I don't have many difficult people, and I have no enemies. I think the only enemy is in the mind. I practice Loving-Kindness on myself: "May you be free of fear." "May you know you are loved." "May you understand thoughts and emotions and be free of suffering." This has helped me to dissolve the enemy and embrace the chaos of this ALS life.

Over the years, I was overly critical about our newer caregivers.

I also still had confrontations with my dad because of his funda-mentalist, dogmatic views. This practice has helped me deal with all that. In a Metta session directed toward a difficult person, Sam Harris talks about how much pain, anxiety, or suffering the person has experienced, and the need to see how this shaped their behavior.

The good thing about my dad is that he is transparent with his pain, almost to a fault. He has shared with me that he walked in on his mom in the act of adultery, not once but twice and that he was slapped over and over again by nuns in grade school. Just like me, he's doing the very best he can. And we can both do a little better. I now understand that *everyone* has a history of pain or trauma, and that their view of the world is based on that pain; that helps me understand that everyone is doing the very best they can. This allows me to love them. The Eastern traditions assert that people's poor behavior is based not on some original sin, but on ignorance. That sounds naive to us in the West, but the best example of this notion I've read is from the author of Luke. Jesus's last words, directed toward those who killed him and who seem to show no sign of repentance, rather they are dividing up his clothes: "Father . . . Forgive them, for they know not what they do."

While this may or may not be historically accurate, his example continues to inspire and motivate me to live more from a place of forgiveness, compassion, and unconditional love.

ONE OF OUR MOST fulfilling service projects is our Gleason Life Skills Sports Clinic. Kyle surprised me with this idea in 2017. Kyle has been surprising me with his ideas since he started with us in 2013. He was a quiet, humble "overnight" caregiver. After a few months, as his shift was ending one morning, he nonchalantly asked me, "Can I try to transfer you?" I wasn't surprised, I was floored. I didn't really know Kyle at the time, and this dude was like 5 feet 9, 170 pounds. Our transfer guys were all over six feet up to that point. I agreed to let him try under supervision of Blair, and it went well. Kyle is now working with us full-time, and is one of the main reasons our family has flourished. Over the last ten years, Kyle has become like our kids' second father, Rivers's baseball coach, and a teacher to me. Infinite gratitude for him may be an understatement. When he comes to me with an idea, I am always interested. I loved the idea of the Life Skills Sports Clinic in 2017, and we've been successfully sharing them with the youth of New Orleans ever since.

I see the clinics as the ultimate service because they're giving the next generation the tools to be resilient in the twenty-first century, which will likely be the most challenging and chaotic time in history.

We use sports—baseball, basketball, football, and volleyball—as a vehicle to teach kids essential life skills that aren't specifically taught or emphasized in schools today. We're even exploring disability sports, martial arts, music, and other ideas. Life skills such as communication, leadership, discipline, attitude, collaboration (teamwork), responsibility, patience, poise, goal setting, sacrifice, focus, gratitude, active listening, and more are all included in our curriculum. We have a great team of high-character coaches and are fortunate to work with the Saints, the Pelicans, Metairie Park Country Day School, and Tulane University to be able to use their facilities.

The Gleason Life Skills Sports Clinic curriculum is uniquely designed and crafted to include hands-on sports skill training, life skill exercises, various aspects of competition, and open communication with parents.

After the COVID pandemic, we introduced the life skill of meditation to the kids. As awkward and uncomfortable as some of the kids, coaches, and parents look when we tell them to find a seat on the ground and prepare themselves for a meditation, the responses afterward are incredible.

In one of my speeches I said, "We know now that gratitude is probably the most important part of learning to serve others. I keep a gratitude and small steps journal, and it has changed my life for the better.

"So, how do we strengthen our practice of gratitude? I have discovered a powerful tool, and that tool is meditation.

"Meditation is not some spooky magic. Meditation is simply the process of training our minds to pay attention to our experiences, without distraction. I like to say, if I'm not grateful for at least three things in every single moment of my day, I'm simply not paying attention to life!"

After the meditation, we guide the kids through a group conversation. When we ask how meditation made them feel, we receive responses such as "I felt wisdom," "I was able to focus more," "It reset me," and "It gave me energy."

"I can use my breath when I'm feeling anxious about my homework." "I can use my breath to help calm myself before a big game." "I can use my breath when my little sister annoys me."

These clinics are the bullseye of service and love for me. Having Rivers involved in these clinics since he was six years old has been one of the best parts of the experience. Gray now comes to help, too. Well, she doesn't necessarily help with the clinic, but she helps bring joy to the kids, coaches, and her daddy! That is a powerful life skill in itself.

To pass on some of the critical skills I've learned to not only survive but enjoy this crazy wonderful life, and then receive feedback from kids and parents, is as rewarding as it gets.

> Mr. Steve,
>
> Thank you for empowering me through the Gleason Life Skills Sports Clinic. Your lesson in active listening and being resilient has changed the way I live. I am forever grateful and have renewed resilience. I look forward to the next camp.
>
> Thanks,
> Adam B.—11 years old

Michel once said, "It feels good to feel good." At the time I smiled at her Yogi Berra–like comment. But at the end of a recent two-day football camp, after reading that letter from Adam B., I had to agree with her. It did indeed feel good to feel good.

19

Fatherhood

I hear babies cry, I watch them grow
They'll learn much more
than I'll ever know
And I think to myself
What a wonderful world.

—GEORGE DAVID WEISS AND BOB THIELE

This chapter is not just about our kids, it is for our kids.

Parenting is difficult. Not just for me, or other parents with ALS, parenting is difficult for everyone who cares about being a good mom or dad. At least for me, to watch our kids experience hardship, failure, or deep sorrow can be more difficult as a parent than perhaps it is for our kids.

It seems that navigating the landscape of parenting is our most important work. As a dad who hasn't been able to provide physically for our kids, this landscape has had some deep valleys.

November 6, 2019, was the low point in my career as a father.

During my morning workout, I started feeling achy, light-headed and feverish. I'd felt like that on and off for the past few weeks.

Also, Windows updated my tablet the previous night, changing how I typed and spoke. It's difficult to understand how subtle yet drastic changes like this are for me. It's like learning to write with your nondominant hand. Or waking up in a foreign country and having to instantly learn the language because no one really understands the language you're speaking. It's not just frustrating, it's isolating.

Since I wasn't feeling well, I decided to go to bed early. While I settled, Michel said that she and Rivers would come watch a Saturday night movie with me in a sec. Before they came in, my tablet somehow lost the ability for me to speak. I was mute.

While I tried to fix the technical difficulty, Rivers ran into the room, danced around, and playfully hopped in bed. He didn't communicate with me at all. He just flipped on the TV and started scrolling through our movie collection. This behavior was unusual; he usually was communicative with me, especially about those kinds of decisions. While I worked on fixing my un-fucking-believably mute tablet, he decided on the movie *Minions*, pushed "Play," and was happy as could be.

While I preferred to watch a movie for the whole family, I was more focused on unmuting my un-fucking-believably mute tablet. I figured when Michel came in, she'd "ix nay" Rivers's impulsive choice.

A few moments later she did indeed come in and asked, "Wait, why are we watching *Minions?*"

Rivers whined a little, then kind of mumbled something. Michel said we should watch something we all wanted to watch, and Rivers, in a very eight-year-old fashion, started to whine and protest.

In her book *When Things Fall Apart*, Pema Chodron says every single human has times when they feel like life is falling apart. The Tibetan phrase for this is *ye tang che*, which translates to "totally, completely exhausted."

That is precisely where I was at that moment.

My tablet finally unmuted. Bursting with frustration at my inability to communicate and my overall sense of *ye tang che*, the first thing I said was not "Holy shit balls, that was frustrating!" No, my first choice of phrases was "C'mon, Mom, he acts like a princess, because he's treated like a princess."

As soon as the words left "my mouth," Rivers burst into tears.

He sat up and yelled, "I hate you, Dad!" Then, stormed out of the room.

"Steve, what the hell?!" Michel said. She saw the expression of anguish on my face and asked compassionately, "What's up, bud? What was that for?"

She patiently waited and gave me a chance to type.

"Fuck, I'm an idiot," I said.

"Steve, I figured you two had talked about what movie to watch and decided together on this," she explained.

Rivers walked back in the room. Michel explained that she thought we had discussed what movie we were going to watch, and she told him we were switching to something we all agreed on. While she talked, I typed a message to Rivers.

"Rivers, I'm sorry for my behavior," I said. "That was a stupid thing to say. I know you're tough. Will you forgive me?"

Rivers crawled over Michel and gave me a hug.

"Yes, Dad. Love you, too," he said.

"Rivers," I continued, "I know it sucks for you that I type and talk so slow. But I'm trying my very hardest to be a good daddy. I just want you to know that."

We settled on the new *Lion King*, with the "real animals." It's a favorite of mine, and as a dad, the parallels to our lives are compelling. I admire Mufasa's (the dad's) amiable and consistent guidance. Of course, it's easier to be a parent in the movies than in real life. But as frustrated and as guilty as I felt, I was still able to marvel at how understanding and forgiving my son could be with me. I knew I had missed the mark that night, but I was committed to learn the lesson.

I have lost so many things in the past thirteen years. Moving, eating, breathing. But the inability to communicate normally, and in real time, is easily the most painful aspect of this disease for me, Michel, and the kids. It's caused me to feel extremely lonely and disconnected from people I love. Like Michel told Peter King in our first TV interview after I was diagnosed, "It doesn't seem fair."

For me, I now believe the pain of this loss *is* fair. It's helped me learn to be resilient, forgiving, and compassionate. But, man, some-times it doesn't seem fair to Gray and Rivers. Or even to Michel.

EARLY ON, the experiences like that—not being capable of being the actively involved and engaged parent that I've always wanted to be—have left me broken and untethered in a brutal way.

When Rivers was a baby, I was still able to do some things with him. Losing the ability to speak to him, hold him on my lap, and spend time alone with him was tough. It was equally painful to watch other people do things with him I couldn't do. At times, it was even difficult to watch Michel parent our kids without my direct involvement. Thoughts and feelings of inadequacy bombarded my mind: "If I were a normal dad, Rivers would be better at math." Or "If I were a normal dad, our kids would have more discipline." Or "If I was a normal dad, I could comfort three-year-old Gray when she is wailing in the middle of the bathroom floor."

I often have to rely on the help of other people to relay any mes-sage to our kids. It is difficult for them to interpret and try to add the emotion I want to communicate.

Our caregivers have always done their best to foster a connection between me and our kids, and I've appreciated their efforts. But I still experienced jealousy and irritation watching them do things in a different way than I would have done. Michel felt the same way about parenting with someone other than me. It's awkward for everyone. The caregivers often find themselves caught in the middle of a family issue. As Kyle once put it, "We have to par-ent, but we are not the parents." How Kyle or Jenni may approach parenting might not be the approach Michel and I take. As a good caregiver, they must have a high level of social awareness without being too overbearing or involved. They are forced to negotiate a never-ending balancing act, walking the line without crossing over it.

In the summer of 2017, while we were on our annual summer trip to the Pacific Northwest, that reality hit me in the face.

At that point, five-year-old Rivers's love for the Pacific Northwest was still evolving. I was eager to see if he would enjoy jumping off a ten-foot rock on the Pend Oreille River. But he didn't love it. He was nervous and afraid. Any normal dad would have been able to express his understanding and coax confidence in their child to give the courage needed for this kind of adventure.

I was not able to properly talk to or comfort my son. He couldn't see the confidence I had in him. He couldn't feel the strength of my energy and love. I couldn't swim with him or bring him to the top of the rock to talk about the emotions he was probably experiencing. I was totally unable to control a situation that I desperately wanted to control. My messages had to come through the letter board, since we were on the boat, and I couldn't use my tablet in the sun.

As I desperately tried to communicate all those feelings, I lost the focus of what the actual goal was for Rivers. Instead of conveying love and strength, I felt and conveyed my own frustration. All I ended up saying was "Don't be a pansy." Luckily, that terrible message wasn't relayed to him.

Despite my clear inability to do things I used to be able to do, at the time I was unable to understand my role on this team. I was hostage to the thoughts and idea; the story of being the dad I *should* have been. My resulting behavior caused frustration and suffering for our team. Rivers ultimately refused to jump off the rock.

BEFORE ALS, I never wanted our kids to feel compelled to play competitive sports. I would have been fine if they were passionate about less obvious competitive sports like snow skiing or surfing, as well as being into music and art. I wanted to help them learn to be wilderness survivalists. But, here we are. I have ALS, and Rivers has become really into sports. Gray hasn't started playing competitively, but I imagine she will. The silver lining is that I know everything I learned in athletics has given me guidance on living with ALS. I've also learned entirely new lessons, experiencing athletics with Rivers.

When he was four years old, Rivers played above his age group in the five-and-six-year-old baseball league. He had a natural swing and batted fourth in the lineup. I was so stoked when he hit his first in-the-park home run. As much as I wanted to be out on the field coaching him like a normal dad, I was still able to help coach him through Kyle. Kyle was a lefty like me and Rivers, and he had played center field in college. Kyle and I would take Rivers out back and teach him all the right mechanics. We used a comparison to one of his karate moves and told him to swing like tia tua. Michel videoed his game at-bats for me so I could analyze his swing and talk to him afterward when I could use my tablet. Still, my inability to be directly involved with him caused a deep sense of insecurity, and there is no question it altered my behavior.

When he turned five, Rivers wanted a baseball-themed birthday party, so we invited his new team. He looked up to a bigger kid on the team, Barry, who was competitive and athletic. However, his swing was not great. Rather than being short and quick to the ball, it was long and loopy. But he could hit the ball hard, and hit fly balls all the way to the outfield, which Rivers clearly noticed. Rivers's swing, on the other hand, caused him to hit line drives and opposite-field line drives, which was great—but did not impress five- and six-year-old boys. A few games into the season, Rivers got up to the plate, took a swing, and whiffed. Swing two, another long and loopy whiff. Same for strike three. I started blinking, no, no, that's not what we've practiced. On his second at-bat, the same thing happened. I could see Kyle, who was pitching, try to remind him to use his swing, but to no avail. By the end of the game, and on the whole way home, Kyle and I were in complete shock at this transformation.

As we prepared for Rivers's birthday party, Michel started laying out the plans and I typed the following sentence. "I don't want to invite Barry to the party." Michel looked at me, mouth agape in amused, perplexed shock. "Steve, are you being serious right now?"

I continued, "I don't want Rivers emulating his swing anymore."

"Steve. THEY ARE FIVE YEARS OLD!"

"Fine," I said, pouting.

If I had all my pre-ALS abilities, I don't think I would have behaved like that.

Being an elite athlete gave me confidence. Fortunately, Rivers and Gray are far more socially adept than I was. Rivers is athletic, fast, and really coordinated. He has incredibly quick feet, a trait that he gets from both of us. Michel is really fast. I can't remember seeing someone with faster quick-twitch muscles than she has. I have concerns that people, society, everyone, will expect Rivers to be like me, so I anticipate that he'll need to be innovative, resilient, and creative as he gets older and if sports become a higher profile part of his life.

I assume football may be thrown at him from every angle, but I want him to pursue it only if he's truly passionate about it. If he feels called to do it, then I will support his decision. Regardless, we have decided that we won't let him play tackle football until the eighth grade, just like me. It's no secret that head trauma is bad and can be a contributing factor in some brain diseases. Recent studies have also concluded that head trauma for young adults can have lasting effects. That's not my opinion. It's a fact. And while he plays several sports and head trauma can happen in other situations, we have enough information to not allow him to play tackle football until he's older. Since Rivers is only a few years away, I'd like to help get flag football as an official high school sport in Louisiana.

ON THE AFTERNOON of September 16, 2020, I sat in my wheelchair a few inches from the massive sliding doors on the eastern wall of my bedroom. Through the glass, I gazed at the sun-soaked oaks in the backyard. I allowed this calming scene to loosen the clenched fist in my mind. I sat with both a newly raw and painful grief. Tears flooded my eyes and spilled down my cheeks.

A few minutes earlier, I was at the dining room table with Rivers and Michel, trying to be an active and involved father. It was homework time. During a math exercise, Rivers was irritated because he didn't understand the problem and Michel was losing her patience, unclear how to teach him. In a fit of frustration with my inability to help with the situation, I typed up and said, "This is like the blind leading the blind!"

As soon as the words left "my mouth," I regretted uttering them. What a fucking ignorant thing to say, dude! I felt shame and regret. Shame for my mindless comment to Mic. Regret for allowing myself to be overwhelmed and being so disrespectful. As we have done over and over in our relationship, I was penitent and apologetic, and Michel quite graciously forgave me. But, gazing out at the oak, I grieved for the body and abilities I once had. Before ALS, I had a real ability to teach in an enthusiastic, encouraging way. That ability has been taken from me.

As the tears streamed, I allowed myself to feel the pain and embrace the grief, deep and raw within me. These were sorrowful tears of mourning, and an awareness came over me. I could feel the pain, but I could also see it from a place where I could almost revel and really enjoy the grief and accept it in peace. I had moved through the different phases of processing pain, from envy, anger, and frustration to acceptance.

As I processed these emotions, Jenni came into the room, and I asked if we could take a walk through the park with Gray. These walks are times of excellent contemplation for me. In Lake Vista, we're surrounded by such wonderful and majestic creation, yet I don't get to physically experience the glory as intimately as I once did. This paradox causes my mind to chatter. "Enjoy this. It's amazing!" And "Fuck, I wish I could walk with Gray, hold her hand, and smell her blond hair." And "Many daughters don't get to walk with their dads like this. Stay present." Pessimist vs. Optimist. I was just starting to learn that the ego self always seems to want more than it has, but if we can train our minds, it seems we can discover contentment by wanting precisely what we have.

As Jenni steered me with Gray on my lap, we wandered through our nature soaked neighborhood, going to Zinnia Lane on Zephyr Park, about a third of a mile from our house. Before the turn at Zinnia we found a familiar oak. We noticed a swing on one of the long, gnarled, and knotty oak branches. We maneuvered my wheelchair through the soft, boggy, rained-soaked grass to play on the swing. At one point Jenni pushed the swing toward my face, and as the swing moved forward, it also moved up toward my eyes. As the swing stretched, Jenni held it in place so Gray's eyes were only about six inches from mine. There was no distance, no separation or space between us. Gray had a no-nonsense look in her brown eyes, and it pierced through my hazel eyes, directly into my soul. I was stunned with awe and wonder. A tide of grace and peacefulness swelled within me. At the Soul of the Oak tree, I swung with my little girl. A moment of union. A moment of eternity.

This encounter with frustration, guilt, and grief during homework was toward the end of several years of brutal wrestling. As a father, it's been a humbling and glorious transformation.

In the summer of 2020, I stumbled upon a podcast with Peter Crone as a guest. Crone is known as the "Mind Architect." He helps people redesign their minds to discover freedom.

He spoke about how people have deep, primal constructs based upon their history that imprison them in fear. Some examples of these deep-seated constructs include "I'm not safe," "I don't belong," or "I'm not enough." His words hit home. Growing up, I believed I always had to do more to belong and be loved. I recognize these fears in my approach to being a dad.

Typically, with these constructs, rather than find the core of our discontent, we exhaust ourselves with an effort to take action to solve the problems in our lives. In my case, this fear of inadequacy as a father caused me to exhaust myself trying to prove my worthiness. This had caused Mic, Rivers, and our caregivers an enormous amount of pain. Since I was introduced to Peter when Gray was less than two, she has been mostly spared, I think.

Peter approaches our fears by working with clients to investigate whether these conditioned beliefs are true or not. And they are "always not a truth." In this way, Peter says, "I don't solve people's problems, I dissolve them."

The aspect of the conversation that most resonated with me was that Peter's mom died when he was seven and his dad died when he was seventeen. To hear Peter talk about being a space of unconditional love, boundless possibility as well as experiencing freedom from suffering with such authenticity, after being orphaned as a child, humbled and motivated me to learn all I could from him.

After hearing this podcast, I thought, Man, religions offer salvation after death, which is a belief that can't be proven or disproven, but this dude is offering something different. Peter Crone is offering salvation in the present moment. That freedom is tangible and experienced in this life. That is what I'm interested in.

I enrolled in the Free Your Mind course on Peter Crone's website and learned things like "True success is when I'm completely free regardless of my circumstance. So, I'm no longer a victim of what's going on around me. I can maintain a sense of peace and centeredness regardless of the circumstance."

This all rang so true for me!

Could I be truly successful?

In a one-on-one Zoom conversation in early 2021, I asked Peter how I could be a better listener. That seemed to be a superpower of his, and something I could greatly improve on in my life.

His answer was illuminating. Essentially, people are typically listening through the lens of self-protection and inadequacy, so the ego self is worrying, How does this affect "me"? Peter told me, "To honor others and let them express their reality, and to truly be with whoever is speaking, is the greatest gift we can give anyone, because that is synonymous with love."

I believe this is precisely what helped me and Mic emerge to the light. We were able to compassionately understand the deep suffering we had both experienced, and we wanted to help each other be free of that, no matter what happened.

While I intended to continue living this wonderful life for decades, I asked if he had any insights into ways that I could share lessons or skills with my family, to strengthen their ability to cope, be resilient, and thrive after my death.

He told me that he had been working on and trying to be a perfectionist, and then someone told him, "You don't understand. . . . Your presence is enough."

I've given dozens of interviews saying that I'm passionate about being active and involved in our kids' lives. But, as parents, are we being superactive and involved in the most important things? Or is being present and loving enough? It's a great question for any parent to ask, regardless of ALS.

"So that would be my reflection to you, brother," Peter said. "Your presence is enough." Hearing those words felt like a miracle. It *was* a miracle! I felt a massive burden completely dissolved. As someone who had been struggling with my identity and purpose in this life, this opened up entirely new possibilities.

Then he said something that felt like he knew what I had been through but I was just learning in the past year or two: "You think so deeply about others and how you can have an impact on their lives but sometimes that impact is detrimental, right? So, the greatest gift you can give them is to recognize that they're taken care of and recognize that they're going to be okay. My parents stepping aside allowed me to step forward.

"Even in the absence of this beautiful Soulful Steve Gleason, they will thrive because that's their destiny. So you can let go of the grip of wanting to make sure they're OK, and know that they're taken care of."

This conversation transformed my entire career as a father, and redesigned my life purpose. I made a commitment that day that presence, to give myself entirely to each moment, is my purpose. In the three years since this conversation, the fruits of my commitment to be present have been bountiful.

This came to light on our most recent trip to the Northwest. On the way to Pend Oreille River, we made a pit stop to the home in Five Mile Heights I moved to when I was twelve.

Upon arrival, Rivers hopped out of the car and started to ascend the steep hill across the street from my old house. The same hill I used to climb as a boy. His best friend, Landry, followed suit. Beau positioned the car so I could kind of see in my periphery.

Shortly after, Gray hopped out and approached the hill.

"Rivers!" she implored. "Wait!"

Rivers waited patiently for Gray to reach him, so they could make it to the top together.

"Mommy, come up here!" Gray yelled.

Michel climbed up, and once they were together at the top, they looked out over the land that had shaped and formed me. They yelled at me, smiling with raised hands.

I felt a rush of miraculous awe that this all happened organically. This was one of the truly sacred places of my youth, and it represented the exploration and growth that follows me to this day. Now our family was stepping forward, traveling on a similar path. Rivers, leading as something of the man of the house, and Gray, right on his heels, thoughtfully remembering Mommy.

I smiled with contentment and gratitude. I wasn't with them, but my presence was within them. Love. And with all the love surrounding them in Spokane and New Orleans, I know they will be OK.

At this point, while I think it's important that kids listen to parents, ultimately it seems kids *become* their parents. This motivates me to be better every day. Small steps. I'm here to be a model of Resilience for Gray and Rivers and love them as unconditionally as possible. That will never change. Ever.

With acknowledging my physical limitations, I'm not a disciplinary teacher-type dad, so I work to experience life with them. I call Rivers and Gray "brother" and "sister" quite a bit, and I tell them that they are ultimately in charge of their lives and decisions. I'm here to grow and learn, fall and fail *with* them. I regularly tell them, "It's good to have high expectations, but wisdom comes from understanding that you are good enough, just being you." One day, our children will be our equal in stature and knowledge and eventually surpass us. It's an evolutionary inevitability. I quite look forward to that moment.

During this journey with ALS, I have been keenly aware of the impermanence of me, but our kids are also very aware that everyone dies. While modern culture works to deny or distract people from the reality of death until they are forced into it (which is too late), Michel and I had no intention of sheltering our kids from the truth of living with ALS. Recognizing the truth and beauty of our mortality can be a doorway to living a better, more fulfilling life.

Rivers and I regularly discuss this reality. On the night of his twelfth birthday in October 2023, he read my birthday letter to him out loud. This is a tradition we started a few years ago.

One part of my letter addressed the topic at hand:

It's so crazy that you're presented with the precious fragility of life at your age, dude. I never really thought about people dying when I was your age. But Rivers, I know this can be a positive development for you if you can explore. When I recently asked you your thoughts on dying, I loved your answer, dude. You said, "I'm not really worried about being dead, but I don't really want y'all to die." I've explored what happens after death a lot in the past 12 years. Remember this, you are safe. The question I like to ask is, What was our experience before we were born? And, there is the fact that the core essence of me and momma, conscious presence, continues in you, Gray, and others. It's also totally understandable you don't want the people you love to die. I know it is OK to feel sad. And I know it is OK to cry. It's so helpful to express our emotions, and to let people we trust know how we feel. And Rivers, like every single animal, and every single plant that is alive, this body will transform and die someday. I am committed to live and love you and Gray and Momma for as long as possible. This is not easy for any of us, but let's love every moment of this wonderful life together. When this body dies, no matter where you go and no matter how you feel, that love is always with you. Revel in this love. That will never die!

Multiple times a day, I tell our kids I'm proud of them, and I love them, how impressed I am by them, rather than finding fault with them. I learned this habit from asking people who have lost a parent really young, what they would like to know about their mom or dad. The response has been mostly unanimous, which was amplified in an interview I did with Eddie Vedder in 2013.

I asked him that question about his father, whom he never knew. He replied, "The first thing that comes to mind, not having the opportunity to have known him, is if he loved me and how much. I get the feeling that he did, you know?" He continued, "And, you know, I wish he was around now. And I think he'd be proud of me."

Still, there are times when I feel a pit in my heart, thinking about the pain our kids might feel when I die. I thought about this when sitting at the first father-son mass Rivers and I attended in 2019 at Stuart Hall School. I imagined Rivers at future masses, without me. The thoughts haunted me. I questioned myself for being so involved. Am I being selfish? Would my death be easier for my kids if I just lay in bed all day, uninvolved? Or if I had died when the kids were younger?

I think about all of the cool things that they are able to experience because of me and how they might miss them if I'm not around. I think about Mardi Gras, and I imagine them missing walking in the parades, and people screaming at them for beads. I think about being near the Saints locker room as the players walk to the field. Or going to Cubs games and getting to throw out the first pitch. We've had such magical moments. The thrill of these experiences can be addicting. It's egotistical to say, but I worry that they'll struggle to get past the feeling of emptiness if I'm not here. Ugh. What have I done?

I wonder how people will treat them when I'm gone. Will everyone tell them, "Your dad was such a hero." Blah, blah, blah . . . Shut up!

I also continue to write journals to Gray and Rivers, sharing with them as many life lessons as possible.

Gray and Rivers,

My ultimate intention is that you have both read this in 10 years, while I'm still alive. How spectacularly satisfying that will be. But, the reason I even began this journal project in 2011 is because I might not live until you're on your own.

Everyone suffers, it's just part of the human experience. I believe that when you're suffering, especially deeply suffering, it's vital to seek ways to help other people, and the world. Everyone needs help in some way. I'm not necessarily talking about helping poor, homeless, addicted, or terminally ill people. All people need help. People need plumbers, architects, musicians, astronauts, philosophers, and artists. Seek ways to help people in a way that is meaningful to you and invigorates you. Seek to help in ways that you see as good, as important and valuable to the world. In this way, you serve what you love. I think the only person who can decide what is good and valuable to the world is you. What do I think you should do? I'd like you to deeply understand this—everything you have is enough. Like our favorite Zac Brown Band song says, "Ain't no dollar sign on peace of mind, this I've come to know."

I believe tragedy and suffering offer us opportunity. Opportunity to inspire, serve each other, explore, grow, and be heroes. I like to think the greater the pain, the greater the opportunity.

When you're feeling like you're at the bottom, take one small step each day, and remember that it takes time. If you're a slow learner like me, a long fucking time. Keep it simple. Keep showing up.

I would add, along with finding ways to love and serve others, when you're experiencing painful emotions, or outright suffering, lean on people you trust, so they can love, support, and even challenge you. So many people love you both. Accept the challenge, and if you can become curious, explore and befriend your pain, you will grow in understanding, compassion, and love for yourself and other people. This has been the most valuable aspect of this ALS adventure for me. Sharing the extraordinary love, challenges, and support from and with others. We're all in this together.

You have a lot of life left to live. I invite you to really stick together. There will understandably be tough, tense times, but my guidance is to let these times go. You are a wonderful duo! I'm within both of you, always.

I love y'all, forever,
Dad.

20

The Beauty of Being Broken

The greatest thing you'll ever learn,
Is just to love and be loved in return.
—EDEN AHBEZ

After my diagnosis in 2011, I endured a few long years of losing nearly everything; I even felt as if I'd lost my identity. Then life became more stable. Stability is so damn seductive, but it's not the truth of life. The truth is that everything changes. As Marcus Aurelius said, "Loss is nothing but change, and change is Nature's delight."

As you know, Jazz Fest is one of my favorite places to share my love for this life. In the spring of 2022, I beamed my smile to friends and family there for hours. Then, later that summer at Rivers's sporting events, I began to struggle to smile on cue. When I wanted to embrace people and brighten someone's day with a smile, I couldn't always do it. As much as I'd lost in the past twelve years, it seemed like losing my smile would be the most painful.

I have an abstract painting in my room that was given to me by a New Orleans friend, Martin Benson, a longtime meditator. It's a picture of the sun with a rainbow around it. It's titled "If the Sun could speak, it would still only shine." I love the picture, but it's the title that inspires me to continue to shine every day. I'm not able to hug or hold people. I shine by smiling. What if that disappears?

It feels like all I have left is my smile. Is it possible to keep shining with no smile?

As always, more change was on the way.

In the fall of 2022, out of nowhere, I started having episodes of "relentless hiccups," as I called them. They would occur multiple times a day and occasionally during the night and sometimes last for an hour or more. Eventually, I figured out a pretty gnarly way to stop them. Before ALS, I used to hold my breath for as long as I could, so I thought I would try the same. I would have caregivers take the hose of the ventilator off the trache, which meant I wasn't breathing. They would keep it off until I would essentially start suffocating, so the muscles in my chest and diaphragm started working, kind of trying to breathe on their own. I really don't know how to explain it, but those muscles were too weak to get enough air. They would eventually exhaust themselves, and my body would be starved of oxygen. I would then look at the caregiver to put the hose back on. Talk about a death practice . . . Barbaric, yes, but the hiccups would stop. After a week or two of this, I got a mild fever, and some lung pain. I was checked in to the hospital. It turns out the sodium levels in my body had dropped to seizure and near-death levels. After some investigation we discovered I was drinking too much water. It turns out I was an aquaholic. I had no idea I could die from being too hydrated! Relentless hiccups saved my life.

We're not sure why or how, but after I left the hospital, I lost the ability to blink, and it would take about ten to fifteen minutes of squinting to close my eyes. At the time, I was completely ignorant of the implications of this latest loss. After one of Rivers's soccer games, I texted our care crew, "Well, it's official: I have ALS face." Saggy cheeks. Half-open mouth. Blank, zombie-ish eyes.

After years of no noticeable symptom progression, it's like life said, "Steve-O! You're rolling along really well, champ. Let's see what you're made of now. It is time for another opportunity to grow!"

Part of these changes was added pressure.

IN JANUARY 2023, our team at the publishing company expressed a desire to shorten our deadline in order to release this book earlier than originally planned. In my naivete, I told our team a mantra I had adopted a few years earlier: "I'm passionately committed, but completely unattached. I'm in. If it happens, great. If not, we can explore other avenues." I increased the time I spent writing each day from a pretty easy and creative three to four hours to a rigorous six to seven hours. I would take a five- to ten-minute eye break every forty-five minutes or so, but the inability to blink combined with typing for that long each day quickly took a toll on my eyes.

We didn't make the shorter deadline.

Since the seventh grade when I started keeping a poetry journal, writing had always been therapeutic and healing for me. But writing this book started to become the opposite of healing. Having a deadline for writing a story about my life, with unblinking eyes, was not therapeutic. If I'd maintained the pace I needed to keep to make the deadline, I would have killed myself. But that was not my biggest fear. I was most afraid of losing the input I needed to tell our story fully and honestly. I feared that I wouldn't have enough time to polish and refine my ideas. There were other fears too. Mic and I had taken risks and been extremely open and transparent about them. Had I offended people? I worried—and still worry—that I've overexposed our kids. I wonder if they'll be treated differently because of my views. Will they be ashamed of or embarrassed by the stories that include them? From my perspective, spiritual growth is the deconstruction of the ego: "To die before you die." But writing a memoir is egotistical and narcissistic. I told my core friends that writing this book was one of the most humbling and difficult things I've ever done, and that it was the worst decision I have ever made.

Once published, my life story would become solid, static, and fixed. That sounded crazy to me, because, as a faithful explorer, my perspectives, philosophical outlooks, and beliefs are dynamic and fluid.

In the summer of 2023, I felt so stressed by the workload and pressure of the book-writing process that I told Michel I didn't think I would be able to go on our annual summer trip to the Northwest. "If I'm going to finish this book with this deadline," I said, "I don't think it's wise to go." I even asked her if we could just stop the process and not publish the book at all. After I said that, she walked up to my chair, turned the tablet, and got right up in my face. *"You are going on the trip and you are publishing this book. What are you most afraid of, dude? It will be OK, Steve-O."*

She was right.

It was time to take responsibility. Ultimately, it was clear that to finish the book, I had to accept all my physical limitations, a total loss of control, and say, "Let it be done." This surrender to the unknown is, at this point in my life, precisely what our motto, No White Flags, means to me.

When the Saints gave me a Super Bowl ring in 2011, I ended my speech with "ALS has fucked with the wrong dude!" I think that message was appropriate at the time. But as things progressed and evolved with the disease, I learned to see the phrase as a message of acceptance and surrender. One of my favorite aspects of No White Flags is that both our kids' names embody this motto of resilience. I am living to discover and show Rivers the true power of being like water. I'm living to discover the freedom and the beauty of the middle way. The path of Gray. May we never surrender our ability to accept the circumstances in our lives.

No White Flags initially was a message of bravado and resistance. Over the course of thirteen seasons with ALS, my approach has changed.

When Michel recently asked me what I feared most about finishing this book, I told her that I have a fear that we haven't expressed the challenges that come with the loss of blinking, which most people are unaware of and do involuntarily 21,000 times a day, and the astounding implications that may impose. One other progression of the disease that has occurred in the past couple of years is that it's now hard for my eyes to quickly and voluntarily look down. That makes typing even more difficult and presents challenges with the letter board and other nonverbal communication.

My typing speed decreased from 15–20 words per minute to about 5–10 words per minute. I had to start taking fifteen-minute "eye breaks" every twenty-five minutes, where a caregiver quickly massaged my eyelids to simulate blinking and applied eyedrops. In the final months of writing this book, I could only write for a maximum of two hours a day. Some days, my eyes just don't work. Even writing these words, my eyes aren't blinking, and they're hurting. At night, if I wake up and use my eyes to do letter board or type to a caregiver, it can take up to thirty minutes of squinting to close them again. Often, I'm not able to fall back to sleep. The silver lining to this latest progression is that I never lose a staring contest!

I'm only a novice at this point, but I'm learning that one of the foundational commitments of the contemplative process is to allow everything to be as it is. This allowing everything to be as it is, is not just radical acceptance, I now call this unconditional acceptance.

This acceptance means my care crew and I have the potential to take appropriate action and create solutions, or if no solutions can be found, unconditionally accept and transform. This *is* Resilience.

We've been meeting with eye doctors, specifically dry-eye experts. I now tape my eyes for my early-morning meditation practice, which is about an hour and a half, then do the same thing out in my sanctuary—nature—for forty-five minutes during lunch. We're exploring new nighttime communication strategies to decrease the use of the tablet or the letter board in bed by taping one or both eyes and using a new system to indicate what I need. So this life seems to be a combination of action and unconditional acceptance, an embodiment of our human dance of doing and being, ego and spirit, person and presence.

I don't share any of these stories to gain your pity. This is my reality, or my view of reality, for me, our family, and other families living with ALS, in real time.

I no longer hope tomorrow will be easier. I no longer pray for relief. That is out of my immediate control, and the antithesis of unconditionally accepting reality as it is. In contemporary culture, hope seems to be rooted in wanting or resisting; so hope is just fear in disguise. If I had merely hoped to make it in the NFL, I would have been out on the streets in no time. I didn't hope I would be successful, I trained to be successful.

If my prayer is anything now, it is silence. It has become clear to me that experiencing stillness and silence have been my greatest adversaries, but mysteriously, my greatest teachers. Life *is* fair. Every breath, my prayer.

During the final months of the writing process, Michael Sork, who, like a percentage of people living with ALS for over a decade, lost the ability to communicate. He lived with minimal communication and connection for a few years, then, in June 2023, made a courageous decision to leave the most difficult life I can imagine. What will I do if this happens to me? If I lost all of my facial expression and I am longer able to communicate? As I draw close to finishing this book, I am aware of this thought: Is this the beginning of the end for me? To explore these existential questions, I now meet with Michel and our team every six months to look at options.

The truth is that every ninety minutes someone in the United States dies from ALS.

I have had multiple close encounters with death, instances where, if things had gone just a little bit differently, I wouldn't be writing this. One of those moments occurred on April 26, 2020.

Mike Gallagher was the caregiver that afternoon. Mike was a twenty-one-year-old nursing student from Lafayette, who we recruited from LSU Health Sciences. He'd been with us for only about a year, so was relatively new to the team.

On this Sunday afternoon, I asked Mike to install a new replacement net for our trampoline out back.

He worked on it while Gray played nearby, and I was set up in my room at the foot of the bed, looking out the slider. I positioned myself so that I could see Gray and watch Mike work. Then I decided to make a move from my spot toward the slider, so I pulled up the Ability Drive program, which takes maybe thirty seconds to load and engage. As I drove between the dresser and the foot of the bed, I inadvertently bumped the ventilator hose against the bed and popped off the vent. The ventilator immediately started beeping—and I stopped breathing.

Overpowering adrenaline rushed through my body and brain. But strangely, there was no fear or panic in my mind. I'd envisioned this exact scenario thousands of times. Similar to an NFL kick-off, I would mentally go through every imaginable scenario. During the play, there was no analysis; it was all instinctual response. Sometimes I succeeded, and sometimes I didn't, but the training and preparation beforehand meant I'd done everything I could to triumph . . . or, in this case, survive. The vent hose had fallen off, been hit, or broken several times in the past, but this was the first time it had happened when no one was within earshot of me.

In these moments, the life-or-death questions are always the same: *Will the caregiver hear the ventilator alert beeping? Can I text the caregiver or tap the beeper to notify them? Will they receive these alerts in time?*

For these reasons, our caregivers are instructed to set the audio settings on their phones at maximum volume during their shifts.

Mike had his phone with him as he worked on the trampoline. I just needed to alert him to the situation—and fast.

Since I was driving, I couldn't type on my tablet, so the first thing I had to do was open the Tobii toolbar, which takes 5–10 seconds. I then closed the Ability Drive app. Another 5–10 seconds. I opened the text messaging app on my desktop to ping Mike. Another 5 seconds.

Ping!

No response.

Type something, anything.

I tried to type "HELP," but in my haste, I only managed "E-L-P."

Ten more seconds.

Through the slider door, I could see that Mike was confused by the first message and didn't understand.

Ping!

Five more seconds.

A second try: "H-E-L-P!"

Five more seconds.

Ping! Ping! Ping! Ping! Ping!

This time, Mike got it. He leaped off the trampoline and raced inside.

"What's going on?!" he asked frantically. "Are you all right?!"

The disconnected vent hose was hidden from his view but the vent alarm was beeping, and he quickly realized what was wrong.

"Holy shit!" Mike said as he reconnected the vent hose.

I'd gone maybe a minute or so without a breath.

When I realized I wasn't going to die, there was an astounding, magical sense of ineffable joy that I was still around to love this miraculous and wonderful life.

But it remains a tenuous existence.

On November 27, 2022, around two in the morning, I woke up to a beeping ventilator. I wasn't receiving any air. The ventilator hose had popped off while I was sleeping. If I hadn't been able to quickly alert our overnight caregiver, India, I would have been dead. Fortunately, I was able to twitch my ear and activate the EZ Switch that rests on the pillow beside my head and ping a text to her. She was able to respond, walk from the caregiver's room, through the kitchen and into my room, and reconnect the hose so I could again receive the gift of breath. Once again my mind was calm, at ease.

It's kind of astonishing to me that I can get so frustrated with non-life-threatening situations, but somehow, I've remained poised and calm in these life-threatening situations. The question is, can I maintain that same poise, be truly successful, in the experience of dying, in its entirety.

Mindfulness practice sessions have become such an important part of my life. Meditation has helped me understand my own mind. To simply observe an emotion like fear, loneliness, or frustration appear then disappear is the greatest skill I've ever learned. While I'm not yet as successful as I'd like to be, the process of watching thoughts and feelings arise then vanish means I'm no longer hostage to the stories of my mind. *This* is freedom. This process has become so important that one day every month I do a "Micro Retreat," spending 8–9 hours meditating in bed with taped eyes. It's my sabbath.

I have an action plan called "The Impermanence Project" to help prepare for the inevitable death of my body. This "project" is a separate document from my living will. While we rarely get the option of choosing exactly how to die, one of my intentions is to detail, if possible, the process of my dying. In the document, I say, *"I know it's most common to dose up on morphine, etc., but I'm interested in being as conscious and present with my dying as possible. I'd like to explore options with our doctors. Obviously, this life is all about acceptance, so let's go with the flow rather than force anything, but I'd also really like to die at home, not at the hospital. Slider door open, if logical."*

Why the hell would I be interested in this idea? It is because the dying process is the last and the ultimate adventure of life. While it's possible or even probable that I retreat and change my mind about using morphine, I'd prefer to fully experience and even embrace this final surrender and transformation. I'm also in the process of creating a dying playlist with meditations and music, two things that are essential to my life.

In "The Impermanence Project," I also explore ideas for what to do with my body. I want to have as "green" a funeral as possible. No casket. I'm not into getting filled up with chemicals. I would like my body to be recycled, to transform and be returned to this miracle of Creation. I'm pretty sure the state of Louisiana is not up-to-date on this kind of procedure so we might have to consider cremation. I love the idea of having an oak tree planted over my body. If that's not possible, I'd like to see if we can plant an oak tree in our Lake Vista neighborhood, or use a current oak, where my ashes can be its nutrients. If the state of Idaho is more open to this practice, maybe my body can fuel the growth of the aspens there. As the molecules of my body are absorbed and digested, eventually I will be exhaled as oxygen to be the breath of life for the people walking the earth. Pneuma.

The most important aspect of "The Impermanence Project" is

writing letters to people who are important to me. Most of these letters are to my family, but I have some to caregivers and friends. I write a letter to Santa Claus every year. These letters are my way of lifting any remaining veil to get heart to heart and soul to soul.

This book is my letter to *you*, my friend. If you're here still, I'd say we're now soul to soul.

Why do I even have "The Impermanence Project"?

Well, if you've read this far, you know, I'm dying. . . .

Just like you.

While I will continue to explore the beautiful truth of the impermanence of the only life I can be sure I have, what I'm really interested in and passionate about is not how to die, but how to live, in the present. I love the guidance from Jesus told by the author of Matthew. He says, "Do not worry about tomorrow, for tomorrow will worry about itself." For me, these words from my homeboy are a call to live my purpose in being human, to be present and love this life, and the people I'm with. To fully appreciate every moment. Right here, right now, even on the fragile precipice.

While the words in this book are static and fixed, I am not. I have discovered strength and beauty within the process of being completely broken. This body may be a prison, but my mind is free. Truly anything is possible in a life we have titled impossible.

As difficult as writing this book has been, it's been rewarding and a true source of growth. Through rigorous introspection, I've gained clearer insight on the priorities for my life. Writing this book has helped reinforce the understanding that I can stay sane and content in the midst of chaos.

Michel and I have been able to deeply connect and collaborate as we relive the peaks and valleys of our life. The process has been arduous. We've both experienced impatience and enormous frustration, all while working to be parents. But it's also made us stronger. The greatest challenges truly are the greatest opportunities.

After I blocked the punt against the Falcons in 2006, people called me a hero, which felt bizarre. I wasn't a hero; I was just a dude trying to do his job. After I was diagnosed with ALS, I said,

"Through adversity, we find our heroes." I think this book shows that if I'm considered a hero, then we all have the opportunity for heroics.

I've been asked hundreds of questions about that punt block, but the most fascinating question I've been asked was from my brother on this ALS journey Brian Jeansonne, a New Orleans native. Like all those who have been impacted by ALS, he and his family have faced more than their fair share of tragedy.

Brian said to me, "This is not meant to be disrespectful. Every Saints fan knows exactly where they were that night and your name became immortalized in one play in every New Orleanian's mind. I'm curious, if you hadn't blocked that punt, do you think your reach and impact on ALS would be the same?" This is the type of question that I've enjoyed pondering my whole life!

My answer was "If I don't block the punt, I am probably not alive."

He was appreciative of my brutal honesty, and his response was "So if you hadn't blocked the punt then I'm probably not alive either." He said, "At the time I was just excited some long-haired surfer dude lifted my spirits after I lost everything in Katrina. But you actually saved my life."

So many people have told us that our foundation's efforts and support have saved their lives. If I didn't block that punt, I'm just another has-been football player. It's probable that I just fade away. I don't see any of this happening.

On September 10, 2023, the NFL asked me and another former NFL player with ALS, Tim Shaw of the Tennessee Titans, to be the honorary captains for the first Saints home game of the season.

I asked permission to have Rivers and Gray walk with me to the middle of the field for the pregame coin toss ceremony, and the request was granted. However, as we entered the field that morning and started to prepare, I realized that I was not able to control the Ability Drive app to operate my wheelchair because of the Superdome's bright lights and my weakened eyes. Typing is sometimes difficult in the Dome, but I've always been able to drive. But now

I was losing that ability in my old office in front of 75,000 people. I had seen this as a chance to show my independence and strength to the world—and now I couldn't fucking drive! I was bewildered and upset.

I kept recalibrating and trying to drive. Jenni was with me, and I used the letter board to tell her what was going on. We sat there for a moment, but the clock was ticking.

Jenni finally said, "Steve, Rivers can do it!"

It was the obvious solution, but I still felt the agonizing loss of my own independence. How badly I wanted to hold on to my own strength.

"I can do it, Dad," Rivers said.

It was time to accept reality as it is.

When the lights dimmed and the crowd started getting loud in anticipation, we were unsure if Gray would leave the safety of Michel's arms to venture onto the field with us. She was feeling scared, not so different from me. I regularly tell her, "It's OK to feel scared, sister, but you are safe." Mic put her down, she reached for Rivers's hand, watched the players storm the field, and bravely climbed up on my lap. What a perfect example for me. I am my daughter's father.

Slowly, along with a couple of Saints players, Rivers drove me and Gray to the middle of the field. Tim and I were announced as captains over the public address system, and the crowd roared its approval. We watched the coin toss, then Rivers stoically drove us back to the sidelines to meet Michel. In the absence of my physical abilities, Rivers and Gray stepped forward to lead the way. To be dependent on our kids was the most beautiful surrender I've ever experienced.

A few months ago, I was writing after my workout, and Michel came into my room and said, "I'm happy you're still with us, Steve-O." I felt an enormous burden lift. To hear that she was happy that I was alive and present was a powerful reminder to reorient my mindset to love.

She said, "The fact that the kids have a dad who is alive and know he loves them is enough. And they sure as shit know he loves them. And the same goes with me. Everything more you provide is just lagniappe."

I replied, "Thank you, Mic. I love you."

"I really feel that, Steve-O. I am so grateful you're here." She said, "You're our constant."

I thought, *My presence IS enough.*

She added: "I don't live in fear of it, but I'm scared about when you aren't here. So thank you for showing up for us every day."

My identity has evolved throughout my life. In the NFL, I identified as a counterculture athlete, but after I retired, feeling like a failure, that story was shattered. When I was diagnosed, I identified as an active and involved father and husband. Story shattered too. What am I really? After all the stories have been shattered, what remains?

The ultimate spiritual growth seems for us to have *no* identity, but I'm inspired by the oak tree. Silent. Still. Ancient. Present. Wise. *Constant.* Rooted in the earth and reaching to the sun.

My body will one day fuel the growth of an oak. In the same way, this book is part of my compost.

—SG

Acknowledgments

Writing this book has been almost impossible. . . . Almost. Without the support and effort of dozens of people, it would have been just that, impossible. This is my offering of thanks.

Thanks to Jeff Duncan for being our head coach, creating the game plan.

Michel Varisco, my wife, the "forensics queen," thanks for collaborating, strategizing, and calling audibles to move us down the field.

During this process, I've confided in close friends and family on what to say and how to say it.

Our "Write On" group thread, thanks for reading, reliving, and even writing the skeleton of many of these anecdotes—Kyle Gleason, Tony Hazel, Frank Relle, Clare Durrett, Jim Salters, Kyle Olasin, Jenni Doiron.

Thank you to Thais Lange and Marion Brannon for their insightful editing.

Robert X. Fogerty, for being on our visual storytelling journey from the beginning until now.

Author and dear friend David James Duncan, for guiding me on the crazy wonderful highs and lows, joys and pains, tragedies and triumphs of being a first-time author. I'm grateful. The love that is alive in us never dies.

Thank you to Sam Rosen, GM at Waking Up. Thanks for your friendship and guidance as I navigated the language of mindfulness to discover a "peace that surpasseth all understanding."

Stephanie Capella, thank you for keeping this team on time and on point.

Thank you to our agent, Chad Luibl, of Janklow and Nesbit, who got us in the game.

Immense gratitude for our editor, Peter "Pierre" Gethers of Knopf, who saw the power of our story and guided us on how to move forward. Additionally, Morgan Hamilton at Knopf, for her invaluable contributions. And special thanks to Andrew Miller at Knopf for his encouragement and support right when I needed it.

A special thanks to all of my friends, colleagues, and family members from New Orleans, Spokane, Gonzaga Prep, Washington State, and the ALS community who agreed to be interviewed for this project.

The amazing staff at Team Gleason, who supported me unconditionally since forming the organization, but also contributed their expertise to the content of the book while I focused on its completion over the past two years. Added thanks to Paul "Pops" Varisco, Blair Casey, Sally Cox, and Suzanne Alford for digging deep for answers and images that helped make this book a reality.

Jenny Lay-Flurrie of Microsoft, whose big-picture guidance helped make a great deal of our crazy ideas and the technology I use possible.

Thank you to the members of the Team Gleason Tech Advisory Committee and the A-Team for their personal stake in advancing technology for people with ALS and beyond. A special thanks to Jay Beavers of Tolt Technologies, whose vision and guidance for the past decade has been lifesaving for me, and thousands of others with ALS.

Publisher Judi Terzotis, executive editor Rene Sanchez, sports editor Perryn Keys, and Saints editor Zach Ewing deserve thanks for supporting the project and allowing my collaborator, Jeff Duncan, the time and opportunity to work on the book.

Special thanks, as well, to Ellis Henican, James O'Byrne, and the "Bretts"—Brett Anderson, Brett Martel, and, especially, Brett Martin—for their editorial expertise and input.

A NOTE ABOUT THE AUTHORS

STEVE GLEASON played eight years for the New Orleans Saints and has become a global inspiration in his post-playing career as a living example of resilience and leadership. Gleason was diagnosed with ALS in 2011 and, along with his foundation, Team Gleason, has been a leader in improving the lives of those affected and raising awareness of the disease. Gleason and his foundation have brought ALS to the forefront. In 2018, both the U.S. House of Representatives and the Senate unanimously passed "The Steve Gleason Enduring Voices Act" to ensure the availability of life-sustaining communication devices. Gleason has been honored with countless awards. In 2020, he was awarded the Congressional Gold Medal, the U.S. government's most prestigious civilian honor. He is the first football player to receive the Gold Medal and only the seventh athlete to receive the honor. Other notable Gold Medal recipients are Mother Teresa, Thomas Edison, George Washington, and the Dalai Lama. Gleason's story was the subject of an award-winning documentary, *Gleason*, that debuted at the Sundance Film Festival in 2016. He has delivered keynote speeches for major corporations like Microsoft and United Healthcare and twice addressed the United Nations Social Innovation Summit. He also has spoken at various universities, professional (NFL, MLB) and NCAA athletic organizations, religious organizations, and major conventions. He was the featured personality on the highly praised and reviewed Microsoft commercial during the 2014 Super Bowl with more than three million views since airing. A native of Spokane, Washington, he was a four-year letter winner and team captain for both the football and baseball teams at Washington State University. In his sophomore season, he helped Washington State win the Pac-10 Conference and earn a berth in the Rose Bowl. Academically Gleason was a four-time Pacific-10 All-Academic selection for football, including first-team honors his junior and senior seasons. He was a special teams captain for most of his NFL career and retired as the club's all-time leader in blocked punts with four. In 2002, he was the special teams Pro Bowl alternate and was named to ESPN's All Pro team. He made one of the greatest and most memorable plays in NFL history when he blocked a punt against the Atlanta Falcons on the night the Superdome reopened after Hurricane Katrina. A bronze statue commemorating the play was erected and displayed outside the Superdome in 2014. In 2009, Gleason started an MBA program at Tulane University, while working as a sustainability consultant at the Shaw Group. He also worked with the Saints, as a community ambassador. In 2008, Gleason retired from the NFL and married New Orleans local, Michel Varisco. He and Michel have two children, Rivers and Gray.

JEFF DUNCAN is a columnist for *The Times-Picayune* in New Orleans. He was a member of the *Times-Picayune* team that won two Pulitzer Prizes for the paper's coverage of Hurricane Katrina. Duncan is the author of three books on the Saints: *Payton and Brees*; *Tales from the Saints Sideline*; and *From Bags to Riches*. A native of Louisville, Kentucky, he has won four Columnist of the Year awards and four Story of the Year awards from the Louisiana Sports Writers Association. Before his stint in New Orleans, he worked as a sports journalist at various newspapers, including *USA Today*, *The* (Louisville, Ky.) *Courier-Journal*, and *The St. Petersburg* (Fla.) *Times*. He is also a member of the Pro Football Hall of Fame Selection Committee and a Saints analyst on WVUE-TV in New Orleans.

A NOTE ON THE TYPE

This book was set in Janson, a typeface long thought to have been made by the Dutchman Anton Janson, who was a practicing typefounder in Leipzig during the years 1668–1687. However, it has been conclusively demonstrated that these types are actually the work of Nicholas Kis (1650–1702), a Hungarian, who most probably learned his trade from the master Dutch typefounder Dirk Voskens. The type is an excellent example of the influential and sturdy Dutch types that prevailed in England up to the time William Caslon (1692–1766) developed his own incomparable designs from them.

Composed by North Market Street Graphics,
Lancaster, Pennsylvania

Printed and bound by Berryville Graphics,
Berryville, Virginia

Designed by Cassandra J. Pappas